MAKING MUSIC MAKE MONEY

An Insider's Guide to Becoming Your Own Music Publisher

ERIC BEALL

Edited by Susan Gedutis Lindsay

Berklee Media

Associate Vice President: Dave Kusek
Director of Content: Debbie Cavalier
Business Manager: Linda Chady Chase
Technology Manager: Mike Serio
Marketing Manager, Berkleemusic: Barry Kelly
Senior Designer: David Ehlers

Berklee Press

Senior Writer/Editor: Jonathan Feist
Writer/Editor: Susan Gedutis Lindsay
Production Manager: Shawn Girsberger
Marketing Manager, Berklee Press: Jennifer Rassler
Product Marketing Manager: David Goldberg
Production Assistant: Louis O'choa

ISBN 0-87639-007-6

1140 Boylston Street
Boston, MA 02215-3693 USA
(617) 747-2146

Visit Berklee Press Online at
www.berkleepress.com

DISTRIBUTED BY

HAL•LEONARD®
CORPORATION
7777 W. BLUEMOUND RD. P.O. BOX 13819
MILWAUKEE, WISCONSIN 53213

Visit Hal Leonard Online at
www.halleonard.com

Printed in the United States of America at Vicks Lithograph and Printing Corporation

12 11 10 09 08 07 06 05 04   5 4 3 2 1

*To my wife Cheryl, who's been with me every step of the journey.
And to my parents, whose love and support made the journey possible.*

Contents

Introduction

So you've written a song. Or two. Or maybe even several dozen, or several hundred for that matter, all recorded somewhere on dusty work tapes stacked in your closet, or on Pro Tools files eating up space on your hard drive. All of those songs, carefully and lovingly created, silently waiting on the answer to the inevitable question: What next?

Now assuming you've taken the time to read the title page of this book, you are probably well on your way to surmising the answer to this question (wonderfully perceptive and intuitive creatures, these songwriters are). Yes, you guessed it—what you need is: A PUBLISHER! You need an effective, diligent music publisher who will share your enthusiasm for your creations, use his or her music business acumen to organize those piles of tapes into a coherent catalog, dip into a bulging Rolodex of industry contacts to put those songs into the hands of the right recording artists, music supervisors, and A&R staffers, and who will then, with the tenacity of a Brooklyn loan shark, collect the inevitable flow of money that results. Simple, right?

Well, maybe. Having spent fifteen years as a professional songwriter, and having enjoyed successful and profitable relationships with several different music publishing companies, I would hardly be the one to tell you that such a goal is out of reach. As someone who has now spent the last four years on the other side of the desk, as a Creative Director for one of the music industry's most successful independent publishers, it would be a little foolish of me to minimize the value of working with a full-service music publishing company. The purpose of this book, as I will reiterate several times, is not to discourage the developing songwriter from seeking to build relationships with established music publishers.

The purpose of this book is simply to let you in on a simple truth that has probably been lurking right under your nose. If it's a hardworking, well-organized, well-connected music publisher that you're looking for, look no further. You already have one. In fact, he or she has probably been around for some time now, having been with you since you penned your first potential hit. Your publisher is your greatest untapped resource, ready to take your **assets** (that's your songs) and put them into **action** (put them somewhere where they can earn . . .) to yield **income** (which is the goal here, remember). Whatever your publisher may lack in experience will inevitably be compensated for with an uncanny understanding of your work, and an unquestionable devotion to your career. So . . . songwriter meet your first, and quite possibly finest, publisher . . .

You.

Okay, I know. It's not exactly what you were hoping for. You were expecting the high-powered, father-figure type, or maybe the nurturing Mother Hen, with deep pockets, a big office, and a lunch meeting in the Sony dining room. Fair enough. Those characters do exist and if you and your current publisher (that's you, pal) do your jobs well, you may someday meet that mythical music business icon. There is a paradox at work here. Until you take ownership of your own publishing company—which exists, at least in theory, from the day you complete your first song—you are unlikely to ever attract the interest of a major publisher, or, for that matter, an important artist, A&R person, or manager. In the beginning, there is you, and what you do will open the doors to all the other parties who will help to develop your career. When an aspiring writer asks me how to find a good publisher, I usually reply, "Become one."

The paradox extends even further. The truth is that the most successful songwriters in any large publishing company are inevitably those writers who have become successful music publishers on their own. They have learned by necessity how to pitch their own material, develop and administer their catalog, protect their copyrights, construct a solid business team, and establish a presence for themselves and their company in the industry. Now their publishing company is a solid independent business entity, and as such, it presents a larger, more established music publisher with an opportunity for a real partnership, a co-venture with an already productive company.

This is the second paradox then. Not only are you most likely to find a publisher by becoming one, you will usually be most successful in working with a major music publisher when you reach the point of not really needing one. Starting your own publishing company is not necessarily a choice to avoid affiliation with a full-service music publisher. Rather, it is a proactive approach to structuring your music career.

I'd love to say that I learned this lesson early in my songwriting career. But I would be lying. In truth, it was only when I entered the publishing world on the business end, thus coming into contact with a wide variety of writers much more successful than I, that the truth began to sink in.

One of the first people to show me the value of a writer taking control of his own publishing was Steve Diamond. As the writer of such hits as "I Can Love You Like That," "Let Me Let Go," "Not a Day Goes By," and many others, Steve is a well-established songwriter whose career stretches over two decades. But what's really impressive is that he has established a publishing company, run primarily by Teri Muench-Diamond (herself a seasoned industry professional, who spent years in an A&R role at RCA), that is in many ways the model of a well-run small publishing firm, with an impressive track record.

When Steve affiliates with a larger publisher the approach is never one of a writer seeking a publisher, but rather of one business owner seeking a co-venture with another. It is understood that Steve's company, Diamond Cuts, is already an established business, and capable of functioning on its own; the larger company is expected to act as a business partner, bringing its own expertise and adding a little corporate muscle. Going into business with Diamond Cuts is not cheap, nor should it be, as Steve and Teri bring a great deal to the table. At the same time, a co-venture with such a company may be less risky for a large company than a less expensive deal with a beginning writer who has not yet learned to operate as an independent publisher. In the case of the latter, the entire burden of success lays on the bigger company.

For better or worse, the old-fashioned "publishing" deal—in which the songwriter received the "writer's share" of all income generated from his or her song and the publisher received the entire "publisher's share" of all income for that song—has largely disappeared. Most publishing deals today are "co-publishing" deals, which means that the writer receives 100 percent of the "writer's share" of income, but also a portion (usually 50 percent) of the publisher's monies. If that seems like a better deal for the writer, it is—but it also leads back to the original paradox: to get a publisher, you have to become a publisher.

Most publishers would prefer to split the income and enter into a co-venture with the writer's publishing company, rather than keep all the publishing income but then have to "create" a viable publishing business with a new songwriter, all on their own. Why? Because they hope that the songwriter's company will bring two important qualities to the business that a larger corporate entity cannot: an intimate knowledge of the catalog (no one knows your songs better than you) and a single-minded focus on pitching your songs (no one wants your songs placed more than you). In that sense, the effective, independent songwriter/publisher is aptly suited to the economic realities of most large music publishers.

A quick breakdown:

In most of the major publishing companies, there are somewhere between fifteen and thirty writers for each Professional Manager—those lucky souls who handle most of the day-to-day, songwriter-related duties at the company. This ratio is the result of simple economics: add up the costs of plush office space in Los Angeles, New York, and Nashville, plus administrative systems, payroll, those ever-popular expense accounts, and those whopping writer advances. Compare that to the amount of profit that one writer can generate—keeping in mind that out of ten writers, perhaps only five will be generating any profit at all—and you'll see that, in order to make money, the modern music publishing business requires a relatively large number of writers and a reasonably lean creative staff.

If we return to that figure of fifteen to thirty writers per professional manager, a little more math tells us that in a fictionally fair world, each writer could receive the undivided attention of the creative director for approximately twenty minutes a day. About long enough to play a song, make excuses for the demo, and hand over your lyric sheet and split letter. And that is very much a "best case" scenario.

From a corporation's standpoint, the advantage of going into business with a self-sufficient writer/publisher is obvious. Such a partnership allows a large company to affiliate with an ever-increasing number of writers, without significantly increasing the burden on their creative and administrative staff. The larger corporate entity can concentrate on those things at which it is most effective, while trusting that the writer's own publishing company is competently handling the day-to-day duties of developing the writer's career.

Let the whining begin:

"But being my own publisher will take time away from my writing . . . "

"I'm no good at being a salesman. I'm a creative type . . . "

"I don't have any industry contacts . . . "

"I need advance money . . . "

"Why should a writer sign with a publishing company if the writer is still expected to do all the work?"

Feel free to add more thoughts of your own. You see, if you bothered to read the author bio at the back of this book, you would know that I am not only a music publisher, which allows me to listen to the complaints of dozens of writers each week, but I was also once a songwriter. So I am intimately acquainted with all of your objections. I have used them myself. And now, drawing upon the wisdom of a twenty-year career in this business, I offer the following response:

Sorry. Life is not fair, and show biz is one of the least fair sectors of life. So there you go. If you like to wax nostalgic for a time when writers spent their time in solitude, quietly noodling away at their piano, while a fast-talking hustler with a heart of gold peddled their songs around town, I can only tell you that those days are gone. I suggest that you read biographies of songwriting legends Irving Berlin, Jerry Leiber and Mike Stoller, or Carole King—I suspect you'll find that those days never really existed at all. Successful songwriters have always been aggressive about getting their songs into the right hands, managing their career, and protecting their work. It was ever thus—and the sooner you accept that fact, the better. Smart businesspeople see the world not as it once was or as they might wish it would be, but as it really is.

Of course, there is some truth in the complaints I mentioned. Will being a publisher take time away from your writing? Yes. You will have to work harder. Aren't some creative people unsuited to "selling" their songs? Probably. But the number is far fewer than those who think they are unsuited to it. The publishing business is filled with former writers (David Renzer, the worldwide president of the Universal Music Publishing Group, for one). Creative genes and business genes are not as mutually exclusive as we like to think. Don't you need industry contacts to be successful? Yes. So you will make them. You didn't have any friends in high school until you went there. You will only make contacts in the industry when you decide to become an active part of the industry.

And what about money? Of course you need it. We all need it. Even the big corporate publishers need it. Which is why they probably won't give you any until you show that you're already earning some. And why should you do the publishers work for them? Because you're keeping half of their money. It's a co-pub deal, remember?

So let's get down to it. This book is not intended to be a comprehensive, technical how-to guide to starting your own publishing company. There are a number of those already on the market. Instead, it is an insider's view of the music publishing business, and offers practical tips toward helping you effectively assume a role as your own best publisher. While this book is clearly directed toward songwriters, I also believe that it can be useful to any music business entrepreneur: manager, club owner, DJ, producer, promoter, and independent label owner. Anyone who regularly comes in contact with new songs and new writers should consider establishing a music publishing enterprise. If done correctly, music publishing is a business that requires a relatively small upfront investment (no one's asking you to build a factory, after all) and offers a long-term business (think "Just the Way You Are" or "Misty") from which you can quietly collect income for many years to come.

Oh, and one more thing. For those readers who are old-fashioned enough to really love music, music publishing remains one of the few segments of the music industry still centered on "the song." Unlike the record business, in which most of the day can be spent mired in discussions about recording budgets, scheduling, tour support, radio promotion, distribution, retail space, you name it, music publishers actually get to spend a good part of their day listening to songs. For most of us who do this everyday, that's what keeps us in the business—a love of songs and songwriters, and an appreciation of the power of a truly great song. It's our job to make sure those songs have a chance to be heard. And now it's your job too.

Welcome to the party.

Acknowledgments

Special thanks to my editor Sue Gedutis, and to Debbie Cavalier and Steve Krampf for getting the ball rolling.

PART I

START ME UP:

GETTING INTO THE GAME

1

What Is Music Publishing, Anyway?

My family has a parlor game we like to play each Christmas. Picture the scene: Mom, Dad, Grandma, aunts and uncles, cousins and nephews, all gathered around the dining room table, as the annual holiday dinner begins. A moment of silence ensues, the joy of the season floods the room, and then it happens.

The Question.

"So Eric, tell us again. What is it that you *do* for a living?"

This has been going on for many, *many* years now. I've tried all the obvious explanations—company names, job title, reporting structure. It means nothing. I've tried analogies:

"A music publisher is to a songwriter what a book publisher is to an author."

"A music publisher is to a songwriter what an agent is to an actor."

Whatever. The truth is, to most of the world outside of the music industry—and a fair amount of the world inside the music industry—music publishing is a mystery.

This is not surprising. As proud as I am of my analogies, they're not all that accurate. Unlike a book publisher, a music publisher doesn't really manufacture anything; the music publisher owns the rights to the song, but not the CD on which the song is sold to the consumer. And unlike an agent with an actor, the publisher's real asset is the song, not the songwriter—a publisher owns the creation, not the creator. Confused? Yeah. You and the rest of my family.

So before you embark on your endeavor to become your own music publisher, a quick history lesson is probably in order.

In the beginning, there was The Copyright. The idea of copyright law in the United States dates all the way back to 1790 and applies to any number of media: books, photos, inventions, and yes indeed, songs. Copyright law dictates that if you create it, you own it—and anyone that wants to use it must gain permission from you. When a songwriter writes a song, that song (or copyright) belongs to him or her, and all rights to use the song will require the permission and presumably the financial compensation of the songwriter. This basic principle of the copyright has held up pretty well since the eighteenth century, although the dawn of the Internet and the phenomenon of file-sharing have put it under fire as never before. We can only hope that it manages to hang on for at least a little while longer. If it doesn't, you and I both have big problems.

But back to the songwriter and his or her copyright. Into this happy union of Creator and Creation steps the middleman—The Publisher. Of course, the publishing business as it pertains to books has a venerable history, dating all the way back to the creation of printing technology in the fifteenth century. With all due respect to the hardworking monks who were writing out music back in the Dark Ages, music publishing has its roots a bit later, around the nineteenth century, when songs began to appear for sale to consumers in the form of sheet music. Then as now, the transaction was relatively simple: in order to make his or her song commercially available to the consumer, a songwriter would assign the "rights" to a publisher, who would then print up the sheet music, sell it (we hope), and then share the money with the songwriter (we hope).

Obviously, the sheet music business continues to be a very viable business to the present day, and most of the large full-service publishers have such a division within their corporate structure. But I want to be very clear—the business of printing and selling sheet music is *not* the subject of this book. Not only do I know next to nothing about it, but what I do know would not lead me to suggest that a wise songwriter would try to act as his or her own sheet music publisher. Unless one really enjoys spending inordinate amounts of time at Kinko's, I think the job of printing up music and selling it is probably better left to the experts.

The subject of this book is contemporary music publishing, which is centered not around the sale of printed music, but on the sale or use of sound recordings. The process begins the same way—a songwriter creates a song (or copyright) and then grants the rights to a music publisher. But now, the music publisher issues a license to a record company, which allows the company to sell a sound recording of the song in return for the payment of a royalty to the publisher. And of course, the publisher then shares that income with the songwriter.

The royalty that is paid by the record company to the publisher and then to the songwriter is called a "mechanical" royalty, which refers to the fact that it comes from the sale of discs and tapes, which are mechanically generated recordings. Mechanical royalties are the primary source of income for most writers and publishers. But it is not the only form of income that the publisher derives from the copyright.

"Performance" royalties are payments made to the publisher by broadcasters, nightclub owners, department stores, you name it, in compensation for the licensing of public "performances " of the song. In short, this means that the songwriter receives a payment each time his or her song is played on the radio, television, in a concert hall, or even in a dentist's office. These payments are collected by the licensing organizations ASCAP, BMI, or SESAC, who then distribute the monies directly to writers and publishers based on the amount of use that any particular song has had (yes, they actually manage to keep track of that). Performance royalties are unique in that they are the only income that flows directly to the writer without going through the hands of the publisher first. Writers and publishers receive equal royalties—so that a song that generates $10,000 in royalties for the writer will also generate $10,000 for the publisher—but the money is distributed directly to each party by the performance rights organization.

"Synchronization" fees (or sync fees) are a rapidly growing piece of the economic pie for music publishers. The term refers to music that is "synchronized" with film, which is a fancy way of referring to songs that are used on television and in movies or advertisements. Unlike a mechanical royalty, which is a rate set by the US government, or a performance royalty, which again is a set amount determined by the performance society, sync fees are negotiable. Sync fees range from very low or gratis to the absurd. (Note to file: if you make a low-budget film, do not plan to use "Satisfaction" in the end credits.) In most cases, a publisher is responsible for negotiating sync fees with the film or television company; the publisher is also responsible for collecting the money and distributing a portion back to the songwriter. What I like best about syncs is that they can provide a significant source of income for types of music that do not necessarily sell large amounts of records. The electronica artist Moby licensed every one of the eighteen tracks on his album *Play* to various advertising campaigns or movies—and it was largely this exposure that drove the album to multi-platinum status in the United States.

In case your eyes are starting to glaze over at this point (which is usually what happens in my family at Christmas dinner), let's look at a simplified, almost-real-life example of the process in action:

The Creation

You, Talented Songwriter, have written a bonafide smash hit, touchingly titled "Your Copyright." At this point, you own the song and all the rights to it. But since you're only on the first chapter of this book, you're not quite sure how to properly publish the song. You need some help . . .

Enter Publisher.

Proving that you are not only talented, but also wise, you engage me, Music Industry Weasel, to publish "Your Copyright," thereby granting to me the rights to license your new ditty. To keep this simple, we will suppose that you have granted me 100 percent of the publishing rights.

Welcome to the record business.

Recognizing that "Your Copyright" is a song that will make an artist's career, a savvy record executive decides to record the song on an album by Soon-to-Be-Very-Famous Artist. I, as the song's publisher, gladly grant the license to the record company, and the song is released on the album. Of course, the song catapults STBVFA to fame, and the album sells (for the sake of easy mathematics) one million units.

What's in It for Us

The current full statutory rate for a mechanical license is 8 cents per song, so the calculator tells us that the gross income that will be paid to me by the record company (remember, I'm the publisher) is $80,000. Half of that amount ($40,000) is considered the "songwriter's share" of the income. I then send to you an accounting statement, which details the sales of the record and the money that was paid to me, along with a check for the appropriate amount. I keep the other half of the money, which represents the "publisher's share."

It gets better.

Everywhere you go, you can't help hearing "Your Copyright" on the radio. This generates performance income, tracked by ASCAP, BMI, or SESAC. Remember, this money is paid in equal shares directly to the writer and the publisher by the performance society. So one happy day, while you are opening your mailbox to find a check representing the writer's share of performance payments from ASCAP, BMI, or SESAC, I am receiving a matching check representing the publisher's share. Isn't this a good story?

And better . . .

"Your Copyright" is in the movies. Due to its now classic status, Hollywood Film Company wants to use the song as the theme of its big summer blockbuster. Again, as the publisher, it is up to me to negotiate the amount of the sync fee (think many 0s) and to collect the fee from Hollywood Film Company. And again, I will give you half of the money ("writer's share") and keep the other half ("publisher's share").

By now, it should be pretty obvious how a publishing company makes money. What may be less obvious is what a publisher is actually doing to earn that money, other than the vague "granting of licenses." What exactly does this "middleman" do to justify earning half the money generated by a song?

Plenty.

It is important to understand that the earlier example simply describes the flow of income from record company to publisher to songwriter. It does not describe the actual job of the music publisher, which is considerably more complex. There are five primary functions that are at the foundation of any effective music publishing operation, small or large:

- exploitation

- administration

- collection

- protection

- acquisition

Exploitation

In case you haven't noticed, songs do not generally find their own way onto record albums, into movies, or onto the radio. (Check those dusty tapes in your drawer for further proof of this.) For most songwriters, the primary value of a publisher is that they are an ally in the never-ending struggle to get songs heard.

Please understand, the word "exploitation" has no negative connotations to a music publisher or a professional songwriter. In fact, it's just about the sweetest word in the dictionary. It simply describes the process by which a song finds some avenue to its audience, where it can begin to earn income for everyone involved.

Perhaps it's because this is what I happen to do for a living, but I believe that exploitation is the most important function of a publisher, and probably the most difficult to accomplish. For that reason, this book will focus dispro-portionately on the various opportunities and strategies for placing your music in money-making situations. It does not diminish the importance of any other publishing function to note that without exploitation, the other roles of a publisher are irrelevant. If the proverbial tree falls in the forest when no one's around, does it make a sound? I don't know. But I do know that a song that sits in a drawer doesn't do much for anybody. A little exploitation never hurt.

In a large publishing company, the primary responsibility of exploitation will usually fall to what is termed the "Creative Department." These people, also referred to as professional managers or creative directors, are generally the ones stumbling into the office late, playing music loudly in their offices, running off to "pitch" meetings, or hanging out with the songwriters. It's a rough job, but someone has to do it.

Administration

This is the original function of the music publisher—the task of "administering" the copyrights. Simply put, this is the process of registering copyrights, issuing licenses, negotiating requests for reduced royalty rates, and sorting through the myriad of "paperwork" issues related to the use of copyrights.

As you'll see when we discuss this function in more detail, the administration of copyrights is a complex process that becomes more challenging as a publishing company grows. The more successful you are at exploitation, the more administration there is to be done. For this reason, many small publishing companies will do "administration" deals with a larger publisher. This sort of deal is generally a simple case of a smaller company shifting much of the paperwork burden to a larger firm. A large publisher might take on the responsibility of all administrative duties related to the smaller company's copyrights in exchange for a percentage (usually around 10 percent) of all the income generated by those songs.

It's never hard to locate the Administration Department in a music publishing company. Just follow the paper trail. When you find the offices with very large stacks of paper everywhere, you've entered the world of administration.

Collection

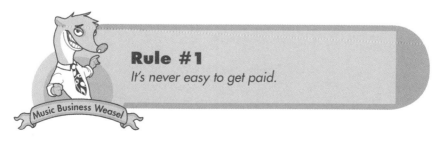

Rule #1
It's never easy to get paid.

Music Business Weasel

With songs potentially earning income in a vast variety of media, requiring royalty payments from any number of different record companies, sync fees from independent producers, film studios, and advertisers, and performance monies from licensing organizations all over the world, it can be more than a little daunting to keep track of who owes what, and where that money is supposed to go.

Needless to say, this is a key aspect of the music publishing business. Remember, the publisher collects *all* the income generated by a copyright (except for the writer's share of performance payments) and then distributes the appropriate percentage to the writer.

Any songwriter who's ever tried to decipher a royalty statement from a publisher will have some idea of the intricacies of this particular function. And any writer who has audited a publisher probably has some idea of how significantly small mistakes can add up.

In a large publishing concern, the task of collecting the money is usually split between the Administration Department and Royalties (or Accounting). Royalty statements are usually issued to writers twice yearly—and when that happy season rolls around, you can spot the Royalty Department by the bags beneath their bloodshot eyes. Or the line of expectant songwriters waiting outside their offices.

Protection

It's a jungle out there. Once you begin to understand the value of a copyright, which can generate income over many, many years, you begin to understand the need to protect that valuable product. The publisher is responsible not only for exploiting a copyright, but protecting it from unwanted exploitation (which is usually when there is no appropriate compensation). This means resolving issues related to reduced royalty rates, unauthorized use of the song, unauthorized alteration of the song, and percentages of ownership between co-writers or co-publishers.

As many writers have learned, protection is not just a matter of protecting your song from those who might wish to infringe (read: steal) it. The accusations can easily flow the opposite way, with other writers accusing you of "stealing" their song. In these cases, it is a publisher's job to protect you and your copyright—to negotiate a settlement, or, if necessary, to defend you in court.

With the prevalence of sampling, some large publishers have now gone to the extent of establishing a Sample Department, which includes expert listeners responsible for uncovering unauthorized "sampling" of their copyrights. Likewise, the creation of Web-based companies like Napster has required publishers to carefully monitor the Internet for copyright violations. These days, you gotta watch your back . . .

Acquisition

You also have to look ahead. An effective publisher is always scouting for new copyrights and new writers, in an effort to keep up with the ever-changing tastes of the listening public. This function requires several skills from a publisher: the ability to accurately evaluate the skill of a developing songwriter or the commercial potential of a particular song; the savvy to know at what price new music can be acquired; and the persuasiveness to convince a songwriter to turn over his beloved copyrights.

Acquisition is usually a function of the Creative Department; it's a job that is at once the most tedious role in the publishing company, and the most thrilling. It means listening to a ceaseless supply of demo tapes (mostly bad), spending long evenings in dingy clubs (mostly smoky and loud), and poring through pages of industry trade magazines (that every week tout the Next Big Thing, which almost never is). It also means every once in a while finding an undiscovered song or songwriter that is truly unique or special—the rough equivalent of a very small needle in a very large haystack. The excitement of hearing a *hit* before anyone else, and having an opportunity to play a part in bringing that song into the world, is what keeps most of us in the business of music publishing.

Exploitation, administration, collection, protection, and acquisition. If you're a songwriter, I know what you're thinking. "What about that part that I like best? The part where publishers pay writers money they haven't earned yet . . . "

Ah, yes. The writer advance. While it is not one of the primary functions of a music publisher, the role of Songwriters Central Savings and Loan is one that has come to define the publishing business, particularly with respect to the very large corporations that dominate the modern music publishing industry. For many songwriters, the music publisher is perceived primarily as a bank, willing to loan money in the form of "advances," which will then be repaid to the publisher from the songwriter's future earnings. Here's how it works:

When seeking to acquire a desirable copyright, or to sign a promising writer to an exclusive publishing agreement (which simply means that the publisher is acquiring rights to all of the writer's copyrights for a set period of time), a publisher frequently finds that personal charm, vague promises of stardom, and a couple of pricey lunches are not enough to close the deal.

In order to convince the songwriter to grant the publisher the rights to the desired copyrights, the publisher must also fork up some cash.

As with almost everything in show business, the amount of the advance paid to a songwriter can vary wildly, from the paltry for a young, unproven writer, to the astronomical, for an established hit-maker or the hot new buzz band. In addition, a publisher may also agree to pay for other items, such as demo recording costs, travel, or equipment rentals; this will usually be labeled an "additional advance." But whatever the amount, a songwriter should remember that any advance is always recoupable. This means that the writer will not be paid a percentage of the income generated by his or her copyrights until the publisher has recovered the amount of the advance. An advance is not a wage or a fee paid to the writer; it is an interest-free loan against future earnings.

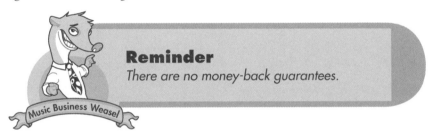

Reminder
There are no money-back guarantees.

Music Business Weasel

A publisher must remember that an advance can only be recouped from future earnings—it will not be repaid by a writer whose songs fail to earn back the amount of the advance. If you're going to be in the banking business, then bankers rules apply—make your loans only to those people you are pretty sure can pay them back. The amount of an advance should reflect what you believe a writer, under reasonable circumstances, can earn from his or her songs. The advance should not be based on how badly you want to sign the writer, or what the writer needs, or what others in the industry would pay the writer. Because of their financial structure, large publishers can sometimes offer an advance that far exceeds what they believe a writer can actually earn. But if you are playing with your own money, prudence is always the better part of valor.

While it is not an integral part of the music publishing business, the writing of an advance check has become such an important part of the publisher's role that we could probably add one more function to the Big Five—let's call it **capitalization**. By advancing money on future earnings, a publisher is giving the writer the money he or she needs to survive and grow the business as they feel necessary. In this book, we will not devote a great deal of space to this particular function, as I doubt most readers are eager to begin handing out thousands of dollars in advances to their songwriting cronies. Nevertheless, it is important to understand that it is a strategy employed aggressively by all of the major publishers. It is also important to understand how you and your fledgling publishing business may someday be able to obtain access to that capital from a larger company wishing to enter into a partnership with you.

Pennies from Heaven

Given the music publisher's role as a middleman in the process of turning a song into a record, music publishing exists somewhat in the shadows of the music industry. And yet, the music publishing divisions of the major music corporations are often much more profitable than their flashier, more media-friendly record label cohorts. In the fiscal year 2001–2002, EMI Music Publishing chipped in 57 percent of the parent company EMI Group's total operating profit—the publishing unit's operating margins were nearly three times that of EMI Recorded Music (the record label).

Sometimes ridiculed as a "pennies" business, publishing is a testament to the truth that pennies add up—if properly cared for, a classic song can continue to generate many pennies worth of income year after profitable year. As the amount of media opportunities for music exploitation continues to increase (think about those 100 channels on your cable box and all the songs that can go on those networks), music publishing is a consistently growing business, with 2001 revenues of $3.5 billion, up from $3.37 billion the year before.[1] While it may not get you the front-row seats at MTV's Video Music Awards, success as a music publisher can nevertheless be highly rewarding. Ask Berry Gordy, the legendary founder of Motown, who sold 50 percent of his publishing entity, Jobete Music, to EMI Publishing in 1997 for over $132 million. Or Herb Alpert and Jerry Moss, who sold Almo/Irving/Rondor Music to Universal Music for over $250 million. And remember, these companies were started by individual entrepreneurs—songwriters who were prescient enough to be their own publisher and build those copyrights into empires.

Now if you can explain all that to my grandmother, you're invited over for Christmas dinner.

---

[1] From *Music and Copyright Industry Newsletter* by Phil Hardy/quoted in *Financial Times*, June 18, 2002

2

It All Starts with the Song: Evaluating Your Catalog

Every great endeavor has to begin somewhere, and if you're going to launch your own music publishing venture, there's really only one thing that will get you started . . .

Songs. You need songs. Preferably good ones, and ideally, a healthy number of them. Because whatever you've got at the moment in that drawer, on your hard drive, or on those DATs, is your catalog. The first step toward becoming your own publisher is to come to grips with what will be the primary assets of your company. Songs.

As I mentioned in chapter 1, this book will be directed primarily toward songwriters interested in developing their own publishing company. So I will assume that you already have a collection of songs sufficient to get you started in this game. However, if you are not a songwriter, you may want to skip way ahead to chapter 24, "Acquisitions." But make sure that you come back to this chapter, because taking stock of your catalog is never quite as simple as it seems.

Ask yourself a few questions:

Do you own the songs?

Of course you do. You wrote them, right? If you write a song, you own that copyright, both the writer's share and the publisher's share. You are not only the writer—you are also the publisher. Unless you co-wrote the song . . .

That gets a little trickier. If you wrote the song with someone else, you now own a portion of the song, which leads to a whole new set of questions:

What percentage of the song did you write?

Many songwriters assume that this is a matter of simple arithmetic: divide 100 percent of the song by the number of writers involved. That is to say, if there are two writers, each gets 50 percent of the song; if there are three, each of them gets one-third. Nice, tidy, and egalitarian. But not very realistic.

Imagine that you wrote a song with the guy who has the recording studio next door. You wrote all of the lyrics and three quarters of the music. Your friendly neighbor programmed the drums and contributed a chord progression that eventually became the bridge of the song. Is your neighbor entitled to half of the song?

Maybe. When I was a writer, I always felt that it was best to simply stick with the easy formula and split everything equally (probably because it was the only way I could manage the math). But many writers would disagree, particularly in an instance as one-sided as the one above. There are many factors that could figure into this, including whether the lyrics and music were written after the drums were programmed (and thus presumably inspired by them), the prominence of the bridge section, and the amount of guidance, suggestions, or hand-holding the co-writer provided while you were coming up with the bulk of the song. You should probably also consider the place of the co-writer in the music industry food chain. If he or she is a big fish (are there a lot of very shiny plaques on the studio wall?), or at least a bigger fish than you, I guarantee that the co-writer is expecting at least half of the song.

Writer splits is a touchy subject, and rarely as straightforward as it might appear. The hard truth is that the percentages on a song are entirely negotiable. I know of one writer who received just 8 percent of a song, which is about the lowest percentage I've ever heard of. Imagine how that writer felt when the song became a hit (which it did). The only way to deal with this issue is through an open and frank dialogue with your co-writer—sounds like marriage counseling, right? You must somehow, some way reach an agreement as to what percentage of the composition is owned by each writer.

Then you *must* get it in writing in a "split letter." A split letter is a simple document that outlines the basic agreement between the writers regarding the ownership of the composition. It should document the date the song was written, the writers involved, and the percentages controlled by each writer and publisher. It must be signed by each writer; each writer and publisher should maintain a copy. (You can find one version of a split letter on page 15.) The verbiage of the letter can vary, so long as it clearly states the correct shares of the song. The crucial point is that it must be signed by all writers, and you must keep a copy of it on file.

If you do not have split letters for the songs in your catalog, you need to go back and get them. Yes, I'm aware that you and your co-writers are friends, and that you're all pretty laid back about this, and that this seems a little awkward, and you're sure everyone will be cool about it if something happens with the song. Trust me on this. I have seen twenty-year partnerships dissolve over petty split disputes. I have also learned that split discussions never become disputes until something good is about to happen with a song. The best time to have a discussion about percentages is before or during the writing session itself; the second-best time is immediately afterward. The single worst time to have the conversation is when it absolutely cannot be avoided, which is when someone is about to record the song. The first step toward organizing your catalog is determining exactly what percentage of each song belongs to you as a writer.

What percentage of the song do you publish?

Didn't we just talk about this? If you wrote 50 percent of the song, then you control your 50 percent of the publisher's share, right? Maybe. Let's go back to that hypothetical co-write with your neighbor. Was that co-write suggested or arranged by another publisher? If so, that publisher may expect a percentage of the publishing for anything written during those sessions. And what about your neighbor's recording studio? If he demoed the song at his studio, at his cost, then he may be expecting a greater portion of the publishing in return.

Or let's look at this from your side. Here you are, preparing to become your own publisher—ready to hit the streets peddling this new song like a professional, while your co-writer retires to the quiet privacy of his studio. Suppose you manage to place this song on a record or in a movie. Perhaps you should be asking to co-publish your neighbor's share of the publishing (this would give you 75 percent of the publisher's share of the song). Come to think of it, that's a pretty good idea. Keep that one in mind.

Again, it is important that you never assume that you know the splits on a song, whether it concerns the writer's share or the publisher's share. I would never encourage you to try to take unfair advantage of a co-writer. That is a surefire strategy for a very short career. Nor would I suggest that you give up your own share of the publishing without reason. But song splits are always subject to negotiation, and you should not be hesitant about broaching the subject. Be sure that the publisher's share, as well as the writer's share, is clearly delineated in the split letter. There is an example of a split letter on the next page.

Songwriter Split Letter

Date:

To Whom It May Concern:

This is to confirm that we are the sole writers of the composition listed below (the "Composition") and hereby agree between and among ourselves to the following writers' and publishers' divisions:

SONG TITLE: _____ _____

WRITERS	WRITERS SPLIT %	PUBLISHERS	PUB SPLIT %

Month/Year in which creation of this work was completed: _____

(month/year)

If any samples are contained in the Composition for which the sampled writer(s) / publisher(s) are to receive a copyright interest in the Composition and/or income attributable to the Composition, then we agree that: (circle one of the following)

all of the above shares shall be reduced proportionately, or

the shares of _____ only will be reduced proportionately.

The following list of samples represent all of those samples which are embodied in the above composition:

SAMPLE TITLE	SAMPLE ARTIST/WRITER	SAMPLE PUBLISHER	SAMPLE LABEL

Your signature below will indicate your agreement of the above.

READ AND AGREED:_____ _____ _____

Name: _____   Name: _____

Signature: _____   Signature: _____

Are you sure that you own the songs?

Let's dig a little deeper. If you wrote the songs by yourself, was there anyone else in the room at the time, perhaps engineering or helping program the track? While you may be quite confident that their input wasn't really part of the writing process, they may be less sure.

How about samples? In many instances, clearing one well-known sample from a major artist can require giving up 75 percent or more, sometimes even 100 percent, of the new copyright. This is not necessarily an argument against sampling, which is simply a part of the modern songwriting landscape. Nor would I necessarily say that you need to clear all samples immediately—generally speaking, you can clear a sample once your song is slated to be released commercially. But be aware that if you've stuck a nice big chunk of a James Brown classic into your "new" song, you own a lot less of that song than you think you do. You might not own any of it at all.

And then of course, there's every songwriter's worst nightmare. "Does this song sound like something familiar to you?" The subject of copyright infringement generally conjures up an image of nefarious behavior, a scoundrel listening through the keyhole as you compose your masterpiece, only to steal it out from under you. In my experience, most copyright infringement cases in the songwriting business are entirely subliminal—a matter of a writer unknowingly reprising a song lodged somewhere in his or her subconscious. It happens.

I know of one songwriter who waited years for a breakthrough hit, finally finding himself with a potential #1 record. On the day that the song hit the top of *Billboard's* Hot 100, he received a call. He was being sued for copyright infringement by a superstar artist, who not coincidentally happened to be the writer's childhood idol. Of course, the writer had spent a lifetime absorbing this superstar's music, listening until he knew each song by heart. Unfortunately, he didn't recognize until that moment that he had just rewritten one of his hero's classic songs. This is to be avoided.

While you can never entirely safeguard yourself against copyright ownership issues, it is essential that in your role as publisher, you try to loosen some of the personal attachment you have to the songs in your catalog and examine any concerns carefully. This is particularly true as it pertains to infringement issues. Don't fool yourself. If something sounds like it might be a problem, it probably is. Many copyright issues can be resolved through negotiation, but you must deal with them sooner rather than later. It's all part of understanding your catalog.

If it seems like I'm harping a bit on this issue of copyright ownership, that's because I am. I've had the experience of working with a large catalog of songs, in which there are constant questions about writer and publisher percentages. I also know from experience that nothing quite makes your day like placing a song on a record, only to find that you don't own the song at all. In the best cases, you will have just done someone a big favor, which will earn you some good karma but not much else. In the worst cases, you will damage your relationship with the record company to whom you pitched the song, and you could find yourself in court with the song's real publisher. This is a business, and the first order of the day is to know exactly what you've got to sell.

Of course, there's more to understanding your catalog than just the question of ownership. The other question that comes immediately to mind is:

Are these songs any good?

Ouch. That cuts a little close to the bone, especially if you wrote the songs. But if the first thing you must establish as a publisher is *ownership* of your catalog, then certainly the second thing is *objectivity* about your catalog. Perhaps the greatest benefit to becoming your own publisher is to acquire some degree of objectivity about your own work, and for a few moments at least, be able to stand on the outside of the writing process and make judgments regarding how your songs will actually function in the industry.

When I first made the transition from writer to publisher, the one question I heard over and over from my songwriter buddies was, "So what's it like on the other side of the desk?" The answer was that I could now see much more clearly how rare a real "hit" song really is. Most writers will write hundreds of songs in their lifetime, and if they write three or four genuine "hits" in that catalog, they probably belong in the Hall of Fame. Of course, writers don't usually think about this—if they did, they'd have a hard time getting out of bed every morning, much less writing a song. But when you become a publisher, you know the truth.

The truth is this: the catalog of any successful songwriter or publisher is inevitably a mixture of about 5 percent genuine, grade-A "Hits"; 45 percent "Good, Not Great" songs, and 50 percent "Misses." If you've written fifty songs and you think you have five or ten hits, you're fooling yourself. Remember, the goal here is *objectivity*.

Success in the publishing business depends largely on learning to maximize the value of not just the top 5 percent, but also the 45 percent of the songs that lie in the middle ground. As for the 50 percent of the songs that just plain miss their mark—there's not much you can do with those. Those songs are why every publisher needs plenty of big, empty file drawers in their office.

Let's take a good objective look at the catalog you're working with.

The Top Drawer

Can you spot the "hits"? Let's hope so. A hit song is a hard thing to define, but if nothing else, it should be obvious enough to stand out amidst the other songs in the catalog. The actual science of what makes a song a hit is something that we'll discuss at length later on in this book—for now, we'll stick with the basics. If you're a performer, what song do you open or close with? Which one can silence a noisy audience? Which one do people request? If you had an opportunity to play one song for someone who could truly make a difference in your career, which song would you play? Those songs are your hits.

Is this a difficult choice? If it is, then chances are, you don't really have any hits in your catalog. Fine. Remember, the objective here is to be objective. Frankly, if you are a relatively new writer, you probably don't have a hit song in your catalog—yet. Focus instead on those three or four songs that you think are the strongest, that best represent what you do. Those songs go in your top drawer.

The Middle Drawer

Now think about the next category: Good, Not Great. These songs are your real challenge as a publisher—in order to have significant success, you need to learn to get the B-level songs in situations where they can generate income. They may never become hits (although with a little luck and timing it can happen), but they can make it onto records and television shows, and into advertisements. As you narrow down the songs that fit into this category, here are a few things to consider:

Tempo

As a general rule, up-tempo songs are always more viable than ballads. Think about it—every album has ten to twelve songs, out of which perhaps three or four are ballads. Every radio station plays at least three or four up-tempo songs for every ballad. Consequently, most labels release two or three up-tempo singles off any album, and only one ballad. If your catalog is made up predominately of brooding, down-tempo material, the numbers are stacked against you.

When you get into the world of television, movies, and advertising, the advantage for up-tempo songs becomes even more pronounced. Action sequences, montages, and comedic scenes all require up-tempo material. In many instances, tempo can become the primary concern for directors and music supervisors.

One of the first steps in assessing your catalog should be to take note of all the up-tempo material, particularly songs that are 116 beats per minute or above. In most cases, an up-tempo song is defined not by the number of beats per minute so much as by its aggressive, rhythmic feel. This is especially true of urban material, where even the most up-tempo track rarely gets above 100 bpm. But songs that are in the 116 bpm and faster category are rare, and can be very useful in instances where the need for tempo is of utmost importance. Unless the song is very weak, anything in that tempo category should probably go in the middle drawer.

Lyrics

Any lyric that breaks a bit from the typical love song mold should also be a part of your active catalog. Songs with inspirational lyrics (think "From a Distance" or "I Believe I Can Fly"), controversial lyrics ("No Scrubs"), or even just silly, non-romantic party lyrics ("Who Let the Dogs Out") tend to stand out in a sea of songs about lost loves and broken hearts. Moreover, they are vastly more appealing to music supervisors and advertising agencies. You need some of these to work with.

Demo Quality

The production quality of a song demo is always a factor in assessing a song's value to the catalog. While you should avoid judging a song by its demo, you do have to be aware that it's easier to get a cut with a record quality demo than with a homemade piano/vocal track. This is especially true when it comes to pitching songs for television projects, where you can often get a great sounding demo placed directly in the show (which means you collect the master license fee, in addition to the publishing sync fee).

The Bottom Drawer

What about those songs that haven't quite found their way into either the "Hits" category, or the lesser but still honorable "Good, Not Great" category? How about that cathartic, five-minute, intensely personal ballad that you never had a chance to properly demo but that still means so much to you? Sorry. The good news is, I'm not telling you to throw it out.

I am telling you to put it in the bottom drawer. Regardless of how special the song is to you, it is part of your inactive catalog—and you probably won't need to get at it very often. I know this hurts, but take solace in the fact that every writer has "misses," and many of the songs in that category are some of the songwriter's personal favorites. But now we are thinking like publishers, and, for better or worse, those lengthy, introspective, personal musical statements simply aren't very useful to us. To call something a "miss" as opposed to a hit is not an artistic judgment; it is a commercial one. Publishing, after all, is a commercial business. To be effective, you need to invest your efforts in those songs most likely to yield a return.

Still, hope springs eternal. This is why you never throw a song away (that's a writer's role, not a publisher's). While the bottom drawer is not choice real estate, it isn't equivalent to being tossed out into the street either. Periodically review this part of your catalog, as you may find that you've judged some songs too harshly, or that the musical fashion has changed and something once hopelessly dated is now back in vogue.

More importantly, you will have instances where that song at the back of the drawer is the ideal pitch for a very specialized project. I can recall pitching songs for an advertising project in which the crucial selling point was the presence of the word "smile" in the song's chorus. When you get those sorts of calls, you need all the catalog you can get your hands on, and that bottom drawer can take on a new allure.

Can you find the songs?

As you begin this process of carefully sifting through each song in your catalog, you may already be noticing the third quality that you as a publisher must bring to bear on the stack of music in front of you: After ownership and objectivity, you must establish *order*.

There is a mysterious but irrefutable sociological characteristic of songwriters that I have been studying for some time now. I first noticed it in myself, back in my halcyon days, and have since noted it among an overwhelming majority of the writers with whom I work. Songwriters never label anything.

Don't ask me why. When I was a writer, I had hundreds of DATs, most of them with only vague scribbled notes on the J-card to indicate what material they might actually contain. I would spend the first hour of every day just trying to find the track on which I was supposed to be working. When I became a publisher, I quickly learned that it's not just me. Inevitably, writers come to meet with me, bringing a stack of unmarked CDs. This means we spend the bulk of our meeting skipping through track after track, looking for the one song they just know I'm gonna love. If only we could find it. Frighteningly, writer/producers are the least likely to label anything—and these are the folks who handle master recordings, rather than just demos.

As a songwriter, how would you feel if every time you called your publisher about a specific song, he spent fifteen minutes looking through his desk: "Umm, here it is . . . no, wait, maybe under here . . . I know I've got it somewhere, just hang on . . . are you sure you sent it to me?"

You see what I mean. What may be a mere eccentricity in a songwriter is something more problematic in a publisher. It is incompetence. Now that you are joining the publishing ranks, order is in fact the order of the day. So grab a Sharpie, or print up some labels, or start a file in your computer, whatever suits you. Because we are about to get organized.

There is a myriad of ways to organize your catalog, ranging from a file drawer and some index cards, to MP3 libraries and office systems like Filemaker—we'll discuss these in more detail in chapter 8. For now, let's make it easy. Each CD, DAT, or song file needs to be properly identified. How you choose to go about this is up to you—if you can't think of anything better, you could try starting an old-fashioned file, and filling out a song submittal form like the one in chapter 8 for each song. This requires the following information:

- title

- writers

- publishers

- date written and/or recorded

- studio

- engineer

- status—is this a master, a rough mix, a work tape?

- any relevant software information—Pro Tools, Logic, etc.

If this feels like overkill, it probably is. But when you get to the chapter about lawsuits, particularly relating to ownership of the copyright, you'll understand why it's helpful to have a record of dates, studios, and engineers for each song. If this seems like a lot of paperwork, you're right. That's what publishing is.

In case you've missed it, the point of our whole discussion of catalog comes down to this: if music publishing is your business, then songs are your assets. Yes, they are works of art, and a means of personal expression, and entertainment, and a magical means of communication across social barriers that can make the whole world sing. But to a publisher, they are assets—not unlike inventory to a store, or airplanes to an airline. And if that's the case, then they should be treated with care. You must know what songs you have *ownership* in and how much of them you own. You must bring some *objectivity* to the management of your catalog. And you must establish *order* within that catalog, so that each song is properly identified, easily accessible, and part of a coherent cataloguing system.

It's a little like cleaning your apartment. Inevitably, you find a few things that you didn't remember you had and a few things that aren't yours at all. You realize that some of your stuff is a lot more valuable than other stuff. Eventually, you get enough things stacked on the shelves or packed into drawers that you can actually find what you need when you need it.

Don't it feel good?

The "F" Word: Focus

There's one more quality that you need to bring to bear on your catalog: *focus*. It's so important that it gets its own chapter.

For some writers, artists, publishers, or entrepreneurs in the music business, the decision to focus their career on a particular genre or subgenre of music is one they hardly remember making. There may be only one style of music with which they really identify, or in which they feel their talent can fit. In many ways, these are the lucky ones. They are specialists without ever having chosen to be so. This doesn't necessarily mean that they don't understand or enjoy music outside of the genre in which they work—but it does mean that they don't feel compelled to personally create or sell *every* type of music that they enjoy.

And then there are the generalists—blessed with a vast range of musical interests and a confidence to match, sure that their career should encompass everything from jazz to hip-hop, with some country songs and a bit of chamber music just to keep life interesting. You don't need to go very far into a conversation to recognize a generalist . . .

Music Business Weasel: "So, tell me, what sort of music do you write?"

Songwriter: "Oh, geez . . . that's a tough one, you know. I mean . . . I can write everything."

Uh-oh. First off, let's get real. Nobody can write "everything." Nobody. Except maybe Prince (or whatever he's called this week). But even the versatility of someone like Prince is based more on his ability to adapt or arrange his songs in a variety of styles, rather than actually altering his own songwriting approach. The song can be put in a number of different contexts—pop, rock, dance, r&b—but it is clearly still a "Prince" song, written in his idiosyncratic style. The same is true of Diane Warren. While she has had hits in virtually every genre, most of these songs are essentially "Diane Warren"-style songs, adapted to fit different markets.

One other thing to notice about Prince and Diane Warren. They didn't start out that way. In the early years of his career, Prince was very much a part of the Minneapolis school of r&b, which he in large part created, but which later included Morris Day and The Time, and of course, Jimmy Jam and Terry Lewis. It was only after he achieved superstar status that he began to branch out into more experimental rock and jazz areas. Everybody comes from somewhere; nobody comes from everywhere. You cannot lay a foundation for your publishing company with a catalog that does "everything."

I once heard Monica Lynch, the former president of Tommy Boy Records and a very savvy music business executive, make this point in a forum attended primarily by developing writers and artists. She simply said that she was not interested in meeting with anyone that claimed they could do "everything." This was not well received. A murmur passed through the audience. How dare she seek to limit their creativity, or impose boundaries on their wide-ranging musical tastes? Isn't that exactly what's wrong with the music industry, with its focus on markets, and formats, and target audiences, yada yada yada?

For whatever reason, many musicians, writers, and artists take a misplaced pride in their own versatility. They are so sure that they can play any type of music, sing any song, write in any style, or record an album that covers the entire range of American popular music, that they miss one important thing:

It doesn't matter. No one cares.

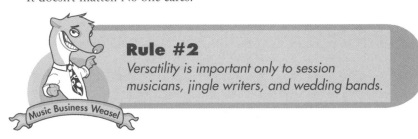

Rule #2

Versatility is important only to session musicians, jingle writers, and wedding bands.

Music Business Weasel

Everybody else needs to **focus**.

What does focus mean to a publisher? It means that as a start-up publishing company, your catalog should be made up primarily of songs in one particular musical genre. This is your focus. A catalog spread over two styles is workable, if the two styles are at least somewhat compatible—for instance, country and pop would be a better combination than country and techno. Within that stylistic focus, variety is both necessary and desirable. You need a selection of songs: up-tempos, ballads, mid-tempos, male songs, female songs, group songs. The idea here is not to limit anyone's creativity—the idea is to harness that creativity and direct it down one specific path.

Of course, there will always be some songs that just fall outside any of your usual musical boundaries. Fine. Have fun with them. The idea of focus in business is no different than the idea of focusing your eye—the point is not to eliminate everything else from your view but simply to direct your eye toward the most important thing. Experimentation is essential and can sometimes lead to the discovery of a new focus, more viable than the previous one. Fine again. Then change your focus—but don't lose it. If someone asks what sort of music you publish and it takes you more than twenty seconds to answer—reread everything I just said. And then continue.

Three Things That Focus Will Do

It will give your publishing catalog an **identity**. Any business, in any industry, needs to establish some sort of identity in the minds of its customers. Call it branding or image building or whatever you like—the fundamental objective is to give your company a specific presence in a crowded marketplace. There is probably no more crowded marketplace than that of the contemporary music industry, with hundreds of established songwriters and publishers, not to mention thousands of mostly unknown companies, all vying for the same opportunities. Why does an A&R person need to speak to you?

When our friend the Music Business Weasel makes the standard inquiry, "What sort of music do you handle?" this is what he or she is really asking, in his or her own moderately polite way: "Who are you?" "Why should I speak with you?" "Do you have anything I need?" If the weasel's opening gambit confounds you, or if you chirpily reply that you handle "everything"(which isn't really much different than not responding at all), you have lost the opportunity to answer these questions. You will probably not get another chance.

Because the music publishing business is not oriented toward the general consumer, but rather to other industry professionals, it is not a business in which massive marketing campaigns are a primary means of establishing a brand identity. Rather, music companies are defined first and foremost by the sort of music that they sell—and the more specific the musical direction, the stronger the image that they can establish in the industry.

Versatility is not a highly valued skill in the commercial music business, which is a specialized business that rewards specialists, not generalists. When you are dealing with an A&R person or a music supervisor, they want to believe that you have a particular expertise that you are selling them, just as they consider themselves experts in their particular field of music. If they inquire about your catalog, and you reply that you specialize primarily in Southern hip-hop, or progressive house, or Christian metal, you have immediately given your company an identity in their mind. Likewise, you have established yourself as having some particular expertise.

But what if the A&R person is looking for Southern hip-hop and you tell them that you handle Christian metal? Isn't that going to turn them off? Sure it will. Having an identity means turning some people off. Sometimes it means turning a lot of people off. This is the same thing that gives you credibility with the people in your genre. A Christian metal band that tried to sideline as a Dirty South rap act would not reach a wider audience; they would alienate their core audience.

My wife happens to work in the luxury retail business, which is to say that she sells ridiculously expensive items to people with more dollars than sense. In her world, 97 percent of the general population falls into the category of "not our customer." Trust me, no one is losing any sleep over that 97 percent. They are busy worrying about maintaining their brand's credibility with the other 3 percent who matter to them. You should be doing the same.

One more thing. You will find that very few music business professionals are put off by learning that you don't handle the sort of music they are looking for. Instead, they recognize that they are talking to another professional who has the discipline and good judgment to stick with what he or she does best. If what you do doesn't fit what they need, most people in the industry will try to lead you in the direction of the person who would be your customer—whether it's putting you in touch with the appropriate A&R person in their company, or a project that they've heard about, or a friend of a friend who might be helpful. If your company has a clear direction, there is at least a chance that they can help you down the path. If you're going everywhere at once, no one can show you the way. And no one will try.

Which leads to the next thing that focus will do. It will give you a **community**. No man is an island. If it takes a village to raise a child, it takes a whole town to make a business. Ask any neighborhood bodega owner—if you wanna be in business, you gotta be part of the community.

Probably because we spent too many of our formative years locked away in solitude—listening to records, practicing our instrument, penning heart-wrenching poems of love and longing—most musicians and songwriters tend to be loners. Now that you're a publisher, it's time to become a team player. If you're wondering who your team is, a little focus will bring them into view…

By establishing a clear stylistic direction for your company, you become a part of that particular musical community, with other musicians, writers, artists, publishers, press, fans, promoters, radio programmers, and anyone else who shares a similar direction. This has been a constant theme in the history of American pop music—a musical community gives birth to a specific style, which, as it catches fire, brings to prominence a whole group of related artists, writers, producers, and companies. Think of the Memphis rockabilly community that spawned Elvis, Jerry Lee Lewis, and Johnny Cash; the Detroit scene that led to Motown; or the Seattle rock scene that spawned Nirvana and Pearl Jam. Think of the Brill Building, the Sound of Philadelphia, or West Coast rap. Most recently, consider the Swedish pop community that fueled the rise of the Backstreet Boys, Britney Spears, and NSYNC. Artists, writers, and companies do not develop in isolation—they grow in clusters, supporting, competing, and learning from each other. But until you focus your business on one particular musical territory, you will find yourself in no man's land—never really at home anywhere.

When I first moved to New York in the 1980s to become a songwriter and producer, I had the good fortune to come into contact with a small group of other songwriters who were also in the process of launching their careers—the group included Alexandra Forbes ("Don't Rush Me" for Taylor Dayne), Shelly Peiken ("Bitch" for Meredith Brooks, "What a Girl Wants" for Christina Aguilera), Jeff Franzel (Shawn Colvin, NSYNC), and Barbara Jordan (former Berklee faculty and president of Heavy Hitters Publishing). While none of us were exactly the same in our musical style, we were all oriented primarily toward writing the sort of mainstream pop material in vogue at that time.

We initially got to know each other through what we called "song parties," at which we would meet to trade leads about who was looking for material, listen to and critique each other's new material, and, of course, trade industry gossip and horror stories. These get-togethers inevitably led to collaborations and friendships, and an ever-expanding network of other writers, musicians, demo singers, engineers, and record executives.

Before long, a fledgling musical community was thriving. If there was an A&R person that I hadn't yet met, inevitably an introduction would come through someone else in our group; if someone else needed a recommendation for a demo singer, or a musician, I might be able to provide one. This is what friends do.

Of course, we were also competitors—all chasing after the same cuts, working on the same projects, and cultivating relationships with the same industry contacts. This is what businesses do—they compete, openly and without apology. And this too is a benefit of being part of a community— competition inevitably makes everyone raise the level of their game.

As any good capitalist knows, healthy competition breeds innovation, better service, and a rising standard of quality. A lack of competition creates

Amtrak and your cable company. Describing the atmosphere working for Don Kirshner in the heyday of the Brill Building, Barry Mann says:

> It was insane. Cynthia and I would be in this tiny cubicle, about the size of a closet, with just a piano and a chair; no window or anything. We'd go in every morning and write songs all day. In the next room Carole [King] and Gerry [Goffin] would be doing the same thing, and in the next room after that Neil [Sedaka] or somebody else. Sometimes when we all got to banging on our pianos you couldn't tell who was playing what. Kirshner was like a father figure to us all. Everyone's first thought, as we sweated over our battered old pianos, was whether Donny would be pleased. The competition, and the pressure, I suppose brought out the best in us.[1]

It's easy to see the same atmosphere within many of the hot hip-hop production companies, like Bad Boy or Murder Inc., in which the competition within the company and the competition with each other continues to push the producers, writers, and artists to be aggressive and innovative. It all starts with defining the musical boundaries of what you do—finding a place you and your business can call home.

But it goes even further. Once you've established an identity for your company, and have become part of a musical community that can help to support and nurture your work, you still need to come up with a realistic plan of attack. Focus is also the key element to developing a **strategy** for your business. We're in Business Management 101 here, and if you've been at this for any length of time, you've probably already noticed a basic principle in action: Until you can clarify exactly what you are trying to accomplish, it is very difficult to figure out how you're going to do it.

You will never know every A&R person at every label, or every music supervisor, or every artist manager. The great news is, you don't need to. As soon as you focus your efforts on one particular segment of the music industry, you only need to know those people who are relevant to what you do. This is a lot easier. You now have an area of expertise, and your role is to make sure that you are fully versed in that particular genre—which means knowing the important players in the game, reading the relevant trade magazines, attending the important conventions, knowing the hot records, as well as the up-and-coming artists and producers, and staying on top of the emerging trends.

It also means studying and understanding the business strategies that have worked or might work in your field. For instance, pitching songs with a simple piano/vocal demo is probably a somewhat viable strategy in the adult contemporary market. In the world of trance music, it's ridiculous. Some

---

[1] *Rolling Stone Illustrated History of Rock 'n' Roll*, "Brill Building Pop" by Greg Shaw

markets, particularly urban music, develop material primarily through a wide variety of writer/producers or production companies. The country market, by contrast, has only a handful of producers that dominate the market, and most of those producers are not writers. By defining the nature of your catalog, you immediately begin to clarify the strategic options that can work for your business.

In subsequent chapters, we will discuss business strategies in more detail, as well as the benefits to developing a business plan for your company. But the planning cannot start until you focus your catalog in one well-defined area—because no single strategy will work across the board for every type of music. Focus is absolutely essential to establishing an identity for your company, becoming part of a musical community, and structuring an effective plan to achieve your goals. Attempting to do "everything" is likely to result in accomplishing nothing.

What to Do If You Won't or Can't Focus

I'm sure this little spiel on "focus" will not go down well with many readers. (After all, I saw Monica Lynch try it with considerably more finesse than I used here.) Musicians and creative souls will forever rail against the segmentation and specialization of the music industry—and certainly there are some negative aspects to the industry's increasing myopia. In the interests of all of you who absolutely refuse to give up the idea of pursuing several disparate musical directions at once, or even those who insist they can do "everything," I offer the following tips:

Keep It Your Dirty Little Secret
Some things are better left unsaid. Given the increasing fragmentation within the music industry, it is quite possible for the musical generalist to conduct his business on a "don't ask, don't tell" basis—if you're meeting with a rock A&R person, simply play him or her your rock songs, and keep that jazz fusion demo to yourself. If you're asked about your current activity, mention only those cuts that would be relevant in the questioner's musical world. Do not think that someone in the pop world will be impressed by your work as a film composer. They will not. Decide instead that what they don't know won't hurt them or you—let them think that whatever sort of music they're looking for is exactly the kind of thing you've dedicated your life to doing.

If this sounds a bit like the guys on Maury Povich that have four wives and spend their days secretly shuttling back and forth—it *is* like that. I never said it was an easy trick to pull off. But it is possible, and it is more a matter

of respect than deception. The people who inhabit each musical subculture
have built their businesses and in many cases, their lives, around one particular musical world. To imply to a jazz composer that you are able to dabble in
his world, while simultaneously striking it rich as a rock star, may not go over
very well—the jazz man is likely to view you as either a shallow dilettante or
an arrogant profiteer. To play pop songs when you're pitching to a country
producer is to waste not just your own time but the producer's time as well. A
bit of reticence about your multiple musical ambitions is not dishonest. It is
simply presenting yourself in a positive manner, as someone who respects the
complexities, nuances, and demands of any specific musical environment.

You Oughta Be in Pictures

There is a special place in the industry where you can pitch a bluegrass song
in the morning and write a power ballad in the afternoon, and follow it up
with an electronica track to end the day. But it's not the record business. It's
the magical world of film and television. Barbara Jordan, whom I mentioned
earlier, has built a very successful business writing and publishing songs for a
vast array of movies and television spots. Her choice to center her business in
this particular world allows her the freedom to indulge a wide-ranging love
of music, and to experiment with the songwriting techniques of different
historical periods:

> I write in every style of songwriting ever invented. If you've ever felt that you missed the
> boat by having been born in the last couple of decades, try writing a song for a movie
> that's set in the 1940s. It's fabulous fun to pretend you're writing a song for Billie Holiday
> to sing, or to imagine you need a new disco tune for John Travolta in Saturday Night
> Fever. I can tell you from experience that it's a terrific songwriting workout, and terribly
> difficult! But well worth the effort, since you will feel like a time-traveler who is picking
> up the best songwriting tools of every decade and bringing them back to your own.[2]

They're Jinglin' Baby . . .

As I mentioned earlier, the advertising business is another area in which
versatility is a plus. With advertisers drawing on every possible musical style
to grab the ear of the listener, anyone working in this field must have the
ability to cross into any genre and quickly assimilate the basic musical char-
acteristics of the style—it is, in many ways, the ideal situation for a writer or
publisher that resists categorization. Be forewarned, however. This business
generally requires not just an interest in several types of music, but an open-

---

[2] *Performing Songwriter* magazine, May/June 1996.

ness to every kind of music—which is a different matter entirely. Yes, there will be days when you can indulge your secret love of Jamaican soca music, but there will be other days when you are trying to come up with something that sounds just like Hampton and the Hamsters. If you live by the sword of versatility—sometimes you die by it as well.

First, Get a Million Dollars . . .

. . .then start a really, really big publishing company. While I'm urging you to keep your catalog focused and specialized, the reality is that the most successful publishing companies in the music industry take exactly the opposite approach. EMI, Warner Chappell, and Universal Music are all distinguished by the vast breadth of their catalogs, which include everything from jazz standards to rock and roll oldies, to current hits. This is an extremely effective approach, as the catalog provides an almost bottomless source of income, allowing the companies to be extremely aggressive in courting new writers who then create the hit catalog of the future. Despite what I may have said earlier, I highly recommend this approach—if you have a lot of money.

These companies have been constructed largely through the acquisition of catalogs, which is usually a high-rollers game—recall that $132-million Jobete deal that I mentioned earlier. If you happen to be independently wealthy or have access to significant funding for such a venture, this sort of acquisitive approach to developing a very broad catalog is a perfectly sensible strategy. In fact, the more broad the better, as a range of songs in different musical genres will protect you from the ups and downs of any one particular market. If there is a fledgling Marty Bandier out there, I recommend you put this book down and pick up your checkbook.

Or Just Wait a While . . .

As your publishing company grows, your focus can widen along with it. That's not loss of focus; that is creative growth. Once you have established an identity for your company and you have become a part of a specific musical community, you can begin to expand your strategy into new areas—hopefully without alienating your core market.

Zomba Music is a good example of this particular approach. Starting in the 1980s with a catalog based primarily on the songs of Robert John "Mutt" Lange (Def Leppard, Bryan Adams) and a small collection of top urban and hip-hop writers, it is now a company that represents almost every style of contemporary music, including country, blues, rap, alternative, gospel, and pop. But this was a gradual progression, undertaken as the company gained prominence, financial resources, and management structure.

If you are viewing your music business as a career, then it's not necessary that you tackle every market at once. Find the one in which you are best equipped to compete, focus, and create a success story. Then move on from there. The differences between the tortoise and the hare were largely those of discipline and patience. Ultimately, it is this focus that will allow you to compete with companies larger and more established than your own.

The primary weakness of the giant music corporations is that they are inherently incapable of focus, precisely because of their size. By directing all of your efforts and energy into one small segment of the music market, your small catalog can actually be competitive with the biggest guys on the block. This has been demonstrated throughout the history of the music business, in the development of virtually every important musical trend, from rock and roll to rhythm and blues, punk, disco, and hip-hop. In each instance, the sound was developed by small, independent companies that were an integral part of that music community. Likewise, in almost every instance, the large corporations neglected what they believed was a niche market until that small business grew too big to ignore. It is by finding and focusing on these sorts of opportunities that the small independent company can gain a toehold in the industry.

You will never be able to compete with the corporate powerhouses by attempting to do everything that they do, only better. But if you choose one specific area of music (ideally, one that the large companies are neglecting) and direct all your efforts there, then you can compete—and also win. The large companies simply can't afford to focus with that degree of specificity. They have too many interests, too many writers, and operating costs that are too high for them to limit the scope of their company in that way. Monica Lynch knew this, because she had been a part of the development of Tommy Boy Records from its inception. Every musical entrepreneur from Sam Phillips to Ahmet Ertegun to Master P has demonstrated the same lesson.

For the small independent company, **focus** is your secret weapon. Don't lose it.

Start Me Up:
The Basics of Business

Okay, let's talk business. While it's theoretically correct to say that anyone who's written a song is also a publisher, we don't live in a theoretical world. And in the real world, most people who own a catalog of songs are not publishers at all, because they haven't bothered to create a basic structure for their enterprise. Just because you have a backyard filled with old stuff doesn't mean you're an antique dealer. Theory only goes so far—to be in business, you need a framework in which to operate, and that means starting a company of your own. Before you hang your shingle outside your front door, there are a few important issues that you need to sort out . . .

The Name Game

Names are a pain. Anyone that's ever tried to come up with a name for a band knows the basic drill—four or five people in a room, all trying to be creative without looking stupid, throwing around a random assortment of words that range from banal to ridiculous. "Maybe we could just like, combine all our names, you know?"

"Yea, or maybe the names of our pets . . . "

"Or we could just open a book, and put our finger down anywhere on the page . . . "

It's a lot of fun. Then, as the atmosphere progresses from initial excitement to utter hilarity to quiet frustration, inevitably someone in the group chimes in.

"Hey man, why's it such a big deal? It's only a name. One's as good as another . . . "

If only. When it comes to naming your company, I cannot offer you any surefire methods for how to come up with a great moniker. But I can assure you that it does matter, and that by no means is one name as good as any other. So assuming you've already gone through the "hey, help me think of a name" brainstorming session, and now have a list of potential candidates in front of you, let's consider the options . . .

Naming the Company After Yourself—L'Affaire, C'est Moi

The viability of this depends largely on your status both within the company and the industry as a whole. If you are a well-established writer or executive, and your name means something in the industry, this is probably a wise move. It makes sense for Steve Diamond to call his company Diamond Cuts, or for Paul Simon to have Paul Simon Music. Be aware however that this puts you at the center of your company's identity, which can be both positive and negative. You are linking your own personal fortunes to your company and vice versa in a very direct way, which can be dangerous if either party's career trajectory takes a sudden nosedive. Think Martha Stewart. Also, by focusing the company so firmly on yourself, you may find it difficult to attract and acquire other talented writers (particularly equally well-established ones).

For the lesser-known writer, I think naming the company after you is something to be avoided. One of the chief advantages to creating a legitimate publishing entity is to be able to shop your songs in a way that doesn't make it obvious that you are sending out your own material. If the Music Business Weasel receives material in a professional-looking package from an unfamiliar publisher, the weasel won't necessarily assume that it's a new songwriter trying to make it past the "no unsolicited material" policy. If the package is coming from Ralph Grimlee Music, the weasel will spot the package's origins right away. In addition, from a marketing standpoint, using your own name is wasting an opportunity to establish an image in your customer's mind. "Ralph Grimlee" doesn't conjure up much of an impression. Go for something with a bit more flair.

The Clever Name—Don't Get Cute

A little flair is good. A lot of flair is just plain annoying. Other than a company named after the songwriter (good ol' Ralph Grimlee Music), the fastest giveaway of a publisher's beginner status is a name that is really, really cute. Too cute. Granted, names that incorporate little in-jokes, goofy wordplay, or quirky personality traits are pretty fun. At first. But after a year, the humor begins to wear a bit thin—both for you (who has to say this name over and over and over), and the executives who see the packages and phone messages coming across their desk. Your name is one of the first opportunities you have to present an image of your business; opt for professional rather than comic.

There are a couple of exceptions to my general aversion to cute names. Some people bring a larger-than-life persona to their business; their big, outsize personality is their calling card in the industry. In that instance, a cute, funny, quirky name probably works—it supports, rather than detracts from the business image. Shelly Peiken's company is called "My Cat Sushi"—and for anyone that's ever met Shelly, it just seems to fit. Nashville publisher Whitney Dane's company is called Mighty Isis Music, and Whitney is exactly that—she once rode through Music Row on a hayride with a gown and tiara on. If you talk the talk, you gotta walk the walk.

The other free pass for clever or quirky company names goes to those operating primarily in the urban market, particularly hip-hop oriented companies. Brand names like Def Jam, Phat Farm, or Roc-A-Fella, have become household names in Middle America—these names are effective precisely because they are clever and trendy, and carry within them an inherent street credibility.

The Safe Middle Ground

When it comes to creative choices, I am not usually one to advocate taking a moderate approach. In fact, I think the greatest weakness of almost all songwriters is a propensity to opt for the inoffensive, low-risk alternative rather than going for something truly daring. But for some reason, when it comes to naming a publishing company, I just tend to prefer the names that sit comfortably in the middle of the road.

Part of this is certainly the repetition factor that I mentioned earlier—this name will be the first thing you say every time you answer the phone, year after year. In addition, it's important to distinguish between a band name or stage name (which is intended to appeal to the general public, and has to cut through the mass media and pop culture), and a publishing company name (which, even if the company is successful, will probably be recognized only by others within the industry). Names that are dramatic, strange, or obscure can work for bands; for a publishing company, such names are bit much, like actors walking around the streets in costume and stage makeup. Understatement just works better.

Now remember, I said understated. Not boring. What is a good name? I like Realsongs, Encore Music, Hitco. Will any of these shock or thrill anyone? No. But they convey a sense of quality, and professionalism and feel as if they can comfortably endure for the long-term—they are not trendy, intrinsically linked to one specific writer, or so dull as to be immediately forgettable. This is what you should strive for.

What you can achieve is a whole different matter. If you think it's hard to think of a name, just wait until you try to clear one. The matter of clearing a publishing name, which means verifying that there is no other company already operating under the name you've chosen or something uncomfortably similar, is best done through your performing rights society, ASCAP, BMI, or SESAC. In chapter 22, we will discuss in greater detail how to go about affiliating with one of these societies. Part of that process will require you to submit your publishing company name, and at least two alternative names, for clearance. Yup, that's right. You've got to come up with not just one, but three, ideas for a company name. It gets worse.

Your performing rights society will then check the names against their database and the databases of the other societies to ensure that your name is sufficiently unique and does not conflict with any other previously established company. If my own experience is at all representative, some time later, you will receive a letter informing you that all three of your names have already been used, and that you should think of three more. Repeat. Try again. Repeat again. It now starts to become painfully obvious why so many publishing companies have such goofy names. Like a singles bar at closing time, things start to get a little desperate. I can't offer much advice here, except to say: persevere, try not to settle for something mediocre, and if all else fails, opt for initials. ABC, NBC, CBS, WEA, EMI—it's not the most exciting approach, but initials do have a certain iconic quality to them, and if you experiment around with surnames other than just the obvious Music or Publishing (try Songs, Enterprises, Tunes) you can usually come up with some combination that works.

Doing Business As . . .

Once you've got a name, you know who you are. But you still don't know what you are. A publishing company? Sure. But what kind of company? There are three primary ways of structuring your business as a legitimate legal entity—it's up to you to determine which format is most appropriate to your situation. Here are your choices:

Sole Proprietorship
This is the business structure equivalent of "l'affaire, c'est moi." It's all about you, baby. In this particular form of business structure, the owner (that's you my friend) is responsible for 100 percent of the business, keeps 100 percent

of the income, assumes 100 percent of the liabilities, and is taxed on 100 percent of the profits. For a control freak, this is a very good situation.

The primary advantage of the sole proprietorship is that you don't have to be an accounting genius to do business this way. There's not much to setting up this sort of company (just hang your shingle, and fill out the right box on your tax form) and not a lot of regulatory or tax issues to work through.

Of course, every yin has its yang, and the downside of the sole proprietorship is that there's not much to shelter the income from your business if things really take off, nor is there much protection if things turn ugly. You are personally on the hook for any debts or obligations incurred by the company. This means your property, savings accounts, and other assets can be at risk if the company goes under. The degree of danger this presents is directly proportional to how much property, savings, and other assets you have. If you're already well off, this is a pretty big risk to take. If virtually everything you have is invested in the company anyway, then you're not exactly going out on a limb. You need to come to a decision as to how much risk you are comfortable with.

The Partnership

It takes two to make a thing go right . . . right? Partnerships come in several different forms:

General Partnership: Pretty much what the name implies. You and your pal or pals are starting a business, and everything you earn, own, or lose is shared according to the percentage of ownership each person has in the company. Everyone has a say in business decisions; everyone gets a share of the profits; and you all go down together if the ship starts to leak.

Limited Partnership: If you've ever seen *The Producers* (either the movie or the Broadway show), you've got some familiarity with a limited partnership. Of course, I wouldn't exactly call Max Bialystock's scheme a textbook example of how to run such a business, but it can give you some idea of how this particular structure works. In a limited partnership, there is at least one partner who acts as a general partner and is responsible for actually managing the company—this would be Bialystock & Bloom, Leo. The other parties are limited partners, which simply means that they cannot have a role in actively running the business. The role of limited partners, like the lonely widows in *The Producers*, is simply to provide capital for the venture—they are investors who will receive a portion of the company's profits.

Customarily, the limited partners are only a part of the company for a set length of time—when that period ends, or a certain return on investment is reached, the limited partner no longer has an interest in the company and the assets belong to the general partner. While the limited partner has no say in the management of the company, they are liable only for losses up to the amount of their original investment. On the other hand, the general partner is responsible for all losses or debts incurred by the company.

Joint Ventures: This phrase gets tossed around a great deal in the industry—usually, it's just another way of saying, "let's do business together." It's really not all that much different than a general partnership, except that it's not meant to last. It is set up to achieve a certain goal (let's say the creation of songs for a specific event) and dissolves once that goal is obtained. You could think of a general partnership as a marriage—two equal partners, both assuming responsibility and risk, and both sharing in the profits. In that respect, a joint venture is like a Hollywood marriage—it looks about like the real thing, but it's usually done for a specific purpose and is short-lived by design.

The Corporation

This one's a bit more like *Frankenstein*. When you structure your business as a corporation, you are creating a new entity, separate from yourself. In a sense, the business has a life of its own. This does not necessarily mean that you need a skyscraper full of partners and/or employees; it is possible to form a one-person corporation, with yourself as the shareholder, the Board of Directors, and the CEO. Even in such a situation, your liability is limited to the amount of money you have invested in the corporation—your personal assets are never at risk. For the small business owner, it may be wise to consider forming a Subchapter S Corporation; this allows the company to allocate its profits and losses directly to shareholders (that's you), which usually comes in handy around April 14.

And the Winner Is...

If you're looking to me for advice as to which business structure you should use for your new publishing enterprise, I will give you some:

Go ask an accountant, attorney, or financial advisor. Don't try to figure it all out on your own, and don't take advice from people like me, who don't know you or your financial situation. Any sort of legal entity is viable as a publishing operation, and each presents benefits and drawbacks. It is worth the cost of a quick consultation with someone who can find a solution to fit your financial situation, your career goals, and your personality.

I've used several different business structures over the years and have my own preferences. Being a simple guy at heart, I like the Sole Proprietorship—it doesn't require a great deal of paperwork (not my forte) and it is relatively simple to account for at tax time. Of course, if your company is generating massive amounts of income, it might not be the shrewdest way in which to handle your taxes—sadly, I've never had that problem. And if you're sued, the sole proprietorship can put you at risk—thankfully, I've never had that problem either.

At one point in my career, I was persuaded by an accountant to create a corporation. It sounded impressive—the whole idea of a corporation seems to conjure images of office towers and long boardroom tables. What it meant in reality was a lot of form filing, record keeping, and tax bills, particularly in a state and city where corporations pay a multitude of different taxes. While it is probably a safer way of doing business than a Sole Proprietorship or Partnership, I found it unwieldy—I'd created a monster. This is not to say that it wouldn't work for other people more organized and structured than I. I would recommend working closely with an accountant when forming and operating this sort of legal entity.

Although I've had business partners, I've never used a partnership structure for my business (remember what I said about writers being loners) I think the General Partnership is probably the most viable entity to consider—particularly if you join with partners that excel in areas in which you are weak. Just as co-writing allows you to find someone that can balance you creatively, a business partnership can provide support and a more diverse skill set for your company. Herb Alpert and Jerry Moss, LA Reid and Babyface, and Chris Wright and Terry Ellis are just some of the teams that have established hugely successful ventures together.

The limited partnership is most effective for ventures in which you are seeking to raise money from outside investors. For most people starting out in the music publishing business, this is a somewhat unlikely scenario—most investors attach a risk factor to the music business equivalent to that of drilling for oil in your backyard. You will probably need a track record of success in the music industry, or considerable charm, to persuade people to take a stake in your new enterprise. Nevertheless, it is worth considering. The advantages of such funding are considerable, particularly given the nature of cash flow in the publishing industry (think slow, very slow).

Now, that your company is taking shape (you've got a name and a structure, after all), it's time to tackle the real work. You've got the "who" part of it down, and you know "what" you are—but the big question remains:

How? How are you going to make this business work? How will you know if it's working? How will you fix it if it's not? How?

Time to make a plan.

5

Do You Know Where You're Going To?: The Business Plan

I'll be honest—I'm not much of a planner. I'm more comfortable getting down to work, seizing opportunities when and where they come, than in devising grand strategies for world domination. Every year I try to make a few New Year's resolutions, and inevitably by the next year, I've not only screwed most of them up, but half of them seem completely irrelevant. My life has changed so much in a year that I can't even remember why I made them. I'm not an X-and-O kind of guy—I prefer to run and gun.

So if you're looking for a thorough guide to business planning, this ain't it. Thankfully, there are a good number of those available. (For one specific to the music industry, I recommend *The Self-Promoting Musician* by Peter Spellman, Berklee Press, 2000.) My intent is simply to show you the thought process that can help take you from point A to B: setting reasonable goals, developing strategies to reach them, and recognizing when you are veering too far off course.

I'm not even going to insist that you write out your plan. I know that's an anathema to every accomplished business planner—but this book is for songwriters, and most of us can't even manage to label our own work tapes. Besides, the music business is such a constantly shifting landscape, with trends emerging and receding faster than any company can respond, that it may be best to keep your business plan fluid, with general strategies and flexible goals. If you want to put it down on paper, that's great. But the important thing is to internalize your plan—so that you carry it in your head, constantly referring to it, reassessing and revising it as needed.

Goals

Before You Start Shooting, Aim

Goal setting is a personal process that very quickly leads to some hard philosophical questions. What do you consider success? Is it measured monetarily? Is it measured artistically? Do you need the approval of your peers, your parents, or a stadium full of screaming fans? Is it a matter of quality of life, or is it found in a specific, measurable achievement? Most important of all, how bad do you want "it"—"it" being success, whatever that means to you. I'm not much for navel-gazing, but these are important questions that will influence every facet of your business planning. It's worth a few hours alone in a quiet place to think these questions through.

For most of us in the music industry, there is a constant tension between what you could call the artistic values (creative satisfaction, critical acclaim, and the like) and the business values (sales, profits, income). While I do not accept the premise that juxtaposes artistic and business success in an either/or framework, I am realistic enough to understand that one does not guarantee the other. You need to decide what balance you are comfortable with between these two core values. Is the fundamental goal of your business simply to sustain you, while providing a context for you to write music you love? Or is this a profit-driven venture aimed at meeting the needs of a specific market?

Don't say, "both." One of the most important elements in this planning process is to be clear and decisive, and "both" will not suffice. Something has to take first place, and whatever that is will determine the answers to all the questions that follow. I'm not saying that it's impossible to achieve both artistic and business success; that is certainly not the case. But it is important to know which is the core value of your company. Pick (a) love or (b) money, but there is no (c) all of the above. There is also no correct answer.

With the big-picture question out of the way, you can begin to think more specifically about what goals should be part of your business plan. Think of these goals as markers along a path—each time you achieve one, you should move further down the path toward your ultimate destination. Anything that leads you off that path is not a worthy goal.

For example, if your ultimate aim is to strike it rich as a pop music publisher, then you should not set a goal of winning a Grammy award. I'm not saying that it wouldn't be nice to win a Grammy. But Grammy awards are given on a basis of peer voting, and are (supposedly) given for artistic achievement. They are also not given to publishers. Winning such an award is an honor, but it shouldn't be a goal, because it doesn't directly relate to your ultimate objective. If you want to make money as a pop music publisher, then set a goal of putting a song in the Billboard Hot 100, or on a platinum selling album. Leave the awards for someone else.

When you start setting goals, make sure that they are realistic, quantifiable, and of real business value. Goals are not the same as hopes or dreams—you should not cue the ethereal music and soft-focus lens when you start talking about them. When you begin to think about your goals, you should begin by thinking of your ultimate objective, and then try to determine the benchmarks that will need to be achieved in order to accomplish your long-term goal. Avoid the warm and fuzzy stuff: "I just want to touch people with my music;" "I want to publish songs that I'm proud of;" "I want to help other songwriters realize their dreams." Lovely. Those are fine sentiments for your Grammy acceptance speech, but good luck trying to build a business around them.

Get Real

To say that your goals should be realistic is not to encourage you to aim low. It is merely to say that nothing in the business is as simple as it appears, and nothing happens as fast as you hope. There is enough discouragement in the everyday life of a music publisher without shouldering the burden of a business plan with goals that are impossible to achieve. What are reasonable expectations for your new publishing company? Assuming this is your first foray into the music business and that you are not yet a well-established songwriter, I would say that a goal of having one song recorded and released by a major label artist would be a realistic target for your first year. This will not make you rich or even profitable. But it will let you know that you are moving in the right direction. Every year, try to raise the bar a little bit higher.

In a business as volatile as the music industry, I think long-term planning is little more than wishful thinking. I would suggest that your goals be set on a yearly basis. Certainly, your ultimate objective should remain constant, at least for the first five years. But the goals that will lead you to your final destination will need to be reassessed and adjusted at least once a year. In that sense, a business plan for the music industry is less like a road map than a navigational chart, which has to take into account currents, winds, tides, and the occasional tidal wave. The constant shifting of musical trends and fashion, the evolution of technology, and changes within the corporate structures of the major record labels could all potentially impact the relevance of the goals you've set.

Pick a Number...

If there's a danger in setting your goals unrealistically high, there is an even greater danger in setting them somewhere in the "gray" zone—that vague area where numbers don't quite apply.

"My goal is . . .

. . . to get my songs covered."

. . . to increase my industry contacts."

. . . to make my business profitable."

All worthy aims. But lousy goals. These objectives are moving in the right direction, but they lack enough specifics to challenge you to reach them, or let you know when you've accomplished them. You need some numbers.

What if you said instead:

"My goal is . . .

. . . to get three songs covered this year."

. . . to make four new industry contacts each month."

. . . to make (x) amount in income this year, against expenses of (x) amount."

Now you've got a target. Even better, now that you have a number in front of you, you can begin to break that target down into manageable chunks. In order to get three songs covered in a year, you will need one song recorded every four months. To make four new industry contacts each month is really just one call to a new name every week. This is about as far as my math skills go—but the point is clear. Numbers give you a basis upon which to build a strategy. They also provide an early warning system if your strategy isn't working. If it's June and you still don't have one cover, you're falling behind—you'd probably better consider changing your tactics to get back in the game.

What's the Payoff?

Achievement of a goal that does not move you closer to your ultimate objective is time wasted. It might feel great, it may impress your friends and family, but all it really accomplishes is to distract you from those things that are necessary to reach the larger prize. A positive review in the local paper, an award from a local chapter of NARAS, or a sold-out gig at the local coffee-house is not a goal—at least not if your true focus is on creating a viable music publishing company. These are achievements that may come almost by accident as you pursue your goals, and if they do, by all means go out and celebrate. But they do not warrant being an objective within your business plan. On their own, they are simply not that productive. Your efforts should be directed toward those things that yield obvious, measurable benefits. It's like sitting through a movie—there's got to be a payoff at the end.

Strategy: Can't Get There from Here . . .

Now it's time to play connect the dots. The dots are your goals, which, if chosen wisely, will eventually create a career picture of success. Strategy is what gets you from one dot to another. Needless to say, imagining where you'd like to end up is not all that tough—getting there is a different story.

In a book like this one, it would be nice of me to simply provide a few foolproof strategies for developing your company—do this, then do that, avoid this, and before you know it, you're there. It would be nice, but I can't do that. Developing strategy for your business is an in-depth, highly personal process that is entirely dependent on your own strengths and weaknesses, and your ultimate objectives. Without knowing what you want your business to become, or the style of music on which you're focused, or the quality of your catalog, any advice I offered would be of dubious value.

All I can do is play Socrates (probably the only time a weasel has attempted to put himself in those shoes), and try to ask questions that will get you thinking in a strategic way about your business. If you take the time to think about these questions, you will begin to see a path taking shape in front of you, and some of the barriers that lie in that path. It's up to you to draw, and follow, the map.

The Music Business Weasel's Pop Quiz

1. What is your primary market?

2. Who is your competition?

3. What are the strengths and weaknesses of the leading companies in your particular market?

4. How can you imitate those strengths?

5. How can you exploit the weaknesses?

6. What strategies have been used successfully in this market previously?

7. What does your target audience look like?

8. Is your market growing or shrinking?

9. In what city or cities are most of the companies in your market based?

10. What are the advantages and disadvantages of your current location?

11. What segment of the market is the most crowded with competition?

12. What is the most under-served part of the market?

13. What reactions are you getting to your songs?

14. What part of the market is reacting most positively?

15. Which is reacting with the least enthusiasm?

16. What are the musical strengths and weaknesses of your catalog?

17. What are your strengths and weaknesses as a business?

18. How can you best utilize your strengths?

19. How can you best compensate for your weaknesses?

20. What information do you need to compete in your market?

21. How can you get that information?

22. More importantly, what relationships do you need to have in order to compete?

23. How can you meet those key people, or people that know the key people?

24. What relationships do you already have?

25. What are you doing now to establish your songs in the marketplace?

26. Is it working?

27. If so, why?

28. If not, why not?

29. What equipment or supplies do you need in order to operate effectively?

30. How much money do you have to spend on your business?

And finally, one multiple choice. This one counts double.

At present, what is the biggest obstacle to your success? Is it:

(a) Creative—Weakness in the catalog or demo presentation

(b) Financial—Lack of capital for business expenditures

(c) Social—Shortage of productive personal relationships and industry contacts

(d) Technical—Need for musical or office equipment or technology

(e) Informational—Lack of knowledge regarding the industry or business in general

(f) Structural—Are you in a declining or nonexistent market?

Whew. Pretty exhausting, huh? The good news is, by now you should be starting to see what your strategy will need to encompass. The bad news is, this is not a one-time process. You should get to know these questions well—review them periodically if necessary, or better yet, absorb them into your way of thinking. This is what I meant by a fluid business plan. Your strategy should be something that you are constantly reviewing and revising in your head. Each time you learn something new about the business, make a new contact, or have a success or a failure, there should be some small adjustment to your thinking.

Which leads to the final segment of the business planning process:

What to Do If Your Plan Doesn't Work

On this matter, I actually can offer you a good and simple answer that should work for one and all:

Change your plan.

One of the positive aspects of business planning is that establishing objectives allows you to measure your company's performance, and to recognize when the goals are getting further out of reach instead of closer. One of the greatest dangers of business planning is the tendency to cling to the original plan, even when it is readily apparent that things are not working out quite the way you expected. Dogged persistence in executing a flawed plan is like driving around in the dark for hours because you're too stubborn to stop at a gas station and ask for directions. Sort of like me finding my way around LA.

The truth is, even the most successful companies are continually forced to alter aspects of their business plan in response to ineffective strategies, changes in the business environment, or shifts in musical styles and tastes. That's why every day someone gets fired and someone else gets hired, and the column in *Billboard* is called "Executive Turntable"—because it's always in motion. To find a flaw in your plan and react to it is not a sign of weakness; it is the ultimate sign of strength. The difference between the best companies and the weakest ones is not in the number of mistakes but rather in the reaction time.

A few final thoughts on business planning:

Listen to Your Phone

When I was a student at Berklee, one of my favorite instructors was Bob Freedman, a top arranger in the music industry. He was once questioned by a student who couldn't decide whether to focus his efforts on being a studio musician, a composer, or an arranger. How should the student make up his mind? Bob replied bluntly, "Your phone will tell you." He's right. And so is your phone.

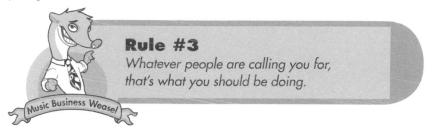

Rule #3
*Whatever people are calling you for,
that's what you should be doing.*

Music Business Weasel

Regardless of your personal assessment of your catalog's strengths and weaknesses, the industry and the public will make up their own mind, and in the world of commerce, majority rules. If people are reacting positively to a certain sort of music, or a particular business approach, don't fight it. Do more of it. To do otherwise is to sail against the wind. When the public speaks, listen.

Hit 'em Where They Ain't

One of the best lessons I've learned from working with Jive Records has been the importance of targeting your efforts toward areas of the market that exist just under the radar of the mainstream music industry. While Jive has had great success over the past few years in the mainstream pop market, much of the label's recent success was built by focusing on the areas that everyone else was ignoring.

When Jive first signed the Backstreet Boys in 1994, teen-oriented pop music was all but invisible. Alternative rock and grunge were at their peak, New Kids on the Block were neither new nor kids, and MTV and radio had no interest whatsoever in a new group of singing and dancing teenage boys. If you were doing a business plan for the group at that time, you would have had to admit that the environment in the industry was a significant barrier to overcome.

What you would also have had to note, however, is that such an environment provided a big, inviting void that was just waiting to be filled. For the screaming teenage girls that have gravitated toward boy groups since the days of the Jackson 5 and the Osmond Brothers, there was nothing out there—no one was providing the music they wanted to hear. From the point of view of the record company, it was a market with little or no competition, relatively low costs, and an audience that, though small at the time, was intensely loyal and enthusiastic. A business landscape that originally looked like a black hole was in fact a big open field, just waiting for someone to throw seeds on the ground. A few years later, Jive did the same thing all over again, using outlets like Radio Disney and Nickelodeon to establish Aaron Carter as a "tween" superstar, before anyone else even knew there was such a market.

It's always best to avoid going head to head in competition with a bigger, stronger opponent. Better to stay out of sight, pick your spots, and exploit any weakness you can find. This has been the most consistently successful strategy for small independent companies in every industry. It is particularly effective in the record business, due in large part to the lemming-like nature of the Music Business Weasel. In a world in which the tendency is for everyone to copy the trend du jour (witness the multitude of boy bands that sprang up after the success of the Backstreet Boys), there are inevitably segments of the market that are abandoned. The trick is to get in early and avoid the crowds.

If You've Got Partners, Put the Plan on Paper

"But I thought you said we didn't have to write our business plan down." Did I say that? Are you sure? Perhaps you misunderstood? That's never what I meant . . .

Communication is a tricky thing. The goals or plans that seem so clear in your own head rarely translate to others with the same clarity. While the sole proprietor or the one-person corporation can get away with a business plan that exists somewhere in the nether regions of his or her psyche, the business partnership requires something a whole lot more concrete.

For those of you entering into a limited partnership, there is no alternative to constructing a full, formal business plan—after all, you're asking people to invest their money and then let you run the show. A snappy spiel and a handshake are unlikely to seal the deal. You are required to provide a professional, formal business plan for the protection of your investors and yourself. I suggest that you speak to a lawyer or a business consultant to help you put your ideas into a proper format.

The general partnership is a bit looser, and therefore probably even more dangerous. A shared philosophy, a few great lunch meetings, and suddenly you're opening a business checking account with your new partner—without much more to show for your planning sessions than a collection of million-dollar ideas scribbled on a napkin. I've seen this movie before—and you won't like the ending.

Almost inevitably, these marriages dissolve in recrimination, and it's not necessarily because either partner is dishonest, disloyal, or inept. It's a simple fact of human nature that none of us understand each other perfectly or perceive the world in exactly the same way. Thousands of years of human comedy and tragedy are built upon this fundamental truth. That's why businesses and other forms of human interaction are built on paper—lots of paper. Don't assume. Don't interpret. Get it in writing.

At the very least, you and your business partner(s) should proceed together through the process outlined in this chapter, including the Music Business Weasel's Pop Quiz. Formulate your answers together, and then put them on paper, making sure that you each have a copy of the plan when you're done. If you want to go through a more formal process, so much the better. The essential thing is that you and your partner have frank, honest, and concrete discussions about your goals for the business, how you expect to achieve them, and the role that each partner will play in the process.

Set a Deadline

You can plan forever. After all, it doesn't cost much, it's intellectually stimulating, and you can never be wrong—at least not until you actually try to make it happen. The process of starting a business—choosing a name, forming the appropriate legal entity, building a business plan—can easily become a full-time job, until you realize that it doesn't make you any money. These tasks are the formalities of creating a business; they are not a business in themselves.

For that reason, I think it's wise to set yourself a deadline to complete the process. Certainly, the amount of time that you'll need for these initial steps will be dependent on the size and scope of the business that you're creating, and the sort of legal entity that you plan to form. A down-and-dirty sole proprietorship, with you as boss and sole employee, shouldn't require more than three weeks to put together. A partnership will take a little longer—particularly a limited partnership, which will require a formal business plan and the courting of potential investors. Figure four weeks for a general partnership and six to eight weeks for a limited partnership. A corporation may also take six to eight weeks to develop, although much of this time can be cut down. It can take up to five weeks to receive an EIN (Employer ID Number) by mail; you can get one much quicker by fax or by phone. Still, there is no reason your business cannot be active before you complete every aspect of the incorporation process.

As I mentioned before, even clearing a name through ASCAP or BMI can stretch on, ad infinitum. Use this time to develop your plan. Begin to put your business systems and catalog in order so that once you have finalized your name, you can hit the ground running. Don't let the licensing organizations or the government or the lawyers lull you into a holding pattern while the process of formalizing your business drags on. Find ways to be productive so that by the time your company officially exists, it's already open for business.

The music industry is not conducted from an ivory tower. It does not diminish the importance of planning to acknowledge that much of a publisher's success depends on fortuitous timing, an aggressive response to any opportunity, and good instincts. Don't waste your time on endless theorizing, introspection, and the details of business structure. If your business plan has focused your thinking, provided a reasonable set of goals, and a gameplan for how to achieve them, then it has served its purpose.

The pre-game show only lasts but so long. At some point, it's time to take the field . . .

Step into My Office: Setting Up Shop

I like my office. Maybe it's because I spent most of my career never having to go to one, putting in my time at recording studios instead. Interestingly enough, I now notice that most Creative Managers who have spent their careers working in an office prefer to spend their time hanging out at recording sessions. As for me—I've had my fill of leather couches and fruit baskets. I like my office.

The best thing about an office is the pure convenience of it. Everything is organized and within reach—files, faxes, letterhead, mailing envelopes. When I was a songwriter, I worked primarily out of my home and could never get around to setting up a real home office. Consequently, I never seemed to have what I needed on hand—the simple task of mailing a CD would take me all afternoon: gotta go get copies made, pick up mailers, run to the post office before it closes. In an office, it takes me about ten minutes.

This is the point of an office. Convenience. Speed. Efficiency. It is not about projecting an image, or flaunting a prestigious address, or having a staff of worker bees to order around. Not yet anyway. For a startup company, the primary function of your office is to save you time—so that the mundane aspects of operating a business do not consume your day. My own experience is sufficient to convince me that you need an office. How and where you set it up is up to you. Here are your three basic options:

The Choices

Commercial Office Space

For most beginning music publishing ventures, this is probably not much of an option. Unless you already have an active catalog or are relatively well funded, the expense of renting office space can be prohibitive. However, it's worth at least considering the pros and cons.

Pros

Space: Any fellow New Yorkers should relate to this one. Somehow, those magazine quality home-office setups, conveniently located in a spare bedroom, or the beautifully renovated cottage in the backyard, never seem to translate all that well to a 400-sq.-ft. studio apartment in the East Village. Probably the greatest advantage to renting commercial office space is that it provides you with exactly that, space—to keep files, office supplies, music and office equipment, and maybe still have room left to provide a spare desk for an employee or intern, or to have a few people over for a meeting.

Work Environment: Beyond just providing a bit of room for your business to grow, commercial office space can also sometimes provide a more productive environment in which to conduct business. While I'm not sure I would describe my office as a sanctuary, it does offer some escape from the distractions of life at home—family, pets, roommates, complaining neighbors or overly friendly ones. Simply by establishing a businesslike environment, an office can prompt you to adopt a more professional, focused approach to your work.

Image: On its own, this is not a good reason to rent office space. But depending on the sort of publishing business you plan to operate, it can be a factor in your decision. If you are planning to actively seek out and acquire new writers, you may find that holding meetings around your kitchen table, or in the diner next door, makes a less than overwhelming impression on your new recruits. Fairly or not, some people are reassured by a nice office or a good address—and as a new publisher trying to convince writers to let you take possession of their beloved copyrights, you can probably use any advantage you can find.

My only advice here would be to find a reasonable balance between the image you wish to project and your financial realities. Renting office space in the worst part of town will probably not cost you much, but it won't do a lot for your image either. Likewise, a luxurious office in the heart of town will look impressive until the bill collectors are lined up outside your door. Look for inexpensive neighborhoods in transition (preferably moving upward) and spaces that are comfortable but not lavish. Then try to inject a bit of style into the mix—this is, after all, a place for writers and musicians, not insurance salesmen. Vibe counts for a lot when it comes to office space.

Cons

Expense: This is pretty obvious. At a time when you're probably struggling to pay your own rent, you now have another check to write. Great. In fact, you have a whole set of checks to write—for phone service, utilities, furniture, cable service, computers. It adds up. This is one big con.

Time and Effort: These are the hidden costs. The weeks of trudging around town, meeting with realtors, looking at spaces. Filling out applications. Moving in. Renovating. All during the time when you could be pitching songs. Or writing them.

Maintenance: It doesn't end there. Now you have to keep all this going. Phones, lights, air conditioning, computers. Maybe a cleaning service once in a while. And security—particularly if you're keeping stereo or recording equipment in the office. It's sort of like having a vacation home without actually being able to vacation in it.

Remember the fundamental criteria here: Convenience, speed, efficiency. Now, let's consider option #2 . . .

Home Office—and I Don't Mean in Wahoo, Nebraska . . .

One of the things I've always found most attractive about the music publishing business is that it can quite literally be run out of a desk drawer. When I first joined Zomba Music Publishing, they didn't yet have an office ready for me, so I spent much of the first week with nothing but a telephone and whatever desk space I could find. It's still about all I really need. For the most part, this is a business that can fit neatly into your home. If you don't mind stacks of CDs. And constant music. And phones ringing. And piles of paperwork. You'll probably need a really, really big desk.

But instantly you're in business. There is no overhead: you can use your own home phone, computer, stereo, television, and furniture at no additional cost (and even write off some of the expense of these items on your taxes). And you don't have to wait for the bus in the rain to get to work. The advantages speak for themselves. The home office ranks high on the scale of convenience and efficiency.

If you can work that way. I say this from personal experience—the biggest drawback to working from your home is usually not your home. It's you. As I alluded to earlier, the comforts of home are not always conducive to a crisp, professional working environment, and it requires a certain amount of discipline and drive to maintain your productivity when your refrigerator and couch are mere steps away. If you find yourself padding around in your pajamas all day, chatting with your neighbors, or trying to look after the kids, the home office is probably not right for you.

There are other negative factors to consider as well. If you are hoping to have some sort of staff or even an intern, are you comfortable having others in your home? Will other people (employees, other writers, weasels) be comfortable in your home? (Note: if you have a pet that weighs in at over forty pounds, the answer should probably be "no.") Are there any apartment rules or zoning issues that restrict the use of your home as a business? Will you be limited in the hours you can work in your home office? If you share your home with someone else, are they comfortable with you operating an office there? If you find yourself moving frequently, will you be able to maintain a consistent address and phone number for your business? The home office is not for everyone . . .

So what's behind door #3?

Mobile Office

I like this idea a lot. I just can't seem to figure out how to do it. The mobile office is a concept that seems to become more prevalent all the time—everybody working more hours, but nobody ever in the office, and nobody ever at home either. This is the ultimate in modernity, the twenty-first-century solution for the global, jet-setting Music Business Weasel—hopping from LA to New York to Stockholm and taking his or her whole world in a shoulder bag. Have international cell phone, Blackberry, I-Pod, laptop, and Palm Pilot, will travel. It's way cool.

I just can't get it right. Every time I travel, I make another attempt to perfect my mobile office, and by the end of the trip, I'm reduced to borrowing someone's phone (my battery's dead) to call Directory Assistance (because I forgot to update my Palm Pilot and I left my Blackberry in the hotel room). Maybe I'm just too old.

I have however seen this done effectively, and it's very impressive. A publisher from out of town comes to my office with his entire catalog of songs on MP3 files, burns me copies of whatever I like from his laptop, calls his partner in Copenhagen on his mobile phone, and has him e-mail a copy of the new mix of a song straight into my office. By this time, I'm in awe. It seems like Europeans particularly excel at the mobile office concept—spending a week in New York, another in LA, heading over to London, and never missing a day's work, or even a call or an e-mail.

In this miraculous age, it is quite possible to run a business while very much on the run. You will need some sort of business address in order to receive mail (royalty checks, hopefully), but virtually everything else can be done from the road, at no great expense. Clearly, the advantage is that you can spend your time and money meeting with people in person, establishing relationships in any number of different music communities, and in many cases, reacting to opportunities faster than your office-bound competitors. If you live in a location isolated from any music business center, or if you are part of a touring band, or if you just like to hit the road, this is an excellent way of doing business. Just make sure you bring your own tech guy to keep everything running . . .

The Setup

Me—I like offices. My wife likes office supplies. She could happily spend a day in Staples, just looking at all the different file folders and colored labels. Not my thing. Unfortunately, as I mentioned earlier, my failure to appreciate the nuances of mailing envelopes and the like was a serious detriment to creating an effective home office. I just could never get the setup right. For anyone setting up an office in any business anywhere, whether in a home or in a commercial space, there are certain must haves:

- computer/printer
- phone with an answering machine or voice mail   try to get one with multiple lines
- mobile phone
- mail service or a P.O. box (if your office is a transient one)
- e-mail/Internet access
- fax (although this is becoming less essential with the prevalence of e-mail)
- letterhead
- business cards
- labels
- mailing envelopes

Then try not to run out of supplies—buy reasonably large quantities and monitor your inventory so that you don't come up empty on labels or mailers at a crucial time (which is the only time you ever run out of anything).

Plan to open accounts with an express mail service and, if you live in an urban area, a messenger service for local deliveries. In today's business climate, everything is expected overnight—unless it's coming from down the street, in which case it's expected instantaneously.

Then there are the specific tools of the trade:

Stereo: Don't skimp on this one. You need a set of quality monitors, and a professional-quality CD player. Remember, it is going to take considerably more wear and tear than the average home stereo. I'd suggest having a DAT player, although it's not essential; I suspect that this particular technology is going the way of the 8-track tape and the vinyl album. But DATs can be useful as a way of cataloguing your material, which we will discuss later. A cassette deck is another bit of technology on the edge of obsolescence. I use mine about twice a year. Not a great investment. If you're going the mobile office route, there are a few other components you need to think about—an MP3 player and a good set of headphones.

Television and VCR: Not essential, but close to it. With the overwhelming influence of MTV on the industry as a whole, and the myriad of opportunities for music placement on both network and cable shows, television is as much a part of the music business as radio. I keep my television on almost all the time I'm in the office, usually tuned to MTV. Most of the time I keep the sound off, as I need to be listening to other music, but it serves as sort of visual radio. If a new song or artist shows up, I can stop what I'm doing and check it out.

CD Burner: Again, make sure you get a professional-quality burner, as the consumer versions tend to wear out rather quickly. If you're doing your job right, you'll go through a burner almost every year. FYI—nobody sends out cassettes anymore. CDs are the industry standard. As I mentioned earlier, if your office is essentially your laptop, then make sure you are set up to burn CDs from your laptop at pitch meetings. This is a big time-saver, and allows the A&R person to keep a copy of the song while it's still fresh in his or her mind.

All of this brings up the question of MP3s. Over the past two years, more and more songwriters and publishers are pitching their songs via e-mail by sending MP3 files, which of course can then be burned onto a CD or stored in a file. It's an extremely quick, convenient, and cost-effective method of getting your music into an A&R person's hands. I anticipate that it will become the predominant means of disseminating music in the next few years.

Having said that, like most new technologies, it is not without its drawbacks in the here and now. In many large companies, the limitations of the company's network server make it impossible to receive and open MP3 files—in fact, this is the case at my own office. The alternative in this situation is for the writer or publisher to post the song on an FTP site, either their own or one controlled by the intended recipient. The song can then be downloaded from the site and stored as an MP3 or burned onto a CD.

For most A&R people, this technology is a godsend when waiting on that final mix of the last track on the album that was supposed to be mastered yesterday, or that hot new song from the Neptunes that's the potential first single on an act you've been developing for nine months. But when some songwriter you've never heard of is just sending you a demo, it seems like a lot of work to have to relay the FTP information, or log onto a Web site, then download the song from there. I know it's not fair, but when you receive fifty demos a week, fairness is not a primary concern. Most A&R people would prefer to receive a CD, unless there's a real time crunch on a specific project. Until this technology becomes the predominant means of sending music, I would offer the recipient (that's "customer," to you) the choice as to whether they'd prefer a hard copy or a file. Trust me, the day is coming when you can junk the CD burners, toss the mailers, and cancel the Fed Ex account. Something to look forward to, anyway.

Alright. Feel like you're ready to open the doors for business? Not quite. There's one more thing you're going to need . . .

7

The Inside Scoop:
Setting Up Shop, Part 2

The real currency of the entertainment industry is information. Hot breaking news, inside tips, gossip, rumors, word on the street—this is what passes for knowledge in the world of show business. People are hired everyday simply on the basis of the phone numbers in their Palm Pilot. With all due respect to the old adage, it is not only what you know. It's how soon you know it, who you know, and how well you know them. Indeed, the quest for inside information is so all-consuming that an entire industry exists to provide it, with a myriad of journals, magazines, and tip sheets devoted to keeping the Music Business Weasel always in the know. Part of setting up your office is getting yourself in the loop.

There are three basic types of publications that you should be utilizing in your business: trade magazines or journals, directories, and tip sheets.

Trade Magazines or Journals

These are the most comprehensive and easy to access of the three types of publications. Trade journals are a part of almost every industry—they chronicle day-to-day business developments, executive changes, political issues, and other news that affects those in the industry. The key distinguishing characteristic of a trade magazine is that it is targeted toward those in the industry, not the general consumer. *Rolling Stone* is a music magazine and informative reading for anyone interested in music. But it is not a trade magazine, as its orientation is toward the general music consumer, not the music executive.

The primary music business trade publications are: *Billboard, Radio and Records (R&R)*, and *Hits*. Beyond that, there are several entertainment business publications that have sections devoted to the music industry, such as *Variety* and *The Hollywood Reporter*. Then of course there are dozens of specialized newsletters and magazines for specific genres and segments of the industry: *Pollstar* covers the concert industry; *Black Radio Exclusive* and *Impact* focus on urban music; *Music Row* passes along all the news in the country music industry; and it goes on and on.

Don't worry. I'm not suggesting you read all of these. Most of them are weekly publications (some have daily editions). Subscribing to—and then reading—even three or four would be extremely time consuming and very expensive. While they all have their moments, most of these mags are not the most exciting reading material you could dig up. I suggest that you sample one issue of any publication that seems relevant to your business, and then subscribe to one or two that give you the information you need.

Personally, I'm a *Billboard* guy. In my opinion, it is the one indispensable trade magazine. It has the most accurate charts and the most thorough reporting. It's also the one that is read by virtually everyone in the business. I have a certain personal attachment to *Billboard*, because it helped lead me to my first gig in the music industry, which I'll tell you about a little later. Frankly, I think anyone who is serious about being a part of the music industry needs a subscription.

Of the other trades, my favorite is *Hits*. Unlike most of the other magazines, it's not available on the newsstand and not easy to subscribe to (they can't even manage to provide a subscription form on request). But it's funny and irreverent, and a very entertaining read. It often has better inside information than its more staid counterparts. And the cartoons on the "Hits Daily Double" are instant classics. *R&R* seems to me to be better suited to people in the radio promotion biz than to music publishers. *Variety* and *The Hollywood Reporter* are directed primarily toward the Hollywood film industry—they can be informative but are probably not essential, unless you are directing your business primarily at placing songs in television and movies. Most of the major trade journals also have online subscriptions available, as well as Web sites that are updated daily.

Directories

While the industry trades can tell you what's going on and who's doing what to whom, they will not usually help you much with the next step, which is to figure out how to get in touch with all those movers and shakers that you're reading about. This can present a problem when you're starting out in the industry, as most execs guard their direct phone number and e-mail with considerable care. Just figuring out how to get in contact with someone can require days of sleuthing. Thankfully, there are a number of published sources that can help you track down companies and executives.

Billboard Publications publishes a number of useful directories, which they make available (at a not-inconsiderable cost) to subscribers. The most valuable is the *Billboard International Buyers Guide*, which lists record companies, managers, booking agents, and other industry suppliers from around the world. I sold my first song when I dropped off a tape at the office of Big Seven Music Publishing, an address I found in the *Billboard Buyer's Guide*. Like I said, I'm a *Billboard* guy.

Hits also publishes a very useful annual "Who's Got Who" listing of artists, managers, and booking agents. It's not a separate directory; it's just included in one issue of the magazine. *Pollstar* publishes a directory of artist management firms.

The most valuable directory of all is the *A&R Registry,* put out by *The Music Business Registry*. (They do a publishers registry and a film and television guide, as well.) This is a very thorough listing of almost all of the major and independent record companies and the key A&R staff. It is updated every two months. Not surprisingly, *A&R Registry* is protective of the information that they supply, so the guide is quite expensive. If you are serious about developing a music publishing business, I would suggest that you pay any price to get this particular publication. It is an essential investment.

Tip Sheets

This is the real insider information—the music-business equivalent to stock tips passed at cocktail parties, or secret passwords whispered through a crack in the door that will gain you admittance to the party going on inside. At least that's the idea. Tip sheets are generally small business operations, available by subscription only, and often require certain professional credentials in order to subscribe. For music publishers, there are two specific types of tip sheets: the "Who's Looking" list, and the "Next Big Thing" list.

"Who's Looking"

For publishers that will be actively shopping songs to outside artists, this is the sort of information worth paying for. Tip sheets like *New on the Charts* and *SongLink International* provide a periodic update on those companies—labels, producers, managers—currently seeking material, along with contact information and a basic description of what type of song is being sought. Inevitably, some of the listings are out of date, and some of the artists are merely development projects in search of a label deal or other opportunity. Many of the leads may not be right for your catalog. Nevertheless, these tip sheets offer some hint as to how to get in touch with people who might actually give your songs a fair and open-minded listen. When you are first starting out, that is no small thing.

Tip sheets are never cheap and are usually over-priced for the information they provide. In another one of those unfortunate paradoxes, they are probably more necessary to those just starting in the business who can least afford to pay for them than they are to those who already have a circle of industry contacts. Still, most established publishers subscribe to at least one or two on the premise that even a few good bits of information each year can justify the cost. I think that premise is certainly true for those just starting in the industry.

Of the two tip sheets I mentioned, *New on the Charts* is oriented primarily toward the American music industry, while *SongLink* can provide tips for artists in the UK and Europe. *New on the Charts* is part directory and part tip sheet—providing a list of current charting producers, artists, and managers, as well as a relatively short "Who's Looking" list. *SongLink*, on the other hand, is all tip sheet, with a large number of new listings each month. I tend to rely more on *SongLink*, simply because it's a greater challenge to stay informed about projects outside the US.

"The Next Big Thing"

There is a multitude of these sorts of tip sheets, varying in quality and consistency. Many are disseminated on the Internet, and some are available at no cost. There are a couple that I receive in my e-mail box that I still can't figure out where they come from. These newsletters exist to spread the buzz about new artists and new bands to the A&R community—as such, they are primarily of use to publishers that are interested in signing singer/songwriters or bands that write their own material. The best of these letters is probably *Demo Diaries*, which has managed to unearth a pretty high percentage of bands that wind up getting signed.

While there is certainly a value to these sort of tip sheets (and if you are in a band, it may be a very wise idea to try to get your name mentioned in one), I tend to think that there is enough free information like this available on the Internet that you don't really need to pay for it. When people understand that you are in the music industry, they'll be all too happy to tell you about the great new artist they've discovered—you'll probably want to pay them to *stop* telling you. With these tip sheets, you are essentially employing the writer of the newsletter as a sort of freelance A&R rep—you have to determine whether you have enough faith in the writer's instincts to warrant the investment.

WARNING: If information is power, then you must be sure not to abuse it. Trade magazines, industry directories, and tip sheets are not mass mailing lists or sales-call fodder, and they were not created for amateurs or hobbyists. The people listed in these magazines and letters are busy professionals trying to make a living in a very difficult business. **Do not bug them.**

In Part II of this book, we will discuss at length the most professional and effective ways of pitching your material. This means using…

. . . **research** to find out what sort of music is appropriate for the person you are soliciting.

. . . **judgement** to determine what songs in your catalog are worth sending out.

. . . **etiquette** to approach people in a way that is positive, assertive, and respectful.

As you look into obtaining subscriptions for many of these publications, you will find that they can be quite expensive, and, in many cases, difficult to obtain without clear professional credentials. As you might guess, there's a reason. Particularly in the case of tip sheets, all subscribers rely on other subscribers not to inundate the A&R people and producers with substandard material. If that pact is broken, then each month fewer quality listings appear, as A&R people grow tired of sifting through low-quality submissions. Remember, the publications I've mentioned in this chapter are the same ones that my colleagues and I use every day. Treat them with care.

Now we've made our way through:

The Choice—that is, determining what type of office is right for your company;

The Set Up—and the laundry list of what you'll need to put your office together;

and

The Inside Scoop—so that you have all you ever wanted to know about the music industry at your fingertips . . .

Have you been keeping a list of what you need? Pretty daunting, isn't it? I said earlier that one of the positive aspects of music publishing was that it was a relatively inexpensive business to enter—and that's true, relative to opening a restaurant, manufacturing airplanes, or starting a cruise line. But it's still a startup venture, and that means spending money that you may or may not have, long before any money is coming in. Which is never easy. If you're wondering how you're going to run out and buy all this stuff for your office when you don't even have any business yet, my advice is:

Don't. I'm not saying, "Don't set up your office." I'm saying, "Don't run out and buy all this stuff." There are many qualities that are required of the successful music business entrepreneur—creativity, confidence, ambition, opportunism. None is more important than this one: **frugality**. You are entering a business with a very high risk factor, many ups and downs, and very slow cash flow—the last thing you need is high overheads. In my experience, almost every successful music business owner is capable of running a business on a shoestring. It's good to be smart, but better to be cheap and smart.

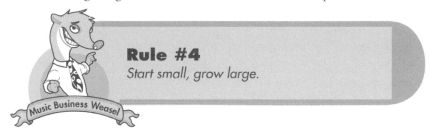

Rule #4
Start small, grow large.

Music Business Weasel

If you think you need commercial office space, can you share it with someone else? Perhaps you could share with a recording studio, music newspaper, or artist management company that might actually attract potential writers, performers, or A&R people to the office. If you need office supplies, can you buy larger amounts with a group of other businesses and achieve some economies of scale? If you're a performer or musician with a reasonably impressive resume, you may be able to get some sort of endorsement deal with a music equipment manufacturer. That means free gear. If you decide to go the mobile office route, scout out the nearest hotel lobby and call it your conference room. Do you need an assistant or receptionist? Consider an intern, who may be willing to work for college credit or just an opportunity to get into show business. If you can't afford to subscribe to *Billboard* or *Variety*, make it a point to visit their Web sites regularly. **If it's cheap, it's good. If it's free, it's great.**

And now that story of my first music industry gig (courtesy of *Billboard* magazine)—and a concluding lesson. Just after I graduated from college in 1984, I happened to read an article in *Billboard* about an organization being formed by Tom Silverman, the founder of Tommy Boy Records. Tom had the idea for an industry trade group, the Independent Label Coalition, that would represent the interests of the many independent record labels that at the time were at the forefront of the budding hip-hop, alternative, and dance music industries. In the article, Tom mentioned with customary subtlety that he was looking for people to volunteer time to this venture and suggested that it would be a fine opportunity for young people looking to get a foot in the door.

I wrote a letter expressing my interest and a few weeks later went to New York to meet Tom and interview for the job (or whatever you call working for free). In 1981, Tommy Boy Records had released the hip-hop and dance music classic "Planet Rock," which was the label's first big hit. By 1984 the company was established as one of the leading indie labels in the country. Imagine then my surprise as I pulled up in a taxi to the address that I had carefully written down—Ninety-First Street and First Avenue (not exactly the heart of Manhattan)—and saw only a tenement building, its door covered with graffiti, and a sporting goods supply store specializing in soccer equipment. No sign. Nothing. I checked the address. The cab driver looked at me, shrugged. I got out. Rang the unmarked buzzer outside the tenement door, and was let in. Walked up the dark, dingy stairwell, also covered with graffiti, to the second floor, above the soccer shop. And there was Tommy Boy Records. The office itself was professional and comfortable, but not lavish. Like every good indie label anywhere, it was full of boxes of posters, 12" promos, and mailers, and manned by a combination of eager kids working for club passes and free records and over-caffeinated staffers working for just barely more than that. It was frenetic, noisy, and just hitting its stride at about 5:30 in the evening. In every respect, it looked, smelled, and felt like the record business—which is a compliment, in my book.

A few months later, having relocated to New York, I went to another meeting, this one in the office of a successful songwriter who was starting a production/publishing company of his own. He was certainly doing it with confidence—a midtown Park Avenue address, reception lobby, a large office space that was spotless (and empty). It had the quiet, gleaming elegance of a financier's office. When I commented on the surroundings, the songwriter-turned-CEO informed me that having been involved with so many different small-time record labels and publishers during his career, he had resolved that his own business would be run in first-class style; he would do things, in his words, "the right way." It was an impressive, if not entirely persuasive, display.

The moral:

This year, Tom Silverman sold his last shares of Tommy Boy to Warner Bros. Records for over $10 million; he had already sold a significant portion of the company several years earlier. By then, of course, the company had relocated to a new space downtown, having long ago outgrown the old First Avenue address. Tom's career included being the head of NAIRD, the National Association of Independent Record Distributors, the founder of the New Music Seminar, and one of the most successful entrepreneurs to come out of the early days of hip-hop. Tommy Boy Records continues to have success with dance artists like Amber, Thunderpuss, and Masters at Work.

The other songwriter's business lasted less than a year. Not even enough time to fit any employees in those swanky new offices.

In the music business, the right way is whatever works. When it comes to setting up an office, cheap is right. Practical is right. Fast is right. Getting your hands dirty is right. Don't get caught up in an office setup that is really just a testament to ego or a television image of a record business "playa." One of my favorite songwriters, Billy Mann, has a publishing company called Tortoise Wins the Race. He's right about that. Your first office does not need to be a showplace. It's a starting point; it's not where you're planning to stay.

8

It's All About the Paper: Setting Up Systems

Recently, in a single day, I dealt with the following issues:

(1) A song slated to appear in a major motion picture, with all licenses issued and all sync fees agreed upon, was suddenly found to have a third previously unidentified writer, and correspondingly, a third publisher. As all publishers must grant licenses in order for a song to appear in a film (which is not the case with records), this meant that two days before locking the music to picture, the movie studio would have to negotiate a license and sync fee with a new publisher, who, being aware of the film company's position, would probably not be particularly easy to please.

(2) It was discovered that a song already released as the single for a major artist was registered with BMI as belonging to an entirely different publisher altogether, and with an additional writer as well. This presented a sizeable problem, as the artist intended to perform the song on five national television shows in the next week, all of which required licenses to be issued by the publishers of the song. To compound the problem, it appeared that BMI's information was incorrect. In fact, even the publisher listed by BMI denied owning the song. Still, someone had to issue a license to the television shows. Fast.

(3) As part of a promotional effort, several compilation CDs were created in conjunction with a major food manufacturer—the plan was to distribute the CDs inside cereal boxes. Most of the songs were licensed by the publishers on a "gratis" basis, which is to say they were free—the theory being that this promotion would benefit the artists featured on the CDs and therefore ultimately help the writers and publishers, as well. Having manufactured several million CDs, it was discovered that one writer of one of the songs had contractual rights to approve the granting of a "gratis" license. This meant

that should the writer deny the request and insist upon a full statutory rate for the use of his song, the cereal company would have to pay over $100,000 worth of royalties, or be forced to destroy the already manufactured CDs.

In each instance, the reaction was the same. Panic. Angry calls and e-mails flew, threats were exchanged, split letters and contracts were frantically dug up out of long-forgotten files, more phone calls were made, and after several hours of mayhem, someone finally 'fessed up. "Sorry, it was all a misunderstanding. Just a minor paperwork error. Not to worry." Conflict resolved. Life goes on.

Is there a point to these stories, other than to illustrate how quickly and often a day can go from good to bad, and when you're lucky, back to good again? Yes. The point is that in the publishing business, "paperwork errors" are not minor. That's because when you get right down to the truth, paperwork is what publishing is. It's like an accountant excusing something as just a "mistake in the math" or a surgeon shrugging off a "slip of the hand." As publishers, we don't have to write the songs, or record the songs, or sell the records. We just have to keep track of who wrote the songs, then issue the licenses, protect the copyrights, and count the money. Accurately. The degree of accuracy is largely the difference between a good and bad publisher.

Off in the distance, the reader groans . . . "Paperwork. Aargh . . . "

I hear you. Trust me, I feel your pain. It's not why I got into this game, either. In any major publishing company, there are people who have devoted their career to the proper administration of copyrights (which is to say, paperwork)—it's honorable and important work, and I have nothing but respect for the people who do it. Nevertheless, I must admit, I fail to understand its appeal. But a day like the one I had last week brings home with painful clarity how essential the administrative process is to the proper operation of a publishing company. We've already touched on issues like split letters and submission forms—now it's time to take this one step further and put systems in place. As you set up your office, you need to put in place administrative systems that will allow you to properly catalog your copyrights, your recordings, and your finances.

Systems? Isn't it a little early for that? Probably. The way to keep the paperwork requirements of publishing from consuming too much of your time and energy is to take the initiative to handle the paper before it handles you. Having a system will not entirely prevent situations like the ones I described earlier (all the publishers involved in those messes had plenty of administrative processes in place), but it will allow you to minimize them, and to resolve them quickly and accurately. In fact, that was another lesson learned during the day from hell. The systems actually worked in the end, and because they did, song no. 1 stayed in the movie, song no. 2 will be performed on television next week, and song no. 3 will probably show up in your cereal box one morning. If the systems had not existed, these issues could have taken months, or even years, to sort out.

Granted, when you're first starting out, the idea of setting up a process to keep track of a small number of copyrights feels like a waste of time. But the truth of paperwork is that you can pay now or pay later. If you start out correctly, investing the time to put systems in place and to stay on top of the work, you will be able to manage your business efficiently as it grows. If you choose not to spend the time now, you will likely find yourself unable to ever catch up, as the catalog keeps growing and issues keep appearing, forcing you to sort through the pile of paper on your desk to try to resolve them, which of course puts you even further behind, until you look up one day and realize that you have spent your entire week on administration issues. As James Brown would say, it's important to get off "on the good foot."

Of course, when it comes to setting up office systems, there are as many variations as there are publishing companies. Clearly, what works for you depends on the size of your catalog, your goals for the business, your access to capital, and your working style. The best I can do is attempt to give you a clear idea of the information you'll need to organize and a few suggestions as to how to tackle the task. It's up to you to customize the systems to your own liking.

There are three primary areas of your business you'll need to organize: copyrights, recordings, and finances. We'll take two different approaches to each—let's call it old school and new school. You can decide which shoe fits . . .

Copyright Administration

Yep, back to those old split sheets. You should have a nice little stack of them by now, right?

Old School
Forms and Files. Every bureaucrat the world over swears by them—if it's good enough for the government, it ought to be good enough for your company. So take that pile of split letters, and let's put together a system . . .

Begin by setting up a file for each copyright. Eventually, this file will contain all the information and paperwork relevant to that particular song. For the moment, the first thing we'll put in the file is the completed split letter. To review, this letter should include the following:

- writers/publishers

- percentages

- date the song was completed

- signatures of writers

The next thing that goes into the file:

Lyrics: Every song should have a lyric sheet, stored either in the administration file or somewhere on the computer. Lyric sheets always seem like a bother—but sooner or later, you always need one. Most importantly, you only seem to need one when there's an emergency at hand. The superstar is at the studio ready to cut the song, but no one knows the words. The song looks great in the movie, but some studio legal-eagle is sure he heard something objectionable in the third line of the verse. Inevitably, the call comes in while you're in the middle of a recording session or writing a song, and you have to drop everything and try to decipher a lyric you wrote two years ago and can hardly remember anyway. Put a lyric sheet in the file.

Copyright Administration Form. The purpose of this piece of paper is to remind you of what you will eventually need to do to administer the copyright, though you don't need to do it right now. There's a sample of such a checklist on the next page.

For the moment, don't worry about the specifics of these procedures—we'll discuss them in detail in part III of this book. The important thing is to have something in place to be sure that you don't overlook a step in the process. You might even want to attach the form to the front of the file folder, so that it's staring you in the face each time you pull out a document. The checklist should include reminders about the following:

Split Letters: But of course you don't need to be reminded about this, do you?

BMI/ASCAP/SESAC Registration: Once you've registered the song with your performing rights organization, you'll receive a copy of the registration form for your records. It should go into the file.

Harry Fox: Again, you'll receive a copy of this form for your records.

Copyright Registration: Many writers (and publishers) register their songs immediately upon completion. Given that there is a fee for registering, I suggest that you wait to register until the song has been placed in some sort of income-generating situation. The reality of most catalogs is that only a few of the copyrights ever really create any income. You can put your money to better use. We'll revisit this subject in more detail later.

Notes: The Notes section of the form should include any information that may be pertinent to the copyright or its use. If you are the only writer

Copyright Administration Form

Forms	Completed (x)	Date Completed
Split Letter		
Lyrics		
Performance Society Registration		
Mechanical License Registration		
Copyright Registration		

NOTES:

REVERSIONS: _____

LIMITATIONS: _____

APPROVALS REQUIRED FOR:

TELEVISION/FILMS _____

ADVERTISING _____

TRANSLATIONS _____

Translations

Language	% to Translator	Fee	Approved (x)	Territories

for your publishing company, then there will likely be very few notes—and those will be the same for almost every song. But if you have several writers signed to your company or if there are outside co-writers that are part of the copyright, be sure that you have all the information you need. A few things to consider:

Reversions: For how long do you own the copyright? Do the rights to the song revert back to the writer at some point in time? Under what conditions?

Limited Rights: Do you have the right to exploit the copyright in any medium without restriction?

Approvals: Do you need the writer's approval to place the song in certain situations? This is the "gratis" license issue that reared its ugly head the other day. Writers often have approval over gratis uses, as well as advertising (particularly as connected to certain products), movies (anything rated R or X), or parodies.

Translations: Has there been a translation of the song for a foreign market? If so, how was the translator compensated—did he or she receive a percentage of the song or a flat fee? Are there any other versions of the song in which the splits may be different than is outlined in the split letter?

These are just a few of the issues that can be addressed in the Notes section. Whatever you think you might need to know when shopping or collecting money on this song, put it in here . . .

Of course, what I've outlined so far is a decidedly low-tech system of organizing your copyrights. But as hundreds of publishing companies before the dawn of the computer era can attest, it will work. And it's cheap. As long as you don't run out of files or filing space, you're in business.

New School

You're still going to need some files for this one—I'm afraid there's not many other ways to deal with that stack of split letters, and the eventual copies of performance society and copyright registrations. But once you've placed the hard copies somewhere safe and secure, you can take that giant leap into the twenty-first century.

There are a number of different systems that can be devised for keeping track of your copyrights on your computer. The most obvious is to simply create forms like the ones already discussed and keep them in a file on your desktop. Or, you may create catalog lists for each writer. The lists can be updated with all the necessary information each time a new song comes in.

Beyond that, there are several software systems that are well suited to managing your catalog's administration. My personal favorite is Filemaker, which allows you to create an index card for each song, which then becomes part of your overall catalog. The great thing about Filemaker is that it allows you to sort by any number of criteria: writer's name, titles with a particular word in them, year of completion, and percentage of copyright.

There is even a Filemaker Pro system that has been created specifically for music publishing. While it may be too expensive for most fledgling publishing houses, it is quite impressive. It allows you to store information about when and to whom the song was pitched, and can store an MP3 of the song within the file. Very cool stuff. Another similar software program that could be useful is Yeah Solutions' "Music Publisher." It includes both a system for organizing your songs and an accounting program.

Music Archives

I'm at war with CDs. They invade my office, overflow my inbox, take control of my desk, fill my cabinets to the bursting point, and still they keep coming. They seem to multiply like rabbits—I have copies of copies, four versions of the same song, samplers, free goods, promos. They're falling behind the desk, underneath the radio, disappearing when I need them, then reappearing six weeks later. I'm at war with CDs and I'm losing.

To control and organize the ever-rolling stream of incoming music is a constant challenge for a publisher, and I'm not sure anyone has found the perfect answer. Whenever I'm frustrated with my own situation, I go visit other Creative Managers at their office and feel much better. My workspace is usually pristine by comparison. At least I don't have any of those sky-high stacks of CDs, leaning like the Tower of Pisa in the corner. (What do you do when you need the song at the bottom of the pile?) Having confessed that I have no easy answer, here are my suggestions for organizing your company's musical archives.

Not surprisingly, it starts with a piece of paper:

The Song Submittal Form

You will remember that we discussed this earlier—this form should be completed any time a recording is submitted. An example is provided on the next page. This form should contain all the necessary information to identify the master tape, where and when it was recorded, and who was involved in the sessions. Again, this should be filed with the rest of the documents relating to that song.

Song Submittal Form

Date of Submission: _____

Date Song Was Written: _____

Date of Recording: _____

Title: _____

Writer	Writer %	Publisher	Publisher %

Studio: _____

Engineers: _____

Assistant Engineers: _____

Format of Submission: (DAT; CD-R; ¼" Reel; Audio File) _____

Description: _____

For Digital Media (e.g. ProTools, Logic Audio, Sonic Archives, etc.)

Software Name: _____

Version: _____

Hardware & Operating System: _____

Types of Files (e.g. Session/Audio/Fades): _____

Sampling Rate: _____

Bit Rate: _____

Additional Comments: _____

_____

_____

_____

_____

_____

Now, the bigger question—what to do with the music itself? Here are two approaches to consider . . .

Old School

I already told you. Get a really big desk with lots of drawers. The primary difficulty I have with CDs is that you can't add to them. You can burn all the songs in your catalog onto one or two CDs, but you can't then add a new song to that CD when one comes in three days later. Consequently, you wind up with a vast array of CDs, each with one or two songs on them. It breeds clutter and disorganization. If your catalog is relatively small, this is not liable to be a problem, and you can simply keep the CD masters in a drawer—properly labeled, of course.

If your catalog is larger and growing fast, you may want to consider keeping your entire catalog on master DATs. With this method, you can add new songs to the writer's catalog each time one comes in, and be able to find them immediately if you need it during a pitch session. Depending on how many writers and songs you have to deal with, you can either keep all the material on a couple of master catalog DATs, or allocate a master tape to each writer.

If most of your masters are on CD, this will mean recording them onto a DAT, which is a slight loss in sound quality but hardly a matter for serious concern. It will also mean taking three to five minutes to dub the song onto the DAT. Personally, I have found this process beneficial precisely because it does require a slight investment of time. So often I have songs given to me in a meeting setting; I find it very difficult to give a good-quality listen in that environment. It's when I'm dubbing the song onto the writer's DAT that I can actually focus on the song itself and begin to think creatively about strategies for exploiting it.

Which leads to the next step in the process:

While you're listening to the song, you should be making notes about where the song will fit in the catalog. Does it go in the top drawer, the middle drawer, or the bottom? Why? Is it an up-tempo or a ballad? Are there any particular artists or projects for which the song seems particularly well suited? Does it need an edit or a new demo? You should set up some sort of document, either in a notebook or on your computer, in which you keep a list of all the songs in the catalog, and the appropriate notes.

Joining a new company as a Creative Director is always a challenge, as it means having to familiarize yourself with a catalog that may contain thousands of songs. When my colleague David Gray (no, not the "Babylon" guy) joined Zomba, he assimilated into the company immediately and miraculously had a full working knowledge of the catalog within his first week or two on the job. I was blown away. One of the techniques David used to accomplish this was to construct a spreadsheet, on which he listed the strongest songs in a variety of styles—ballads, teen pop up-tempos, urban, dance—and included notes to remind him of anything particularly noteworthy about the song. This allowed him to immediately begin having pitch meetings with A&R people and responding to requests for material, even as he was still learning the catalog.

When someone is sitting in your office and asking for a certain type of material, you don't have much time to decide what songs you are going to suggest. You probably only get three or four chances to hit the mark. It can be very difficult to remember every song that might fit the bill—it's essential to keep some sort of easy-to-access document that will give you a quick analysis of each master you have on hand. Scrolling through each DAT while the A&R guy sits across from you shaking his head in frustration is not acceptable.

New School

Goodbye CDs, goodbye DATs, and hello MP3 files. I'm a recent convert to this system, which seems to be growing more and more popular among publishers—that is, keeping all your music archives stored in files on your computer. You can then use a system like Real Player or Winamp to play the files from your computer through your stereo. You can store hundreds of songs in the system, set up separate files for each writer or style of music, and have not one CD or DAT tape to stack in your office.

From a song-pitching point of view, the appeal of this archiving system is that you can flip quickly through a large selection of songs, with no time wasted looking for the tape, scrolling through the DAT, or taking the CD out of the case, putting it in the CD player, and so on. This may sound like a small thing, but the small things add up. Our Nashville division was the first office in the company to switch to this sort of system; they estimated that it saves perhaps ten or fifteen minutes in every casting meeting. That means probably three or four more songs that you have time to pitch. Organizing your catalog in this way can also make your preparation time for meetings much more efficient. Rather than sifting through dozens of different CDs or tapes, you can quickly scroll through a few seconds of each song, determine if it's appropriate for the meeting, and save it on the playlist of your Real Player or Winamp.

Even better, this technology adapts easily to the mobile office approach. With all your music stored in the computer, you can take your catalog in its entirety to pitch meetings outside of your office, either by transferring the files to an MP3 player or by simply bringing your laptop to the meeting. Anyone who has ever made the record company rounds with fifteen CDs in a shoulder bag will be an instant convert.

The only downside to the MP3 system is the potential for reduced sound quality. You must be sure to use sampling rates of no less than 44.1. No matter what anyone tells you, the reduction of sound quality at lower rates is not only perceptible but detrimental. Don't ever compromise on sonic considerations.

Warning: Safety First!

One other warning when it comes to archiving your music—and this one applies to both the old school and the new. No audio technology is foolproof or indestructible, and no publisher is beyond losing a tape or CD every now and then. **Always keep a safety copy!** If you use the DAT or MP3 file system, it's easy just to keep the original hard copy as a precaution—put it in a closet somewhere in case of disaster. There is nothing more depressing to a writer than having a publisher lose one of his or her songs. Even when it's an accident, it always seems to register as an insult. As a publisher, you do not want to ever call a writer to say that you have lost a tape. And if you do make the call, you will be told that the lost song was recorded in Spain with a guy who has since disappeared, taking all his masters with him, and no one knows where to find him . . .

While I'm on the subject, here's something that is simply too stupid and basic to mention, but somehow still needs to be said:

Never send your only master out to anyone in the industry, expecting to get it back. To do this is to send a telltale sign to the Music Business Weasel that all but screams: Amateur Alert! Most of the time, you will not get your master back, nor will you get a sympathetic hearing when you call the weasel's office to explain your plight. You should fully expect that anything you send out or leave in an office will get lost, filed, or thrown in the trash.

And now, on to happier subjects. Counting your money. This is paperwork that you've got to get right . . .

Show Me the Money!:
Financial Accounting

Depending on the nature of your business, your financial recordkeeping can be relatively simple or extremely complex. The primary determinant of the type of accounting system you need is whether you will be the sole writer represented by your company or you will have several writers signed to you.

If you are the sole writer, then it's probably not necessary to break down your expenses or income, as there's only one writer to whom they can be assigned. If you wish, you can go through the process of paying royalties to yourself (and charging yourself for recoupable costs). An accountant can probably advise you as to whether this is necessary—it will depend largely on the structure you've selected for your company.

If you have several writers on your roster, you will need to set up a system to assign income and expenses to each writer. You will have to keep track of each writer's account balance, determine whether or not royalties are due, and charge the writer back for any recoupable expenses. Before we get into the details of setting up an accounting system, let's take a second to understand the basic economic structure of music publishing and the path that a song's income stream will take from record company to publisher to writer.

This gets more than a little confusing. I recommend that you follow the scorecard in this chart.

The Income Distribution Game

FIRST QUARTER: The Kick-Off (Advances)

Writer	$10,000	Income	Advance
Publisher	($10,000)	Expense	Writer Advance
	($7,500)	Expense	Demo Costs
	($2,500)	Expense	Travel

SCOREBOARD			
Writer	$10,000		
Publisher	($20,000)		

SECOND QUARTER: The Return (Income)

Writer	$10,000	Income	Performance Royalties
Publisher	$15,000	Income	Mechanical Royalties
	$10,000	Income	Performance Royalties
	$5,000	Income	Sync Fee

SCOREBOARD			
Writer	$20,000		
Publisher	$10,000		

THIRD QUARTER: The Hand-Off (Distribution)

Writer	$7,500	Income	Mechanical Royalties
	$2,500	Income	Sync Fee
	$3,750	Income	Mechanicals (pub share)
	$5,000	Income	Performances (pub share)
	$1,250	Income	Sync (pub share)
Publisher	($7,500)	Distribution	Mechanical Accounting
	($2,500)	Distribution	Sync Fee Accounting
	($3,750)	Distribution	Mechanical Accounting
	($5,000)	Distribution	Performance Accounting
	($1,250)	Distribution	Sync Fee Accounting

SCOREBOARD			
Writer	$40,000		
Publisher	($10,000)		

FOURTH QUARTER: The Final Charge (Recoupment)

Writer	($10,000)	Expense	Writer Advance
	($7,500)	Expense	Demo Costs
	($2,500)	Expense	Travel Costs
Publisher	$10,000	Recoup	Writer Advance
	$7,500	Recoup	Demo Costs
	$2,500	Recoup	Travel Costs

FINAL SCORE			
Writer	$20,000		
Publisher	$10,000		

How to Play the Game

The game kicks off when Publisher gives money to Writer, giving Writer a significant head start. Publisher pays advance to sign Writer: $10,000. Pays for $7,500 worth of demo expenses. Forks up another $2,500 in travel costs for a writing trip.

Income to Writer: $10,000

Total expenses to Publisher: $20,000

In the second quarter of the game, the income begins to roll in. Publisher receives $15,000 in mechanical royalties for copyrights belonging to Writer. Publisher also receives $10,000 in performance royalties generated by those same copyrights, and pulls in another $5,000 in sync income for having put one of the songs in a movie. And keep in mind, if the publisher received $10,000 in performance royalties, the Writer has also received his or her own check from the performance society for the same amount. As we discussed earlier, performance payments are made directly to writers and publishers, with each receiving an equal amount from BMI, ASCAP, or SESAC. This is why Writer did not receive a portion of Publisher's performance income— Writer had his or her own check in the mailbox.

Total income to Writer: $10,000

Total income to Publisher: $30,000

But wait. Go back. Now we have to determine how this "income stream" is actually assigned. This is the third quarter of the game.

Let's assume that Publisher's contract with Writer is a somewhat typical co-publishing agreement, which means that Publisher controls half of the publishing share and Writer controls the other half. This means the income stream for the song is apportioned as follows:

50 Percent to Writer: Remember, the writer continues to own his or her writer's share; this share always represents half of the entire pie. The publisher collects all the income for the song, but the writer never (or almost never) has less than 50 percent of the "income stream." Credit Writer $7,500 (half of mechanical income) and $2,500 (half of sync income). Writer takes $10,000 total.

25 Percent to Writer's Publishing Entity: This is the nature of a co-publishing agreement. The writer keeps the entire writer's portion, and takes a split of the publisher's share. Credit Writer's Publishing Entity half of the remaining mechanical income ($3,750), half of the performance monies ($5,000), and half of the remaining sync income ($1,250). Writer's Publishing Entity takes a total of $10,000.

25 Percent to Publisher: This is what Publisher keeps, no matter what the writer's account balance looks like. Publisher pockets the remaining mechanical income ($3,750), the other half of the performance income ($5,000), and the remains of the sync fee ($1,250). Total take: $10,000.

Seems pretty equitable, right? Three entities—Writer, Writer's Publishing Entity, and Publisher—all running neck and neck. Or are they?

Let's tally up the score:

Writer has already received a $10,000 advance, a $10,000 check from ASCAP or BMI, and is now credited another $10,000 in income. Writer moves up to $30,000. Then, add in the take of Writer's Publishing Entity: $10,000. Writer just keeps rising—total score: $40,000.

Publisher on the other hand is still digging out of a hole. Having paid $10,000 in advance, and another $10,000 in expenses, Publisher starts the game $20,000 down. Now, having played three quarters of the game, Publisher has $10,000 in income to show for the effort.

Uh oh. Things may look rosy for Writer, but they look decidedly dire for Publisher, who is $10,000 poorer than prior to getting into the game. But wait. It ain't over 'til the fat lady sings—and in the final quarter of the game, a new rule is introduced:

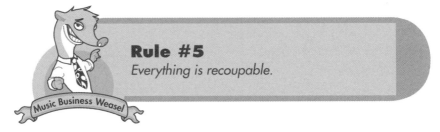

Rule #5
Everything is recoupable.

Music Business Weasel

The Big Payback: Accounting Systems

RECOUPABLE. Say the word again. How does it feel? You will learn to love it. Every weasel does. This is what it means:

Every expense incurred by Publisher on behalf of Writer—this includes advances, demo costs, travel expenses, mailing costs, equipment rental charges, and almost anything else Publisher can think of—can be recouped by the publisher. This is to say that Publisher can charge back, or deduct all recoupable expenses, against Writer's account. Recoupable expenses are deducted from the amount due to Writer, not from the total income received by Publisher.

The concept of recoupable expenses is at the core of almost every music business contract, whether it's a recording agreement or a music publishing agreement. It is also at the center of most accounting disputes, and plenty of flat-out chicanery, as well.

The general principle, outlined in most contracts, is that any expense paid by the publisher specifically on behalf of the writer is recoupable, but general business expenses incurred by the publisher (office costs, salaries to employees, T&E expenses) are not recoupable. Personally, I think that recouping mailing costs and the like is somewhat tacky—but that's easy to say when you work for a relatively large, well-established company. When starting a small independent publishing company, you will probably need to be as aggressive about recouping costs as is legally acceptable. Just remember, any recoupable expenses will need to be identified specifically on the writer's accounting statement, so at some point, you may have to defend them directly to the writer. Be aggressive, but honest.

Given that this book is directed primarily at songwriters, and probably a fair number of artists, you will likely experience the concept of recoupable expenses from the opposite side of the ledger book, as well. My advice here is fundamental: if anyone in this business "gives" you anything, you can be sure that it's recoupable. This includes stuff that seems sort of necessary, like $200,000 video budgets and the A room at Hit Factory, and some stuff that's just plain cool, like that BMW rental car, or the first class flight to London. It's never a gift. Read your contract, make sure you know what your rights are to approve expenses, and then read your statements carefully. And try to live humbly. Don't take candy from strangers or Music Business Weasels.

Now back to the game. Let's tally the score again, playing by the new rules.

Writer still has the $10,000 advance, which no one can take away. But Writer now has to pay back $20,000 in recoupable expenses. Even with the credit of $10,000 in income— Writer is $10,000 in the red. Thank goodness for that $10,000 income from the Writer's publishing entity, which leaves Writer even—still up the $10,000 advance, but no further along than at the beginning of the game. Until...

Writer's Performance Payment (whis is paid directly and, therefore, cannot be recouped against) adds in another $10,000. Writer up $20,000.

But look at the comeback by Publisher. Publisher now erases the $20,000 debt, adds in $10,000 of income, and finishes $10,000 ahead. The two sides just got a whole lot closer. Which is the whole point of recoupable expenses.

So here's the challenge:

How to devise an accounting system that will allow you to keep track of all income and expenses (recoupable or not), properly credit the writer's account and the writer's publishing entity, and properly deduct the recoupable expenses from those accounts. And remember, you'll need to be able to generate coherent account statements for each writer twice a year.

Old School

A ledger book always works. Using a separate page for each copyright, you can simply list in columns each credit for income received or debit for each recoupable expense. Then, in the adjacent columns, note the nature of the payment or expense, a description, and the amount assigned to the writer.

Remember, in a standard publishing agreement, the total income stream of mechanical and sync income is divided 50 percent to the writer and 50 percent to the publisher. Performance payments go directly to the publisher. In a co-publishing agreement (in which the writer retains a portion of the publisher's share), the mechanical and sync income will be split 75 percent to the writer, and performance payments will be split 50 percent to the writer and 50 percent to the publisher.

At the end of each accounting period (June and December) you will add up the accounts for each song, then total the amount due to the writer. The writer should receive an accounting statement (due in September and March) that lists the total income for each song, and the percentage due to him or her. It will also list all recoupable expenses being charged to the writer's account.

Of course, all statements received from ASCAP, BMI, SESAC, Harry Fox, and sync licensees that detail income should be copied and filed, as they will be needed for your own accounting purposes and any possible audits by writers.

You will probably need a separate ledger or set of files for your company's general expenses, like phone, utilities, travel, and expenses. While these costs are not recoupable to the writers, they are nevertheless legitimate business expenses that can be deducted from your taxes. Of course, this part of the record-keeping process is integral to the operation of any sort of business. If you need more information about how to set up this sort of accounting system, consult any general-business book oriented toward setting up and operating your own company.

New School

There's a myriad of options for creating income/debit statements. Probably, the quickest and most obvious is a simple spreadsheet, using a software program like Excel. On your spreadsheet, you can enter any income generated by a specific copyright, register any recoupable expenses incurred, and let the spreadsheet determine what is owed to the writer and the writer's publishing entity. Best of all, you can easily print out the spreadsheet and use it as the basis of your accounting to the writer.

If you're looking for something more specifically geared to the music publishing industry, I would suggest Yeah Solutions' "Music Publisher." There is a plentitude of software programs that provide basic accounting systems for small businesses, including systems like Quicken and Oracle. Any of these can be adapted to meet the needs of your company.

If this chapter has left you feeling more like an accountant than a creative executive in the music industry, I sympathize. Music industry accounting is not exactly straightforward, and never seems to entirely please either the corporate bean counters or the creative community. But there are two important points that should be gleaned from the preceding discussion.

The first thing that becomes apparent is that the complexities of the accounting process increase greatly when you begin to take on writers other than yourself. The more complex the deals are that you make with additional writers, the more headaches you will have. If you structure similar deals for all of your writers, either on a copublishing basis (you keep half of the publisher's share) or, even better, on a full publishing basis (you keep all of the publisher's share), you can set up administration and accounting systems that continue to be effective as you acquire more and more catalogs. If each writer's deal is completely different, it will be very difficult to construct an accounting system to accommodate all the variables. In the eagerness to sign a particular writer, it can be very tempting to negotiate agreements that are unworkable in practice . . .

"We'll do a full-pub deal, but only on new copyrights. Any of the old catalog will be done on a co-pub basis, unless we get the song cut, at which time our share will go to 40 percent of the income stream, or if we put it in a movie, at which time we'll take a full-pub share, but only on the resulting sync fee . . . "

I see these sorts of deals done all the time. Sometimes it's the only way to get a writer to sign the contract. But it's an administration and accounting nightmare that usually leaves everyone in the Copyright and Royalties departments scratching their heads for months after the deal is in place. For a small company, I recommend that you keep your deals simple and standard—and make sure you factor in the accounting work when you negotiate exceptions to the rule.

The other point that should be glaringly obvious is that without the principle of recoupable expenses, it is very easy for a publisher to watch a writer grow wealthy while the publisher goes broke. Though creative people forever complain about the insatiable greed and general shadiness of the Music Business Weasel, the truth is that many entrepreneurs in this industry started as idealistic fans who just wanted to help foster the music they loved. It was only when they realized how difficult it actually is to keep a company solvent while retaining just 25 percent of the income that they became the hard-nosed skinflints that we know today.

Our quick study of the income stream makes it quite clear: If the publisher fails to charge back the expenses incurred on behalf of the writer, the writer is likely to find himself or herself without a publisher to complain about. This is a high-risk business. If you intend to survive, generosity is not a quality that will serve you well. Your first priority must be the fiscal health of your company. Every deal you make and every deduction you take should reflect that ultimate objective. "Dishonest" is not a compliment in this business or any other—but "tough" is.

Welcome to the jungle, baby.

10

We Are Family: Putting Together Your Team

Even when you're in business by yourself, you should not be in business alone. When you're entering the jungle, it's good to have friends out there—particularly among the natives. The first step is to find those people and organizations already established in the industry that can help steer you down the right path. In addition to becoming part of a musical community, as we discussed earlier, you should also be in the process of building a team that can support and, in many cases, promote your company to the larger industry.

The Lawyer

For better or for worse, and I would argue that it is largely for the worse, the music business in the past ten years has become dominated by lawyers. They are in top positions in many of the largest corporations. They have expanded into artist and producer management roles. They are wedged in the middle of every music business interaction. Many companies now have a policy requiring that all outside material (that is, demo tapes) must be submitted through managers or lawyers—and indeed, I receive more demos from lawyers than from anyone else.

If that sounds like a strange role-switch (what exactly would qualify a lawyer for a role as talent scout?), remember that the smart businessperson deals with the world as it is, not as it might be. This is my way of saying, "Go get a lawyer." There's certainly no shortage of them out there. But how do you choose? Here are the basic criteria:

Knowledge

Yes, of course. You need someone with a solid understanding of entertainment law, which is a relatively specialized field. It is not sufficient to try to get by with a family lawyer, a friend with some general legal knowledge, or a business lawyer with an interest in expanding into show biz. You need someone whose entire practice is devoted to entertainment law.

But let's be real. Most of the issues handled daily by music business attorneys hardly require intricate legal knowledge. Very few major music business lawyers have achieved prominence because of their vast command of contract law. It just ain't that kind of gig. Like everyone else in the world of show business, lawyers are prized for the contacts they bring, the people they know, the doors they can open, and the deals they can command. You need someone with . . .

Contacts

Keep in mind that lawyers are well aware that their value is measured in part by their ability to open doors. That means they work hard to develop relationships and contacts and will not treat them cavalierly. A good music lawyer will want to become familiar with the sort of music you do, make some judgments regarding the quality of it, and probably see some positive activity before he or she starts placing calls or setting up meetings. This will not happen right away. But the key is to find an attorney that has access to the people you need. A couple of things to consider:

Location

Generally speaking, it makes sense to have your lawyer in the same city in which you reside—but there are exceptions. If your business is based outside of one of the music industry centers (New York, Los Angeles, Nashville, Atlanta, Chicago), then it is even more important that you find an attorney who is based in one of those cities. Likewise, if you are based in a city that is not the center of the sort of music that you do, consider finding an attorney who can give you an industry presence in the heart of your particular business. If you're living in New York, but pitching songs primarily in the film and television world, find an attorney in LA. If you're an urban writer in Nashville, find a lawyer in Atlanta or New York. At the very least, make sure that the law firm has offices in one of the other music capitals.

Specialization

While music industry lawyers do not limit themselves by genre in the way that a writer or producer would, it is only natural that most of them find themselves focusing predominantly on two or three specific areas. As we discussed earlier, it's a very big industry and it's impossible to know everybody. Consequently, most people concentrate on finding their niche. There are distinct differences in the way business is done in each segment of the industry—you don't want a New York lawyer from the hip-hop world negotiating a country publishing deal in Nashville. Trust me, you just don't. Try to find an attorney who is experienced in the genre in which you'll be working.

Availability

It's easy to get caught up in big-name hunting when you're looking for a lawyer. You can contact the prestigious firms, the people you see written up in the "Wheels and Deals" column in *Hits*, or the attorney who represents your favorite artist. If your story is compelling enough, they may be willing to represent you. This is great news and a perfectly sound strategy—with one caveat: Make sure that they will be reasonably accessible to you when you need them.

If you are new to the industry, you need a lawyer that is willing to invest a small amount of time on spec (that is, without an hourly charge). Many of the issues with which you'll need help are not things that generate significant income for a law firm. The problem with high profile, big-name lawyers is that they are very busy people and naturally gravitate toward the high profile, big-number deals. You need to be confident that your lawyer, or at least an associate within the firm, will be available to you when needed and able to complete deals in a reasonable amount of time. If you need a little help with a sync license, you don't want to wait six months while your attorney wraps up the Whitney Houston contract renegotiation.

A bit of corresponding advice: Never take more of your lawyer's time than you absolutely require. Remember, lawyers are used to working on the clock. Their time is, quite literally, money. Don't call to chat, don't ask questions that you could figure out yourself, and don't expect negotiations or contracts to be completed overnight. (It will never happen—and it won't happen any faster if you call every day to see if it's happening.) If your lawyer likes you so much that he or she calls you to chat, make sure you're not being charged for it.

Affordability

This can be a hard thing to determine. Begin by understanding that if you judge a lawyer's hourly rate on the scale of a musician or a songwriter, or even a producer, no decent lawyer will ever appear to be affordable. The hourly rates of most attorneys in New York and LA make rock stars look underpaid. The good news is, most lawyers don't work solely on an hourly basis. In most cases, they will structure their charges to be a percentage of whatever amount the prospective deal is ultimately worth. Obviously, this encourages the lawyer to be as aggressive as possible in negotiating on your behalf. Likewise, it gives incentive for the lawyer to be reasonable as to how much time he or she puts into the process relative to the potential pay-off. One of the things that I admire most in an attorney is an ability to read the terrain in advance, decide how much money is potentially at stake, and structure negotiations accordingly. You don't want a lawyer spending three months on a $5,000 single-song deal.

Here's a quick word to the wise for the dangerously naïve. If your lawyer is willing to invest time on a speculative basis or for a fraction of his or her regular fee, by all means take advantage of it. But be aware; if and when you hit the big money, your lawyer will expect you to pay the full hourly rate and then some (charges for faxes, long distance calls, you name it). This is not unfair. I believe the legal term is "quid pro quo." It's life.

Trust

This is even harder to determine, not because lawyers are inherently difficult to trust (of course not), but because there are competing forces at work. While your lawyer is working for you, he or she is also working for the law firm that pays them and, ultimately, for themselves. It is impossible to ever determine exactly what someone's highest priority is, but a cursory knowledge of human nature would suggest that in this instance, it's probably not you. It is conceivable that there may be times when your lawyer's interests, relationships, or the law firm's relationships could compromise his or her negotiations on your behalf. It's not common or accepted, but it isn't unheard of either. Try to find someone with whom you feel comfortable and who you feel will make your welfare his or her primary concern.

But what if you're wrong? If you can't trust your lawyer, then who can you trust? You. Read your contracts, learn as much as possible about music business law, and when in doubt, ask questions. If you have misgivings, voice them. If you still have misgivings, don't sign the deal. Never sign something you don't understand. When it comes to lawyers or anyone else in this business—trust, but verify.

The most common method for finding a lawyer is old-fashioned word of mouth. You can get recommendations from other writers, publishers, or industry execs--the most useful information will come from those who've had success in the same market in which you'll be working. Another alternative is to study the industry trade magazines and keep tabs on the attorneys who are at the center of the action. I think *Hits* and *The Hollywood Reporter* are the best sources for this information. Finally, you can read the label copy on your favorite artists' CDs. It's amazing how much useful information can be read in the fine print. There's usually a credit to either a manager or a lawyer (or both)—if necessary, you can usually call the management company and inquire as to the artist's legal representation.

The Accountant

I went a long time without ever involving an accountant in my business—I even did my own taxes. I can't say I'm the better for it. While it is possible to run your business without any assistance on the financial side, it's useful to have some expert advice, particularly when the end of the year rolls around. If you are incorporating your business, I think it's essential. As soon as you begin making any significant money from your music publishing operation, it would be wise to have an accountant as part of your business team.

But not as an everyday player. Unless you are involved in a very complex partnership or an audit of some kind, you shouldn't need your accountant more than a few times a year. A few phone calls when issues arise and one session around tax time ought to do the job.

Personal referrals will probably be the best method for finding an accountant—your lawyer can probably be helpful in this regard. It's useful to find someone with experience in the music industry, rather than just a general accountant. But this is less of a name game than the search for a lawyer—you don't need an "industry player" or someone with a long list of prominent clients. Quiet, trustworthy, and accurate will do just fine. Local is also a big benefit, as tax laws differ significantly from state to state.

Don't over-reach when it comes to managing your money. You need an accountant, not a business manager. A number of financial advisors in the music industry offer what is essentially full-service financial management, usually to superstars who are too busy (or too oblivious) to handle their own vast income. The business managers write checks, manage budgets, parcel out living expenses to their wealthy charges, and manage the star's investment portfolio for what is understandably a substantial fee. If you are so large that you require a separate employee just to manage your income, you hardly need to read any advice from me. But here's some anyway. Keep your eyes wide open and reread the previous section on "trust." These sorts of arrangements have been known to go extremely sour—just ask Billy Joel.

The Performing Rights Organization

We've already talked about the primary role of BMI, ASCAP, and SESAC, which is to collect the performance income from radio, television, live shows, restaurants, and any other venue where recorded or live music is used, and distribute this income to the songwriters. These organizations have other roles in the music community as well. One of the performing rights society's most important functions is to act as something of a support network within the songwriting and publishing community. This is a role that is not necessarily central to the organization's purpose, but it's something that all of the societies have embraced.

ASCAP offers a variety of songwriter-oriented programs, including the ASCAP Foundation's Pop Songwriting Workshop, the Disney Musical Theater Workshop, and an extensive scholarship program, with awards in the name of Abe Olman, Leiber and Stoller, and others. Not to be outdone, BMI also provides a wide spectrum of showcases and workshops, including BMI's Contemporary Professional Songwriting Workshop (in New York), BMI Songwriter's Workshop (in Nashville), the Lehman Engel Musical Theater Workshop, the Demo Derby, monthly Roundtables in New York, LA, and Nashville, and the Legal Series, which is a great way to become familiar with both the legal issues involved in music contracts, and the lawyers that appear on the panels. SESAC sponsors the New York Music Awards, the Songwriters Circle in New York, and the Songwriter's Showcase in LA. Many of these programs are open, in varying degrees, to new, unestablished songwriters and publishers, and are intended to help writers and publishers become more effective—hence, making more money for ASCAP, BMI, and SESAC to collect. No one's happier to hear your song on the radio than your performance organization. Except you.

In addition to the myriad of programs, panels, and other events provided by the societies, each of the groups also has a staff of writer/publisher relations representatives, whose primary responsibility it is to keep the writer and publisher members happy, and to encourage new writers and publishers to affiliate with their organization. These people are the great unsung heroes of the songwriting community. They go to endless shows, buy hundreds of meals, listen to thousands of tapes, and meet with countless writers every year. They do it not only because it's their job, but because they genuinely care about songs and writers, and they enjoy seeing new writers and companies develop into success stories. In an industry where you do not necessarily have a large number of genuine advocates, these people are the real deal.

"Great!" you say. "Someone wants to help. Where do I join? Who do I join?" Hold up. Not so fast. Unless you have a song that is out on a record, actively being played on the radio or television, or being performed in some other major venue, you don't have any performance income to collect. This means you don't need to join a performance organization yet. In fact, in some instances, you will not be allowed to join the society until you have a song commercially released. This is not a bad thing.

We will talk about the process of choosing a performance society and the process of affiliation in chapter 22. Right now, you're in the dating stage—which means that you try to meet as many people from each of the three organizations as you can, develop relationships with anyone who takes an interest in what you do, learn as much as you can about the differences between the groups, and see where it all leads. The object is to see what organization takes an interest in your company, what writer relations reps are willing to offer help or advice, and what programs are of benefit to you. The fact that you are unaffiliated is a plus in this respect, as it allows you to get the best of all three worlds. At this stage, you're free to "play the field."

As a publisher, this freedom will not necessarily disappear once you have a song that's generating income. As a writer, it is necessary to join one specific organization. While you can move from one to the other, you do need to choose one society to license your material. On the other hand, a publisher is permitted and, often, required to have an affiliation with each of the three societies.

If you are the only writer represented by your publishing company, then your publishing company will need to be affiliated only with the society that represents you as a writer. For example, if you join ASCAP as a writer, your publishing company will need to be affiliated with ASCAP. But if you represent several writers, you will likely need to have publishing entities at each society. To elaborate on our initial example, if your company were to add a second writer who was already signed with BMI, your publishing firm would need to create a second publishing entity (just a name really) that would be your BMI affiliate. Any major publisher will have an ASCAP, BMI, and SESAC affiliate—this allows the company to publish any writer, regardless of the society to which the writer belongs. For instance, Zomba Music Publishing has Zomba Enterprises Inc. (the ASCAP entity), Zomba Songs Inc. (BMI), and Zomba Melodies (SESAC). As a publisher then, you will likely maintain relationships at all the performance societies in a way that you might not as a writer.

And again, the warning:

If you handle yourself correctly, the folks at BMI, ASCAP, and SESAC will be your friends (not all of them, but at least a few). But remember that they do not work for you. They are not your manager, lawyer, or PR agent. This is to say, be grateful—not greedy. A call to your contact at the performance society once every four or six weeks with a question, update, or invite to a show is reasonable. A call once a week is annoying. A call every day is abuse. These people are the best advocates that songwriters and publishers have—don't disillusion them. Treat them with the respect that they deserve.

Interns

The same goes for interns. The entertainment business is one of those industries that is fortunate enough to have a healthy supply of bright young people willing to work for college credit or, in some cases, nothing but experience, a foot in the door, and some record industry swag. The smart companies learn to use interns wisely and effectively, and smart interns use the opportunity to make an impression and find a way into a difficult and exclusive industry.

I'm not sure that anyone's done a survey, but I'm guessing that at least two-thirds of the people in the music business found their first opportunity in the industry through some sort of intern position. Before the days of million dollar, Cristal-popping videos, even Sean "P. Diddy" Combs was an intern for Uptown Records CEO Andre Harrell. We've all been there.

The position that first brought me to New York, at the Independent Label Coalition, was an internship of sorts—which is simply to say that I brought very little experience to the job and was paid (or more precisely, not paid) accordingly. Nevertheless, it was an invaluable opportunity, allowing me to work with a variety of record labels, helping to develop contacts that led directly to my first publishing deal, and providing a crash course in the music business, taught by some great independent music entrepreneurs, including Morris and Adam Levy, Eddie O'Loughlin, Juggy Gayles, Joel Webber, and Tom Silverman.

For a small company with little room for payroll costs, the effective use of interns or other volunteers can be crucial. Much of the day-to-day work of a publisher requires minimal expertise, and can easily be done by someone other than you. Mailing packages, answering phone calls, running copies, researching contacts, and filling out forms is not the best use of your time—particularly if you are already trying to balance the dual role of writer and publisher. It only makes sense to tap into the supply of people eager to break into the business, for whom this work can provide experience and a means of making those first contacts in the industry. Contact your local colleges and trade schools, or try putting an ad in a local music paper. Then hire with care. The fact that you are not paying a salary doesn't mean that any set of hands will do. A good intern is invaluable, but a bad one exacts a sizeable cost. Find someone that you believe can develop into a real partner in the business.

Then it is up to you to make that development happen. If you have something at stake, so does the intern, who is expecting this opportunity to be productive, enjoyable, and educational. Just because the intern is working for free does not make them your servant. Don't bark orders—explain what you need and why. Don't guard your contacts jealously—introduce your intern to them, and let them know that you view the intern as part of your team. Don't leave your intern sitting idle until you think of something you need –think strategically every day about what your intern can be doing to contribute, and have tasks set up when he or she arrives. Better yet, empower the intern with enough information, knowledge, and autonomy to decide what to work on. The more you invest in your employees, the more you get back. This is likely your intern's first foray into the music business. It should be an education, not a hazing.

The ability to effectively build, nurture, and maintain an effective team is often underestimated, particularly by the independent types that gravitate toward the music business. I've heard it said derisively about executives, business owners, producers, and even writers—"they don't really do much, it's their _____ (fill in the blank: co-writer, engineer, business advisor, assistant) that really made the success happen . . . ," as if the only legitimate claim to success was to single-handedly control every aspect of your business. The real leaders in any industry are those who can spot talent (whether it's business or creative), develop a team, inspire the troops, build allies, and preserve relationships. I'm not impressed by soloists. Give me the guy who can lead the band.

Because now it's time to strike it up . . .

PART II

EXPLOITATION:

THE REAL WORK OF PUBLISHING

11

Someone's Knocking at the Door: Welcome to the Land of Opportunity

And so the fun begins. Now that your office is set up, all systems are go, your catalog is a model of organization, and your team is in place—it's time to get down to the real work of music publishing. I'm not sure if exploitation is really the most important aspect of the music publishing business, but it is the function that starts it all. Without it, nothing happens. So what is our first goal as music publishers?

Make Stuff Happen

Make what happen? Well, at this stage, anything. Stuff. Pitching songs is not an exact science; it's not really a science at all. It's more like the chaos theory of the universe—everything in motion all the time, setting off reactions that trigger further reactions without any predictable pattern or logic to govern it all. (Didn't think I'd get that sophisticated on you, did you?) The point is, action is always better than inaction, and any small opportunity that allows your song to be heard has the potential to lead to bigger and better opportunities somewhere else. Of course, you want to find the best and most lucrative placement for your song, and I'm not suggesting that you sell your catalog short. If you have a real reason to think that Faith Hill is going to record your song, don't be too quick to give it away to a new artist on a tiny indie label. Duh.

What I am suggesting is that many opportunities arise simply from putting your songs in play, and when first starting, there is almost no opportunity not worth pursuing. It's easier to pick up speed when you're already moving than when you're standing still. So what kind of stuff are we talking about?

Records

This is the big one. While there are other placement opportunities that are becoming increasingly lucrative, this is still the primary money-maker for music publishers—in part because having a song on a record opens up other doors as well. If your song is recorded by an artist on a legitimate record label, the song then has a chance at getting on the radio (generating performance income), and from there, becoming a hit. If your song becomes a hit, it has a better chance of being placed in a movie or advertisement. Although the balance of power in the industry is changing, the record business is still more often than not the driver that puts the process in motion. Whatever style of music is represented in your catalog, it is always beneficial to get your songs on commercially released records.

Artist or Band Demos

Not nearly as lucrative as having a song on a record, but you gotta start somewhere. If an artist, band, or producer wants to record your song as part of a demo package to shop for a record deal, it may be an opportunity to get in early on a project that everyone will be clamoring to work on a year from now. One of the biggest hits I had as a writer was a song called "Nothing My Love Can't Fix," which was written with the artist Joey Lawrence and my songwriting partner Alexandra Forbes. The song was one of the first that Joey wrote, several months before he obtained a record deal. The song managed to stick on the project all the way through the making of the album, and eventually became the first single. Sometimes the early bird really does get the worm . . .

Radio

Every successful writer remembers hearing his or her song on the radio for the first time. Of course, the obvious way to make this happen is to place the song on a record, and let the label worry about getting it on the playlist. But that's not the only way. Listen to the radio, and pay attention to *all* the music you hear—there's a lot more music out there than you think. Jingles, background music in commercials and promo spots, parodies for the morning show audience, underground, DJ-only "white label" tracks for the Saturday night mix shows, and local band feature spots are all opportunities to get your music on the air.

I recently had a situation in which a song was licensed to a music library, which is a business that provides "background" music for use in local advertising, television, and other venues. The song was plucked out of the library by a radio station in Amsterdam, who used the music in an on-air promo for an upcoming concert festival. Strangely enough, the song became quite identified with both the festival and the station, to the point that we received a request to commercially release the song in Amsterdam, as it had become something of a local summer anthem. Like I said, it's chaos theory, not rocket science.

Television

As I mentioned before, television has become as much a part of the music industry as radio—if video hasn't killed the radio star, it's certainly wrestled him to a draw. In the past two decades there has been a real role-reversal between television and radio, with cable service allowing television to drastically increase the diversity and range of its programming, while radio finds itself increasingly at the mercy of vast conglomerates, who systematically enforce ever-more-restrictive formats on their programmers. Remember, when we're talking about television, we're talking about all the stations on your cable box, not just the major networks. If your music isn't appropriate to any single show on any one of those hundred channels, you may be a bit too unique for your own good.

Movies

Again, don't set your focus too narrowly (think wide-screen). The movie business is not just about the features at a local cineplex near you, but also independent features, foreign films, direct-to-video movies, documentaries, short subjects, and student films. Even if you're issuing a gratis license to a small-budget production, you're building relationships and getting your copyright some exposure. There's no telling where that can lead. The old Elvis Presley song, "A Little Less Conversation," originally appeared in his 1968 movie, *Live a Little, Love a Little*—and was promptly forgotten. It resurfaced more than thirty years later in the George Clooney/Brad Pitt movie *Oceans Eleven*. That exposure then led to a placement in a Nike World Cup Soccer advertisement, for which it was remixed by Dutch producer JXL. And only then did the public finally catch on to the version known as Elvis vs. JXL, which became a massive hit in the UK and America. I couldn't make this stuff up.

Advertising

Talk about a growth market. When I first started in the music industry, there was a very clear distinction between what were known as "jingles," which is to say, music written for an advertising campaign, and pop songs. Most "jingles" were written by "jingle houses," which were companies made up of composers and producers whose primary career focus was to provide advertising firms with catchy theme songs. The money was great, the work was plentiful, and the writers and musicians that did the work usually found that jingle writing provided a much more comfortable lifestyle than the weasel-run record business. Seldom did the two worlds meet.

I had lunch recently with an old friend who owned one of the leading jingle houses in New York back in the day. In our conversation, he bluntly confirmed what I had been suspecting for some time. The jingle business has almost vanished. Turn on your television, and you'll wait a long time before you hear one of those catchy "sing it with a smile" sort of theme songs—"you deserve a break today" and all that. Instead, what do you hear? The Beatles' classic "When I'm Sixty-Four," "Days Go By" by Dirty Vegas, or "Lust For Life" by Iggy Pop. Pop songs of all ages and styles have become the primary source for music in advertising, and this is good news for publishers. Rather than paying a jingle house to write and produce a thirty-second piece of music, usually on a work-for-hire basis, advertising companies are now licensing songs, and at times, master recordings, to give their product a hipper, more "cutting edge" identity. The best part is that, in many cases, the songs selected are not necessarily huge, recognizable hits. Songs like Groove Armada's "I See You Baby . . . " or "Days Go By" are selected in part for their underground credibility. The stigma that was once attached to lending your song to an ad campaign has largely been erased, as well. After all, the Beatles probably need the money less than you do . . .

Live Performance

This is not necessarily a big money maker, but remember: the idea is to get your music in front of people. Obviously, if you are a singer/songwriter or part of a band, you are performing your songs already, as often as possible, in whatever venue you can find. Whether it's in a club, bar, festival, coffeehouse, open mic night, a street corner, or someone's living room, performers need to perform and songs need to be heard.

Beyond the obvious venues, think about other events that can incorporate a musical performance. David Nicoll, one of our Zomba writers, toured the country last year performing his song "Biggie Bounce" at WNBA half-time shows. Sports events, corporate meetings, political gatherings, and church and school activities can all offer opportunities for songs to get the exposure they need.

If you are not a performer, there are other opportunities that may allow you to get your songs in front of a live audience. Seek out local artists, bands, or theater groups that can give your songs a voice. One of the most interesting ideas I've heard recently came from my research assistant Stephanie Delk. She suggested approaching local dance troupes or studios that may be willing to use your songs in performance. This not a profit-oriented exercise—remember, this is Step 1. Make stuff happen. Preferably in front of an audience.

Stores, Restaurants, Clubs

Okay, so it's not exactly an audience. It's more like a group of bystanders. But bystanders are people, and if they aren't exactly listening, they are at least aware of the music playing as they shop, eat, drink, dance, whatever. While many stores use music programs provided by companies like Muzak (another place you can pitch your songs to), there are always small boutiques that may be willing to throw your CD on the stereo and maybe even put a copy up front, near the cash register. Likewise, restaurants, bars, and clubs are all about vibe, and if your music fits their market, they may be more than happy to put your music in the mix. It's not the most straightforward method of pitching songs, but come to think of it, it's probably easier to find weasels hanging out in a bar than to get them to take a meeting in their office.

Needless to say, what we've been discussing thus far is a scattershot approach to exploitation, a sort of jumpstart in the song pitching process. It will be impossible to pursue every possible opportunity, particularly if you are running this publishing company on your own. But it makes sense to explore as many outlets for your material as possible and to use the reactions of each market to develop your overall strategy.

In the end, much of that strategy will be determined by the song catalog itself. Depending on the nature of the music, some markets will be viable, others less so, and some not at all. If your catalog is all death metal, you probably don't need to sink much time into sending CDs out to advertising agencies. Follow the path of least resistance, and go where the music leads you . . .

12

This Is How We Do It: Understanding the Musical Marketplace

While it's impossible to discuss every type of music that may be represented in your catalog, here's a quick overview of some of the largest genres, and the strategies that are most effective within those particular worlds:

Pop

The hardest part of talking about "pop" music is trying to define what "pop" is. Is it just a shortening of the term "popular" music, referring to anything that enjoys mass appeal? Or is it an actual style of music, something not quite rock, and not really urban, and not genuine country, but "pop"? The answer:

Both. Certainly, there is an actual style of music that can be defined as pop, which encompasses vocal groups like the Backstreet Boys and 98°, female superstars like Britney Spears, Christina Aguilera, or Madonna, international acts like S Club 7 or A Teens, or male artists like Enrique Iglesias or Justin Timberlake. There's no other way to describe the music of those artists, except to call it "pop." At the same time, "pop" music also includes a large number of artists or bands that did not start off pop, but simply became so popular that they now enjoy an appeal that stretches beyond the genre from which they came. Nelly is hip-hop, but he's also pop; Shania Twain and Lonestar appeal to fans far outside the country music audience; the Goo Goo Dolls are a rock band, but also a pop act. Get popular enough, and there you are. You're pop.

Because mass appeal tends to mean massive royalties, the pop market is always one of the most competitive and difficult markets to break into, whether you're an artist, a label, a songwriter, or a music publisher. When you're out there pitching pop songs, you are up against the Diane Warrens of the world—writers with long discographies and plenty of platinum records on their walls, most of whom are represented by large corporate publishers. Almost all of the artists in the pop world are on major record labels, are represented by large management firms, and are very difficult to get songs to. If you do manage to get a song in the mix, there are usually forty or fifty other songs on hold for the album. When you're playing in the pop game, you are in the big leagues. Be prepared for the challenges you will face.

So am I telling you to avoid the pop market? No. Despite all the drawbacks, the pop world remains one of the most viable markets for songwriters, for two obvious reasons. First, many of the artists in the pop genre are not self-contained—they don't write all their material. Even those stars who are involved in the writing will often co-write with other songwriters or producers, or will cut two or three outside songs on an album. The pop market then is a good fit for either pure songwriters or writer/producers; it's less suited to singer/songwriters. Which leads us to the second reason that the pop genre remains a viable publisher's market . . .

Pop music is all about HITS! While a successful rock act may be able to make an interesting album that sells despite a lack of radio singles, or a country artist like Willie Nelson may remain viable long after his hit-making days have disappeared, even a superstar pop artist is dependent on a hit single to reach a mass audience through exposure on the radio and MTV. Every pop album needs at least three cuts that are potential hits—and hits are what songwriters and publishers are supposed to provide. One of the most frustrating aspects of developing a pop act is this constant need for that elusive, all-important hit song that will break your artist. You'll hear it everyday from every weasel in town—"We're still looking for that first single." "First single" is just a less intimidating way of saying *hit*!

So now you see why you keep your hits in the top drawer of your desk. Because that's what everyone's looking for. To be more precise, what they're really looking for most of the time is:

- something up-tempo (two-thirds of radio singles are up-tempo)

- something with an interesting, perhaps provocative, but certainly attention-grabbing, lyric

- a big, dramatic chorus that jumps out melodically and repeats at least three times in the song

- an aggressive, dynamic track with a lot of energy and some sort of instrumental part that functions as a secondary hook

If that sounds like a formula, it is. The greatest "pop" songwriters tend to be formulaic writers. They have a recipe that they follow again and again, using their creativity to infuse each song with something fresh, but sticking with a tried-and-true structure that works consistently. Holland-Dozier-Holland, Leiber and Stoller, the Brill Building writers, Pete Waterman, LA and Babyface, Diane Warren, Max Martin—they all have a very precise idea of what it takes to make a hit, and they make sure that every song they write has the required elements. Pop writing is a discipline, and to succeed at it, you have to embrace, rather than resist, the formula.

If pop music is one-half formula, the other half of the equation is fashion. Pop music, more so than almost any genre other than urban music, is a slave of fashion. Rhythms, grooves, sounds, production elements, and lyrical subjects all reflect the times that we live in, and consequently, are constantly going in and out of style. Part of the art of pop songwriting is learning to understand music as fashion—to know what things are about to be cool, which ones are still cool, which things are no longer cool, and which things are so old they're almost cool again. Songs that are dated or out of step with popular culture are missing one of the essential qualities of pop music. It must be timely and relevant. Sure, it's often trendy, but it's the soundtrack to our lives, and it's inevitably of the moment. The trick is to always be ahead, rather than behind, the trends.

If you are going to focus your publishing company on the pop market, you've got to have hits in your catalog. A collection of interesting, personal, introspective ballads will not work. It takes a certain killer instinct to be a pop writer—at Jive Records we like to call it "going for the jugular." The pop market is not a place for quiet, unassuming subtlety. Remember, you're writing songs for artists who want to sell millions of albums all over the world. You need songs that make big statements, in a big way, no holds barred. Irv Gotti, the mastermind behind Murder Inc., has turned urban stars like Ashanti, Ja Rule, and DMX into pop stars. He explains the philosophy that fuels his pop sensibility:

My whole thing is, I want to win. If someone calls me (to do a track), I'm giving them 110 percent, because I want to make hits—and that's it! That's the only thing that matters. Either you make hits in this game or you get the hell out of this game, and I don't want to get out yet.[1]

---

[1] From "Behind the Boards," Rap/Hip-Hop Section, *Billboard* (November 2002)

Of course, the upside to the pop market is the pay-off. A big pop hit is the musical lottery jackpot—it doesn't get any better in this business. In addition to generating huge mechanical and performance payments, a pop hit can easily be placed in movies, television shows, advertisements, juke boxes, and just about anywhere else. Someone might even do a parody of it. Nobody parodies an album track on an underground rock album.

Urban

We're casting a pretty wide net with this terminology—urban music can refer to rap and hip-hop, and all the subgenres within that world, as well as r&b and all the varieties of that genre as well. Everyone from Jay-Z to Destiny's Child to India.Arie to Tweet to Luther Vandross can fit under this umbrella. Not always comfortably, but they'll fit. Of all the genres that feed into the Hot 100, urban music is the one that just keeps growing—artists like Usher, Missy Elliott, or Eve are mainstream superstars that transcend any racial or cultural barriers. Certainly at the present moment, you'll hear a lot more urban music on a pop radio format than you will hear "pop" music.

Not surprisingly, then, urban music is a very good area in which to be a publisher at present. That's because the music is enjoying increasing commercial success, and also because it's one of the most vital, fast-changing, entrepreneurial areas of the music industry. Young businessmen and women like Sean Combs, Rodney Jerkins, Pharrell Williams, Chad Hugo, and Missy Elliott have made their mark at an extraordinarily early age, and have become symbols of success that inspire other young writers, producers, and executives to pursue their dreams. This is a very competitive market with a number of young, superstar writers and executives at the top of their game. But it is also a dynamic and growing market that always remains open to something new and fresh and hot.

The urban market is largely dominated by writer/producers who find talent, develop it, write the songs (or at least co-write them), and produce the records. The Neptunes, Darkchild Productions, Murder Inc., Timbaland, and Missy Elliott are all good examples of the sort of writing and production camps that are the primary source for songs in the urban world. There are also writers that specialize in lyrics and melodies, although it's usually helpful for these writers to be associated with a particular production house as well. Except for certain exceptions, R. Kelly being an obvious one, urban music seems to be largely a team sport, and it's important to be part of a specific musical community. Many of the top production squads have several writers associated with them. These writers work their way up the ranks, learn the craft, and then, once they find success, break off and form their own companies.

The key to success in the urban market hasn't really changed much since the early days of rhythm and blues. As you might gather from the term "urban" music, this genre rewards those who are able to keep their ear to the street. Success in the urban market always grows out of an intense awareness of the community that the music serves and the constantly shifting tastes of what is certainly the most progressive audience in popular music. Rapper AZ breaks it down: "Keep your ears to the street. It's inevitable after that. Once a record is hot in the 'hood, it's like cancer—it's gonna spread."[2]

For all its dynamism, urban music does pose some unique challenges. Particularly on hip-hop tracks, the prevalence of sampling can cut the owner-ship of a copyright down to an amount hardly worth administering. The standard of production expected for demos is very high—you'd better be sure that you or your writers have access to a quality studio in which to record. No excuses allowed here. The tracks have got to be bangin'. The lyric subject matter of many urban hits can sometimes limit exploitation opportuni-ties—while film opportunities abound, television and advertising is trickier. It's hard to put "My Neck, My Back" on a prime time television spot. And finally, there's not much comfort zone in this market. Fashions change in the urban market faster than anywhere else. You can go from cold to red hot to cold again very, very quickly. Sustaining a long-term career in this world requires at least nine lives.

Country

Things are tough down on Music Row. Slumping sales, tightening playlists, increasing promotion costs, and an endless succession of mergers and acquisi-tions have combined to make the current situation in country music a little too similar to one of those old time gloom-and-doom country songs. "If it weren't for bad luck I'd have no luck at all . . . "

Having said that, there are still more successful independent publish-ers in the country market than anywhere else, primarily for one important reason. For the most part, country music artists don't write their own songs. There are many exceptions to this, of course. But unlike the pop and urban markets, where the artist is often at least a co-writer in the process and usual-ly takes outside material only for potential singles, many country artists will have eight or nine outside songs on an album. You don't have to crunch those numbers very hard to see the amount of opportunity that this opens up for writers and publishers. This is why Nashville has always been a song town. Unlike New York and LA, there is a real appreciation for songs and for the craft of writing and music publishing. You can find more songwriters in the Noshville Diner at lunchtime than in all of New York.

And these guys are good. Real good. Nashville songwriters are the consummate professionals—disciplined and extremely well-versed in the craft of writing a song. This means everyone writes music, lyrics, and melodies, and most of 'em play a pretty mean guitar, as well. Such competition makes this a very tough town to break into, but it also tends to make for long careers. Many country writers stretch their success over two or three decades.

On the publisher's side, it's a similar story—the country market is the last bastion of true, old-fashioned music publishing. Unlike their LA and New York counterparts, who tend to focus on the banking aspect of the gig, Nashville publishers still develop writers, critique songs, suggest rewrites, and then run the songs around town until they get them cut. I called the head of a major Nashville publisher recently and was told he was "out playin' some songs for people." That don't happen much in New York or LA. If you want to truly learn music publishing from the ground up, Nashville is the place to do it.

And if you're gonna take on the country music market, Nashville is where you need to be. While there are a number of cities that have viable country music scenes, the business is still very much centered in Nashville. Ultimately you will benefit by the exposure to other writers and publishers, as well as the A&R community. The toughest part of the country business is breaking into the close-knit, and yes, sometimes closed-minded Nashville establishment, made up of longtime label execs, a handful of record producers, and the prominent artist managers. The sooner you acquaint yourself with the beast and begin to understand it, the sooner you can take it on.

In many respects, Nashville is the direct opposite of the urban market. While urban music is dominated by writers who are also producers, country music tends to draw a very distinct line between those two functions. Most country writers do not produce the songs they write. Instead they pitch their songs to a handful of well-established producers who control the majority of projects in Nashville. Most of these producers are not songwriters.

Because of the emphasis on a distinctive production sound, most demos in the urban market have to be virtual records; in Nashville, it is still possible to convey a song with a simple demo. And while the urban market is a wild ocean of constant change, the country market by comparison is a slow-moving stream. In Nashville, everything lasts for a good while—singles stay on the charts for months, artists can stay popular for a decade or more, trends last for four or five years, and writers can keep churning out hits for several decades. Memories last a long time down there as well—as do grudges, feuds, and burnt bridges. It takes a lot of patience to break into the country club, and a great deal of care and feeding of your relationships to stay in it.

Despite the shrinking number of new releases each year by country artists, records remain the primary focus of most song pluggers in Nashville. But the real value of having a song recorded in the country market is not mechanical royalties, but the possibility of radio airplay, should your song be selected as a single. The economic realities of the country marketplace are that top albums often sell less than a million records, which doesn't yield a huge return in mechanical royalties. However, a country radio single can be extraordinarily lucrative, as there are more country music stations than any other format in the US. Country singles often spend as long as a year in regular radio rotation. That makes for a mighty big ASCAP or BMI check.

At the same time, the Americana appeal of country music makes it well-suited to advertising (check out Lonestar's "What About Now" on the Toyota truck commercials) and the movies (witness the overwhelming success of the *O Brother, Where Art Thou?* soundtrack). Live performance is another means of establishing a writer in Music City, where the famous songwriter "circles" can provide an opportunity for new writers to showcase their songs in a casual environment, in front of an industry crowd.

Personally, I believe that the country music market is in much the same position that the pop music market was back in the early '90s. It's just waiting for a few great acts, a few exciting new writers, and a few dynamic entrepreneurs to revitalize what has become a somewhat stale business environment. There is simply too much talent among the writers and artists in country music, and the appeal of the music extends too deep into the American psyche for this genre not to make a comeback in the near future. Get in while the gettin' is good . . .

Rock

This can be a very challenging publishing environment. Because the rock market revolves primarily around self-contained bands and singer/songwriters, most rock publishers focus primarily on trying to sign bands or artists that either have obtained a major label record deal or are on the verge of doing so. Even this strategy, which sounds like betting on a sure thing, carries with it considerable risk. Most publishing deals in such situations are quite expensive, requiring six-figure advances and the expectation of promotional support as well. The chances of success are frighteningly low. Very few bands that are signed to major labels will sell enough records to earn back their advance. Unless you are working with a very large pool of capital, or are focused solely on underground, developing bands, it can be extremely challeging to acquire viable writers.

I'm guessing that most readers working in this genre are not as interested in acquiring other catalogs as they are in representing their own work. If you are a singer/songwriter or an active writer within a band, the challenge you face as a publisher is not unlike the challenge you face as an artist. First and foremost, you need a record deal. In the rock market, mechanical royalties are still the primary source of income for a publisher. Radio airplay is much more limited in this market than in pop, urban, and country, and depending on the nature of the music you write, advertising and television opportunities can be limited as well. It's tough to fit a Tori Amos song into an advertisement. Ditto for a Mudvayne song. It's hard to put Puddle of Mudd on a sitcom. Not impossible, but you don't want to build your business on it. You really need record sales.

Certainly, part of your role as a publisher is to supplement the efforts of your manager or whoever is out there trying to generate a record deal. In many ways, the job of a rock publisher can be more like an artist manager than a traditional music publisher. Publicity, tour scheduling, club booking, and do-it-yourself radio promotion can all fall into your job description.

Now let's make this even tougher. What if you're a rock writer, but not a performer? Wow. That one almost stumps the panel. Pitching songs to largely self-contained bands or singer/songwriters is just about the toughest proposition in the music business, but that doesn't mean it hasn't or can't be done. Most of the writers that have been successful in this endeavor are also producers—the expectation is usually that the producer will write with the band, produce the record, and hopefully provide the hit single that the band was unable to come up with on their own. People like Glen Ballard (Alanis Morissette), Desmond Child (Bon Jovi), Mark Hudson (Aerosmith), and Mutt Lange (The Coors) are known as the producers who can help to shape an artist or an album, and who can provide the hit song that allows an artist to cross over to mainstream success.

This is a different business than pitching a finished song—you're really pitching the writer and his or her ability to work with the artist to come up with the right song. In order to sell yourself in that way, you are going to have to show some sort of track record of success.

This means starting small and slowly moving up the musical food chain. Find an unsigned, developing artist to work with, try to write some songs together, see if you can produce the demo, and help them to land a record deal. Next, go out and find a signed band that's struggling—maybe their first album didn't do as well as expected, or they're an older group in need of reinvention, or a new act that the label just can't get a handle on. Again, if you can give the project shape, and provide a hit song in the process, you can take the next step up. It's a long climb to the Aerosmith or Santana gig. But hey, that's rock and roll.

In the meantime, your role as a rock publisher is to find any of the exploitation opportunities that do exist for the type of music that you do. In most cases, movies are the most viable market, and in many cases, film producers will be open to using a relatively unknown artist, or even one without a record deal, if the price and the song are right. In addition to generating sync fees, this can be a major step in getting you or your band signed to a label, particularly if the movie will have a soundtrack album. Lisa Loeb and the Calling are just two examples of artists whose first breaks came from a film opportunity. Rock publishers are a fixture at film conventions like Sundance, hyping their artists to movie producers and directors.

If your music is somewhat pop-oriented, television can also offer placement opportunities—*Felicity*, *Dawson's Creek*, and MTV shows like *Real World* all tend to use rock songs and give them enough prominence to provide a real promotional opportunity. If your music is too hard for those sorts of shows, you might consider the sports networks like ESPN or extreme sports shows, which often go for more alternative, high-testosterone music.

When it comes to advertising, it's all a question of lifestyle—what sorts of things does your audience buy? Sports gear, computers, video games, cars, and beer usually make some sense. Insurance, dishwashing liquid, and investment accounts—not so much.

My other advice to publishers specializing in the rock market: consider diversifying. I know I said all that stuff about focus and now here I am telling you to broaden your horizon . . . Sorry. This is a really tough market. And you may find that there is another genre in which your songs can be effective, without making drastic changes in your musical approach. There's no shortage of examples here—Rob Thomas has penned singles for Santana and Willie Nelson; Desmond Child goes from Aerosmith to Ricky Martin; Mutt Lange has had some success with a country girl named Shania. You may find that the contemporary Christian rock scene can offer you an alternative environment in which to explore another side of your catalog. You might also consider opting for a more global approach. Outside the US, rock artists are not nearly so self-contained, particularly if they are making an English-language album. Don't be afraid to try something a little outside of your own frame of reference—you may find a secondary market that can sustain you until that big record deal comes your way.

There you have it. Pop, urban, rock and country. Which leaves only about 36,785 genres and subgenres in the contemporary music world that I've failed to mention. Let me guess—what you do falls into one of those neglected categories. Okay, fine. Let's take a look at a few more markets, but we'll keep it short and sweet. Here's a thumbnail summary.

Dance: Compilation albums, movies, and advertising are the key here. And this is pop music in the rest of the world, so make sure you take a global view.

Adult Contemporary: Similar to country, in that airplay is the big money earner. Right now, adults are buying records in ever-increasing numbers, so this is a growing market for the first time in many years. The goal is to write a classic song. If you do, you can get it cut a dozen times.

Latin: Another booming market. Best of all, many of these artists will make albums in both Spanish and English, so there tend to be a fair number of projects going on all the time. Writer/producers tend to fare best in this world. Miami is where much of the action is.

Instrumental Music: Many of the opportunities here tend to be in the film, television, and advertising worlds; consider contributing to music libraries as well. There may be some income in print music—consider partnering with a sheet music publisher to exploit those markets.

Enough already. The point here is that the rules of the game change drastically depending on whose field you're playing on. You must adapt your approach to fit the market you're in.

In the following chapters, we'll discuss at length the role of a Creative Director within a publishing enterprise—and the various strategies that can be employed to exploit copyrights for fun and profit. Depending on the genre in which your catalog is based, some of these strategies will be more useful than others. Don't get caught up in specifics, and don't be too quick to decide that a particular approach won't work in your market. Remember, until a visionary like Moby came along, no one thought dance music had much use in advertising. Try to understand the general concepts and then adapt them to your company's specific needs. It's always easy to see what doesn't work. Only experimentation will show you what does.

13

My Name Is:
The Creative Director

Now that you've got your very own publishing company, have you given yourself a title? It's a little weird right? Especially if you're the only person in the company. But what did you go for? President? Impressive. CEO? Very corporate. Manager? A little bland.

I've got one for you . . .

Creative Director. Because whatever else you are—accountant, office manager, secretary—this is what you really need to be. This job gets a couple of different titles in publishing companies—sometimes it's Professional Manager (which is probably the vaguest title in the entire corporate realm), or Creative Manager (which is okay), or my first title, Creative Services (which is just plain weird). But whatever you want to call it, this is the job that you signed up for when you became a publisher. A good Creative Director is a music critic, producer, song-plugger, PR person, coach, and cheerleader, all rolled into one. Being all of those things is what Part II of this book is all about.

When I first started in the publishing business, I had very little actual job experience and not much knowledge of the complexities of the industry. Thankfully, the one thing I did have is songwriting experience. Having been signed to several different publishers, I had the opportunity to work with a variety of top-notch Creative Directors, all of whom approached the job in slightly different ways, but all of whom provided invaluable guidance and direction to this wayward songwriter. I just wish I had listened to them more closely at the time. I did know this much about the gig: I was supposed to **make stuff happen**. Since then, I've learned how and what . . .

There are three primary functions that should occupy the Creative Director's day:

- getting the music right

- getting the music out

- moving the writer up

In that order. Put a note on your bulletin board, or tear this page out of the book and frame it on the wall (just kidding). Keep these three things in mind at all times. Now that you have recognized their importance, it is a fundamental law of the universe that all forces will conspire to continually divert your focus from these three things. Paperwork, business affairs, accounting questions, and copyright problems will always be there lurking, ready to rear their ugly heads. You can't ignore these other issues, but you can control them and keep them in their place. Remember your job title. First and foremost, you are a Creative Director. Get the music right. Get it out. Move the writer up.

Getting the Music Right

First things first . . . and in the music business, getting the music right *should* always come first. Before strategies are in place, before calls are made, before schmoozing is done, and before CDs are placed in the mail, the music must be right. As a Creative Director, you simply cannot put yourself in the position of pushing songs that you don't believe in. You may not always have a smash hit to pitch for every project, but every song that you send out must meet your professional standards. When an A&R person or a producer listens to the song you've sent them, it's not just the song being judged. It's also you, the sender. These professionals are judging your taste level, your musical standards, and your ability to understand what they are looking for and to provide it. If they think that you are trying to sell them material that you know is substandard, they will be insulted and rightly so. If they think that you don't even know the material is substandard, they will write you off entirely.

Your first role then is that of music critic. As I mentioned earlier, one of the chief benefits to acting as your own publisher is to afford you a certain distance from your own songs so that you can critique them with objectivity. Songwriters often work in a rush of creativity that makes it easy to overlook inherent problems within a song or musical shortcomings in the demo. The Creative Director's role is to step in after that initial burst of energy, recognize a song's strengths and weaknesses, and make suggestions as to how to fix the elements that aren't working. The Creative Director must have the discipline to send the writer back to the studio (even if the writer is you) as many times as it takes to get it right. You are your publishing company's Quality Control Department. Nothing goes out until it receives your stamp of approval.

Here's a test for you. Put your most recent demo in the stereo and hit play. Now close your eyes, and imagine that you're sitting across from Clive Davis, pitching your song. Are there things you want to make excuses for? Then those need to be fixed. Is there a lyric line that makes you wince? Change it. Any notes in the vocal that make you cringe? Tune 'em up. Is it getting boring halfway through the second verse? Add something to the arrangement. As the song ends, try to imagine Clive's reaction. Is he bouncing out of his chair, waving his arms with enthusiasm? (That's a pretty funny picture actually.) Is he nodding half-heartedly? Is he checking his watch?

The point is simple. When you play a song for anyone in the industry, you should be able to do so with confidence. No excuses, no explanations, no imagination required. Ultimately, a song is going to have to do a lot more than pass your quality test in order to get cut—it's going to have to blow people away. Quality control is the minimum standard.

Of course, the difficulty is that songs can be maddeningly hard to judge. Anyone that's been in the business for long has been fooled at least once, and either rejected a song that became a hit, or recorded a song that was a sure smash, only to see it flop. And of course, everybody who hears a song has an opinion, for whatever that's worth. But if you listen to enough demos every-day, you start to develop a pretty clear picture of what's important in a song and where most songs tend to go wrong. With allowances then for a certain subjectivity and gut instinct that is part of the process, I offer you:

The Song Quality Checklist

(This should be fun, huh?)

1. Does the title sound like a "hit"?

I can almost invariably tell whether a song is any good simply by looking at the title. Real "hit" songs have "hit" titles—interesting, provocative, funny, and unique. "Genie in a Bottle," "Stutter," "Pass the Courvoisier," "Sk8r Boi"—these titles stand out. Most of the time, it's obvious which songs have single potential just by looking at the titles on an album.

The king of great titles is Mutt Lange. While my general rule is that one- to three-word titles work best, Mutt's titles are so good they can break all the rules. "Man, I Feel Like a Woman," "Pour Some Sugar On Me," "I Said I Loved You

(But I Lied)"—these titles have sold the song before the music has even started. Conversely, titles like "Without You" or "You Are the One" are all but D.O.A. I can tell by the title that I've heard this song too many times before.

Fixing a title is tricky—it's a little like fixing the framework of your house after it's already been built. But sometimes it's just a matter of adding or subtracting a word or two, or even changing the punctuation. Britney Spears' ". . . Baby One More Time" is more interesting than "Baby One More Time." Try to picture how the title of your song would look on the Billboard chart. Would it stand out?

2. Is there a concept for the song?

A weak title is usually an indicator of a more serious problem. Songs called "Without You" are not really about anything, or at least not anything very interesting. There's not an original idea at the core of the song. Take a look at the hit titles. You can see that there's an idea, a concept behind every song. "Stutter" by Joe is about a girl who starts to stutter when she has to explain where she's been. That's an idea worth writing a song about. "Without You" is not. Most songs miss the top drawer because the core idea of the song is simply not compelling. If the concept is weak, it's very hard to rescue the song, no matter what you do with it musically or lyrically.

3. Is the lyric effective? Appropriate? Convincing? Singable? Appealing? Cliché free?

It's the eternal debate between composers and lyricists—do lyrics matter? I'll settle it for you here and now. Yes. Of course it's possible to come up with examples of songs in which a banal lyric is redeemed by a great track, just as it's possible to come up with a lyric that has made something special of a relatively standard melody. There are an awful lot of songs out there—you can find an example to prove almost anything. But as someone who listens to songs everyday, I will tell you plainly, lyrics matter. A lot.

This is not to say that there's anything wrong with a simple, direct lyric. In many cases, particularly in dance music or urban music, that's the only kind of lyric that will be effective and appropriate. "Music Sounds Better With You" is a great lyric—one interesting line, repeated over and over. It's exactly what the song needs. Conversely, a lyric that sounds false or forced can kill a song on the spot.

The words have to sing. If there's a line in a song that makes you cringe, it's usually because the lyrics feel awkward; the melody and words are out of sync with one another. This is a job for Creative Director. Find those clinkers and get 'em out of there. Also, the singer has to want to sing the words. Lyrics function not only within the song but also within the context of the artist's image. Songs that put the singer in a poor light are tough to get covered. Most artists prefer to present themselves as strong and independent, rather than needy and whiny. (They save the needy and whiny stuff for offstage).

Finally, one quick word about clichés. Stock rhymes, like "fire" and "desire," or trite, predictable metaphors drive A&R people nuts. When you're writing a song, it's easy to pass these clichés off—after all, the line sings well and it's only one line . . . but when you listen to hundreds of songs a day, it's not just one line. It's the same stupid, clichéd line that you've heard on ten other songs already today. I once listened to twenty songs in a catalog, and found that eighteen had references to birds flying, and nineteen mentioned rivers running. You start to notice that sort of stuff. Spare me. Spare us all.

4. Is the song structured correctly? Is there a natural build and release within the song structure?

There are endless ways to structure a song, but only about three that actually work:

Verse/B Section/Chorus/Verse/B Section/Chorus/Bridge/Break/
   Chorus Out (?)
Verse (with hook line at the end)/Verse/Bridge/Verse/Break or Bridge
   (repeat)/Verse (or half verse) (?)
Chorus/Verse/Chorus/Bridge/Verse/Chorus Out

The form I see quite often, particularly from singer/songwriters is this one:

Verse/Verse/Verse/Bridge/Verse

Sometimes, if I'm lucky, the title will show up somewhere in there, buried in yet another verse. This is not a structure. This is a stream of consciousness expression. Song structure works on basic principles: use the best parts more than once, don't take too long to get to the best parts, and have at least one section that comes as a bit of a surprise. Try the Clive Davis test. Note if or when you start feeling bored. You just found the weak part of your structure.

Often structural problems can be fixed with a few simple edits. Cut out that boring part, move the chorus sooner, or go straight into the out choruses after the bridge. As the Creative Director, you should feel free to experiment with any options you feel move the song along more effectively—and help to bring it in at less than four minutes. Fact: if your song can't be performed in less than four minutes, it's probably not going to get on the radio. So you might as well make the cuts now. There's no reason for a five-minute demo.

5. Does the arrangement serve the song? Does it enhance the song?

People often speak about arrangement and production as if the two were synonymous. I prefer to distinguish between them. Arrangements are concerned primarily with musical parts and structure, while production is centered around sonic and performance considerations. A drum pattern is an arranging issue; a snare sound is a production one. A background string line is an arranging element; the fact that the strings are out of tune is a production problem.

The first rule of arranging is that nothing should detract from the listener's focus on the melody and lyric. Background parts should not clash with the vocal, and the instrumentation and tempo should fit the mood of the lyric. Most songwriters are protective enough of their song that this is usually not a problem. Lyricists particularly tend to be ever-vigilant about anything that might obscure their favorite line. (Every line is a lyricist's favorite line.)

More often, the problem is that songwriters fail to use the arrangement to enhance the song. Too many demos are nothing but drums, bass, some sort of pad laying down the chords, maybe a string part, and a few orchestra hits, repeating the same patterns until the fade.

On any classic record of almost any style, there is some sort of instrumental hook built into the arrangement of the song—the bass line in "Billie Jean," the string lines in "Yesterday," the guitar riff on "Johnny B. Goode," the pan flute melody on "My Heart Will Go On," the surf guitar and horn lines on "Livin' La Vida Loca," the organ part on "Like a Rolling Stone"—these elements support the song and give it a unique identity. They can also add a sense of dramatic development, providing a jolt of surprise when they first appear, a sense of change when they disappear, and emphasis when they reappear.

Listen to your demo and identify the instrumental hooks. If you're not sure your song has any hooks—then the song isn't done. Go back to the drawing board.

6. Is the tempo right? Does the song drag?

You never really understand the importance of getting the tempo right until you play your song at a pitch meeting. Suddenly, the up-tempo groove that felt so in-the-pocket when you heard it in your office seems to plod, and the ballads seem to run out of gas entirely, stalling to a dead stop somewhere around the second verse. Something must be wrong with the CD player. Take it from a veteran of this syndrome—do not adjust your stereo. There is nothing wrong. Nothing, that is, except the song's tempo.

In my experience, you want to push the tempo up to the breaking point and then pull back just slightly from that. You'll hate me for it until you get to the pitch meeting. You can thank me later.

7. Is the production of the demo "dynamic" and "in your face"?

Production is one of those vague terms that can encompass almost every element of a recording, from the instrumentation to the vocal performance to the mix. My primary concern here is sonic quality and musical performance. Are the sounds fashionable, fresh, and interesting? Are the reverbs, delays, distortions, and other effects used effectively? Is the mix properly balanced (keeping in mind that what constitutes a proper balance differs radically from genre to genre)? Are the instruments and vocals in tune and in time? Does the recording have drive and excitement?

The impact of music is not just emotional or intellectual. It's also physical. If you don't know what I mean, crank a little Nine Inch Nails on your stereo. You get it now? The drums and bass should be a physical force that almost literally pushes the music along. You should feel the bottom of the track in your gut. Snare drums should crack with energy. Demos that have this sort of power immediately set themselves apart from 80 percent of the music that comes across an A&R person's desk, most of which is tidy and pleasant, and also soft and mushy. Don't be timid. Try to blow those weasels right out of their chairs.

8. Does the demo fit clearly into one specific genre? Is that the appropriate genre for the song?

For many songwriters, the creative process is one of complete freedom— an impulsive act of imagination unrestricted by commercial or marketing considerations. That's great. But it's not how it works for the Creative Director. It's your job to figure out where this particular piece could possibly, maybe, hopefully fit in the giant puzzle of the music industry—and then make sure that it fits there. Often it requires more creativity than was used in writing the song.

Sometimes the only way to figure out where a song belongs is to narrow it down, step by step. What type of artist would sing this lyric? How young or old would the artist need to be? What rhythmic feel and tempo works best for this particular melody? I try not to get too caught up at first in chord progressions and the instrumentation on the demo, as those elements can sometimes deceive you. If a song's melody, lyric, and rhythmic feel really fit better into a genre different than the one in which the song was originally conceived, it's always possible for a writer to restructure the chord progression and redo the demo.

For example, if a ballad needs to be sung by an older male artist, it's in three-four time, and it's a lyric about the tragic loss of a loved one—it's a country song, no matter what the writer thinks. That's about the only genre where you'll find an older male artist or in which radio will play a ballad in waltz time, particularly one with a tear-jerking lyric. Go back to the studio, add guitar and fiddle, and take out the five-note chords.

It's often up to the Creative Director to figure out what a song truly wants to be, then to imagine where it could possibly fit in the market, and then somehow reconcile those two realities. That's why you get to have "Creative" in your title.

9. Does the song have the potential for mass appeal? Is it the right size?

No, I'm not talking about the length of the song—that stays under four minutes, no matter what. I'm talking about something much more conceptual, something . . . big.

This is something I was never much aware of as a writer, but it's become increasingly apparent to me as a publisher. Most writers write small, rather than big. So many songs are like lovely little miniature paintings: a melancholy little lyric, with a little hook buried at the end of each little chorus, with a lot of little chords and a melody that never really strays too far from a little six- or seven-note range. In the end, the listener is touched by a little emotion and reacts with a little smile, a nod, and then, in very little time, forgets about the song entirely.

I remember seeing U2 on MTV's *Total Request Live* a year or two ago, when they performed "Beautiful Day" on the balcony of the Viacom building, beamed into Times Square on the giant Jumbotron screen. That's what I mean by BIG. One of the great things about U2 is that they write BIG— BIG, GRANDIOSE ANTHEMS WITH BIG LYRIC IDEAS AND BIG MELODIES AND BIG GUITARS AND BOOMING DRUMS MADE TO BE PLAYED IN BIG PLACES FOR BIG CROWDS. A U2 song can be an event. So can a Springsteen song. The same is true of songs by Jam and Lewis, or Eminem, or Missy Elliott. They are capable of working on a large scale. They can move the crowd.

Now there's nothing inherently wrong with a small song. They can be intimate and touching, and quite satisfying to a coffeehouse full of friends and family. But if you want to reach a large audience and to create a song that has the potential of becoming a classic, you're going to have to think bigger. I recently heard an interview with Eminem, who talked about his primary challenge as a young performer being that of learning to come out of his shell, to lose his self-consciousness, and project the larger-than-life persona that he has today.

This is where the cheerleader aspect of the Creative Director comes in. One of the most important roles a Creative Director can play is to encourage his or her writer to paint on an increasingly large canvas, to move from miniatures, to portraits, to murals. Or to the Times Square Jumbotron.

Obviously this is tougher to do if you are not only the Creative Director but also the writer. Still, the truth is that we all talk to ourselves all the time—writers more so than most everyone else, except for the crazy guys on the subway. Your work as a Creative Director should be reflected in your interior dialogue, and the conversation should be one of a tough but supportive coach—not tolerating any attempt to take the easy, safe way out but rather demanding that you set your sights higher and aim for greatness over mediocrity. Most songwriters fail to leave an impression simply because they think too small and aim too low. Go for the BIG hit.

Wow. A checklist for songs. That felt very creative, didn't it? Sort of like checking a car for defects when it comes off the assembly line. Wouldn't it be easier to just go by gut instinct and decide whether you like the song or not?

Maybe. There's no question that many songs succeed better when listened to than when analyzed. "I Want It That Way" by the Backstreet Boys was probably one of the best pure pop songs written in the last decade, despite the fact that it starts out by rhyming "fire" and "desire," and has a lyric that I still haven't been able to make any sense of. But it also has a can't-miss melody and a brilliant arrangement and production. It just works. Of course, it's easy to follow your first impression and give a song the old "make it or break it" test. No need to dissect the thing—you either like it or you don't.

The problem is that as a Creative Director, your job is not to decide whether you like or dislike the song. It's to figure out how to fix it. Or improve it. Or improve the writer. A quick gut reaction is not going to accomplish that. A writer needs to understand what works and what doesn't, and be offered some constructive suggestions as to what can be done to make the song viable. In order to provide that, a Creative Director has to learn to look at songs in an organized and thorough fashion. "Nah, I'm not really feeling it," is just about the most depressing thing you can say to a songwriter—not because it's negative, but because it implies that the song is hopeless.

As you practice listening to songs in a more precise way, you will also start to find that things are often better than they first appear to be. A few lyric changes, a new drum pattern, or a new demo singer can reveal that there was more potential to a song than you might have initially thought. A careful consideration as to where a song fits in the market may reveal that it has potential in more than one genre. If nothing else, a consistent approach to looking at songs in this analytical way will help you, as Creative Director, to better understand your writer and his or her strengths and weaknesses—even if you and the writer are one and the same person. By maintaining an unrelenting determination to get the music right, you will begin to figure out what it will take to move your writer up . . .

14

We'd Be So Good Together: The Art of Collaboration

Analysis is easy.

In case you haven't noticed, there are plenty of people in this world who are happy to tell you what's wrong with something. There are far fewer who are interested in trying to help you fix it. What if you figure out what elements in a song need to improved, and you send your writer (that is, you) back to the drawing board . . . and the song comes back no better than before? What if you simply hit a creative wall and every idea starts to fall into the same old rut? What then?

First of all, don't panic. This is not unusual. It's never easy to rewrite, and everyone has those moments when everything they do starts to sound the same. Secondly, don't give up trying to get the music right. The standards of the industry don't change just because you're having trouble reaching them. Step 3—pick up your phone and call someone who cares:

A co-writer.

When I was a songwriter, it always seemed that Creative Directors spent most of their time setting up collaborations between writers. I always suspected that this was because it's a lot easier than going out and trying to get songs cut. I was right.

For a good Creative Director, setting up co-writes is an easy, low-risk proposition—a couple of phone calls to another Creative Director ("Why don't we have your guy write with my guy? How's Tuesday?") and in no time you've made something happen. If the collaboration goes poorly, who can blame you for trying it? It's like your Mom setting you up for a date with her best friend's son or daughter.

The strange thing is, often enough, it actually works—which is probably more than you can say for Mom's attempts at matchmaking. Done strategically by a competent Creative Director, co-writes can be productive both musically and from a business standpoint. Co-writes can help shore up a writer's weaknesses, increase his or her presence in the community, provide an entrance into new markets, and often, just keep a writer from growing stagnant or frustrated. Sometimes a new face in the studio and a different perspective is enough to break a dry spell.

Shortly after I signed my first publishing deal as a writer with Zomba Music, I ran into what was the most difficult case of writer's block I've ever experienced. Even now, twenty years later, I can recall the terrible mix of emotions—the pressure of wanting to prove myself to my new business partner, the desperation as deadlines for projects grew ever closer, and the absolute inability to generate one simple idea, either musically or lyrically. I was completely dry.

What finally brought me out of this ordeal was a trip I made to the UK to record the one song that I'd managed to eke out. While I was over there, Zomba set me up with several UK writers to work on material for various projects that the record label was developing. At that time, I wrote primarily on my own. I had written with one or two people in New York, but I was hardly an experienced collaborator. (I was hardly even an experienced songwriter.) Suddenly, I was in someone else's studio, in a different country, with a co-writer staring back at me, expecting me to do something creative. And almost immediately, I could feel the clouds in my head begin to clear.

I have never forgotten the experience and think of it often in my work now, when I see one of my writers sliding into a funk. Writing can be a tremendously lonely experience. Sometimes a writer just needs some company. It's amazing how easily another writer can walk in and solve a problem that has been perplexing you for days. "Why don't you just go to this chord, and then have the chorus come in like this?" Eureka. Sometimes getting the music right means getting the right people in the room together.

Finding Collaborators

Alas, getting the right people in the room is sometimes easier said than done. For readers located in a music center like New York, LA, Nashville, or Atlanta, finding other songwriters should not require much sleuthing. If you can't find someone to write with in Nashville, you'd better take the boards off your windows and doors and start getting out a little more. In all of these cities there is a full calendar of events sponsored by the performance societies, NARAS, and other organizations like the Songwriters Hall of

Fame or the Nashville Songwriters Association International. These events are intended to provide information and professional advice to songwriters, as well as to offer them a chance to get together and develop relationships. If you're feeling brave, you can also check community newspapers like the *Village Voice* in New York, which carries advertisements by musicians and songwriters seeking collaborators (although I'd make sure you hear some music before setting up a personal meeting). A more obvious approach is to simply immerse yourself in the local music scene and begin to approach those writers who interest you.

Once you find someone with whom you click, the number of other interested parties will likely grow. Every songwriter knows at least one other writer, and writers have been known to gossip every now and then. You can also begin to utilize your A&R contacts to find collaborators. Within the conversation at a pitch meeting, try to get a sense of which writers the A&R person is working with right now or which developing writers he or she is excited about.

Or, you can always ask another Creative Director. As I said before, they usually like to set up co-writes. Be prepared to offer some sort of description of what you do, who you've worked with or who recommended you, and, if possible, what projects you are currently writing for. You should also expect to be asked for a compilation of some of your work. You can request the same for any writers suggested to you. Writers and publishers work in a variety of ways—some Creative Directors take a hands-on approach to managing their writers' calendars and will book every appointment, while others may just give you a phone number for a writer and suggest that you get in touch directly.

It's important to remember that the collaboration is between not just the writers, but the Creative Directors as well. Follow up with the other Creative Director after the writing session to let them know how it went, thank them, and tell them when to expect the demo. Once the demo is in, you can follow up again to get his or her reaction and brainstorm as to where the song could be shopped.

If you are far outside of any music business center, then all this gets a bit more challenging. If you are in a city that at least offers a vibrant local music scene, you can simply focus on trying to develop relationships in that community, using local writers groups, songwriting associations, music festivals, and other events as an opportunity to get to know the active songwriters in your area. But if you are in a more remote location, without any local music scene to speak of—well then, I'm afraid you'd better pack your bags.

No, not to relocate. But you are going to have to hit the road every now and then. Find the location best suited to your particular style of music and plan a trip. Ideally, plan to divide your time between writing sessions and A&R meetings. You may want to consider scheduling around an industry event or conference—CMJ or the Billboard Dance Conference in New York, the ASCAP, BMI, or Grammy Awards in LA, or the Country Music Awards in Nashville. This gives you a reason for being in town and an event to fill your day if you're not able to book a full calendar of writing sessions. It also helps to ensure that most people will be in town when you are.

Unless you have a significant track record, it can be very challenging to break into a new music community in this way. Plan your trip a reasonable time in advance and don't set your hopes too high—you will build contacts here the same way as anywhere else, one co-write at a time. You need to emphasize to the writers and Creative Directors with whom you're working that you will be making regular trips, then try to find ways to keep the writing relationships active even when you're back at home. Perhaps you can send lyrics or tracks back and forth to write to.

With the ability to send MP3 files via the Internet, it has become even easier to exchange ideas over long distance. I have one writing team in which one member is in Denmark and the other in New York. They actually mix their demos together by sending Pro Tools files to each other. If you choose to live outside of a musical community, you have to accept that you will probably not have the opportunity to write with dozens of different writers. Instead, the key will be to find one or two collaborations that can be built into real relationships and then do whatever is necessary to develop those partnerships.

As a Creative Director, it's important that you do your homework thoroughly before scheduling a writing trip. This means identifying the key writers that you want to make contact with, finding out who books their writing sessions, securing a place to work (hotel room, studio, writing room), understanding how the co-writers like to work and what they consider their strengths and weaknesses, and managing the calendar so that there is enough time with each collaborator to be productive.

Working styles are very different from one city or one genre to another. Nashville tends to be very businesslike, with writers keeping something approximating banker's hours and booking writing sessions four to six weeks in advance. Most writing sessions in Nashville are done either at someone's home or in a publisher's writing room (which usually includes some sort of crude recording equipment for making a quick work tape). Conversely, New York and LA writers think a noon start is early and are usually hard-pressed to tell you what's on their schedule next week, much less four weeks ahead of time. You'll need to be more flexible in these situations and should probably have backup plans in case of a last-minute cancellation. Country writers tend to book sessions with different writers every day; pop and urban writers usually need two or three days together to work effectively.

And then of course there's that old wild card, "chemistry"—a lack or a surplus of which can throw even the best-laid plans askew. It is one of the great mysteries of human existence: Why can two people meet and within minutes be finishing each other's sentences, while another two are in a screaming match in the next room? Why do some people write well with people they can barely tolerate, while others find it impossible to work with their best friend? Why is Jagger so much better with Richards than anyone else? Or McCartney with Lennon?

Matchmaker, Matchmaker . . .

You've now entered the realm of the great human experiment—the artificial union of human beings based on abstract and possibly random criteria. Matchmaking. I'd love to be able to offer you the Ten Steps to Setting Up Successful Collaborations, but I have no idea what they are. All I know is that the formula for good co-writing chemistry is based on some strange combination of personalities, artistic temperaments, musical tastes, and complementing strengths and weaknesses. And a lot of it depends on what mood the writers are in on that particular day.

Nevertheless, after setting up hundreds of collaborations, and having been a writer/guinea pig in dozens of others, you do start to develop some instincts as to what sort of things will work and what won't. I think there are three primary considerations for a Creative Director in assessing whether a match-up makes sense.

Musical Compatibility

First of all, note that music, as always, comes first. It would be nice if all great musical teams got along happily on a personal level as well, but they don't. And they don't need to. After all, this is a job for everyone concerned, and it's reasonable to expect a writer to deal with a little personal frustration if it yields good work. If the music is great, it's worth all the pain and suffering.

Likewise, you should never be in a position of setting up co-writes solely for business purposes. Too many Creative Directors treat their writers like pawns who can be placed here, there, and everywhere in the interests of a larger strategy. They set up co-writes to develop relationships between companies, or as paybacks for favors rendered on other projects, or with the hope of finding an in-road into an otherwise inaccessible project. Certainly, these strategies are all part of the game, but they cannot be the driving force behind a collaboration. If you don't think two writers belong together musically, then do everyone a favor and don't put them in the same room.

So what else makes a musical collaboration work?

Complementary Strengths and Weaknesses

Composers need lyricists, and lyricists need composers. Melody and lyric writers go with track-oriented producers. Two composers together give you an instrumental track and two lyricists give you a poem. This may sound obvious, but I have seen many co-writes where the two writers arrived to find that no one in the room played an instrument. Or three writers arrived only to find that there were two track guys and a melody writer, and no one brought a pen and paper because no one wrote lyrics. First and foremost, a Creative Director must understand what each writer in the collaboration does and what their limitations are. And you better be sure that those add up to a finished song.

That's the easy part. The greater challenge is to use the collaborative process to compensate for weaknesses a writer might not even be aware he or she has. Not everyone who writes both music and lyrics is equally adept at both. Not everyone who can write music knows how to put a track together. Some people can sing incredible melodies but lack the harmonic knowledge to construct a proper chord progression, or the lyrical sophistication to come up with a great commercial concept. Just as you have taken a cold, hard, objective view of your own catalog's strengths and weaknesses, you must do the same with others' catalogs—and then figure out if you can provide the missing elements. Lennon added an edge, and a bit of salt, to McCartney's sweetness. I still haven't figured out the Jagger/Richards thing.

Shared Tastes and Differing Influences

I once arrived at a writing session while my soon-to-be collaborator was finishing up a phone call. The writer asked me to make myself comfortable in the living room and assured me that she'd be off the phone shortly. While I waited, I began to look at my co-writer's CD collection in the cabinet. Of course, I already knew what sort of music she wrote, but I was curious as to what she listened to (which is often very different). As I looked through the CDs, I began to get a sinking feeling in my stomach. Her entire music collection was the sort of music I hated.

When she finished her phone call, she came into the living room, and we commenced with the customary small talk that usually takes up more of a writing session than the writing. As we talked, she asked me what sort of music I was listening to. I listed off a few current favorites, and now it was her turn. Her face grew worried. She hated every record I'd mentioned. I think we both knew at that moment (although we spent the next few hours proving it) that this particular collaboration would never work. Today, we both remain good friends and admire each other's work. And we laugh about the impossibility of writing with someone whose musical tastes are antithetical to your own.

Conversely, some of the most successful co-writes that I have set up have been those between two writers from two very different genres. When Eugene Wilde, one of our urban/pop writers, went to Nashville to write with Jason Blume and George Teren, whose backgrounds are in the country market, they came up with two songs for Britney Spears. A similar result arose when the urban artist Joe wrote with country writers Gary Baker and Wayne Perry—they penned "No One Else Comes Close," which appeared on both Joe's album and the Backstreet Boy's *Millennium*. Go figure.

I think the key to musical compatibility is the right combination of shared musical tastes and different musical influences. As I mentioned earlier, most writers have a knowledge of music that extends far beyond the type of music they happen to write, and almost every writer has strains of several musical influences running through his or her work. If you compared the record collections of two collaborators, you'd like to think that there would be a least a few commonalities. If you played both writers ten records, you would hope that they could agree on the merits of at least five of them.

At the same time, too much agreement isn't always positive either. While collaborations between two similar writers in the same genre will seldom result in disaster, such efforts don't always generate the creative sparks that you might hope for. Part of the value of co-writing is to draw each writer out of his or her own comfort zone into a world where each is creatively challenged. This is why it works to put Elvis Costello with Paul McCartney, or Masters at Work with George Benson, or Rob Thomas with Willie Nelson. Of course there is common musical ground, but each writer comes from a very different place and brings with them a distinct musical point of view. These collaborations present a challenge to the writers involved. They are probably a bit awkward at first, requiring both writers to stretch outside their own world. That's often when co-writing yields the most exciting results. Vive la difference.

Personal Compatibility

I like songwriters. Having met with hundreds over the years, I can comfortably say that most songwriters are pretty nice people. If nothing else, they're a good hang. So when I'm talking about personal compatibility, I'm not just talking about avoiding writers who are arrogant, rude, disorganized, or suffering from drug and alcohol problems or the like. Although that's probably not a bad rule.

Like the question of musical compatibility, the real challenge of personal compatibility is not only to find two people who can sit in the same cramped writing room for four hours without killing each other. The challenge is to understand how each personality will add something to the equation. For example, I like to combine older, more experienced writers with younger ones. I think the older writers bring discipline and a larger perspective, while young writers bring fresh energy and a cutting-edge sensibility. Two young writers together can sometimes (not always) be a bit too unfocused and experimental. Two veteran writers together can sometimes be too comfortable and safe. I like to combine experience and energy. Even if the song doesn't turn out well, the younger writer will have learned something about life and the business from his or her exposure to the older writer. And the old pro will have gotten a jolt of excitement and youthful perspective from the up-and-comer.

It's also wise to consider the work habits of the writers you are putting together. Some writers are flighty, undisciplined, and easily distracted—they need co-writers who are patient but forceful, and who can offer them clear, firm direction. Other writers are highly insecure—they need partners who are supportive and confident. And some writers have a tendency toward laziness and complacency—they need someone who's going to light the room up with ambition and push them beyond what they're used to. Just as you assess a writer's musical qualities, a Creative Director must also understand a writer's personal qualities and take into account how they will affect the collaborative process.

Keep in mind, though, music first. Not every co-write has to be a love match. Frustrations, arguments, screaming matches, even fistfights are not necessarily a sign of a bad collaboration. In fact, those situations are probably preferable to two writers sitting in dead silence or happily having a three-hour lunch together when they're supposed to be writing. A little tension can be productive. At least it's a sign that each writer's comfort zone has been breached. A Creative Director is part matchmaker and part agent provocateur.

Business Compatibility

This is when a Creative Director has to think strategically. To the novice, collaborations are simply about two writers writing a song together—a pure, unfettered expression of a shared musical experience. Sure. But to the savvy Creative weasel, collaboration is also a networking opportunity, a resume item, and a thinly veiled song-plugging opportunity.

Each time you set up a co-write, you increase your network of contacts substantially. You now have a relationship with another writer, his or her publisher, manager, or record label, and potentially, anyone to whom the other writer and his office shop the song. Your writer is exposed both to the co-writer and, more often than not, to the co-writer's circle of other collaborators, singers, musicians, engineers, and friends. It's like the old "Six Degrees of Separation" game—the more collaboration you do, the wider your reach in the industry becomes. When you know someone who knows someone who knows Kevin Bacon, you can stop and go back to writing alone.

You can also begin to climb up the ranks of the musical food chain simply by association with a more established co-writer. While you don't get into the pantheon of A-level writers without being directly involved in a hit song, you can sometimes make it into the B-level just by working with an A-level writer. When an A&R person inquires about what a writer has done, the mention of a few well-known collaborators can confer immediate credibility.

Finally, a smart Creative Director can use a co-write as an entree into an otherwise closed shop. There is no better song plugging opportunity than collaborating with an artist or producer for a specific project. Rather than casting around in the dark, you can now tailor-make something from scratch with someone who knows exactly what is needed—and even better, who now has a vested interest in using the material. If the artist or producer thinks they were part of writing the song, it can only help. Often artists and producers intent on controlling a project will be more open to co-writing than listening to your finished songs. Fine. Do whatever it takes to get in the door . . .

The key to using collaborations for business purposes is to make sure that in most instances your writer is writing "up" rather than "down." Pair your writers with people who are more experienced, more successful, or more connected. If that sounds cold and opportunistic, it is. I never said the weasel was an attractive beast. Nevertheless, it is important that the Creative Director seek to use the collaborative process to a writer's advantage by connecting with already successful writers (whose work is presumably in demand), with writers who are affiliated with strong publishers (giving you another active partner in pitching the song), or with producers or artists that are involved in specific projects (giving you the inside track in developing songs for the album).

And now, a word to the songwriter in you. For many writers accustomed to writing on their own, the suggestion of a co-write can be almost insulting. "Are you saying I can't write lyrics?" "What's wrong with my tracks?" Toughen up. The ability to examine your own talent and identify the strengths and weaknesses is a sign of maturity—the inability to do so borders on self-delusion. Richard Rodgers and George Gershwin collaborated with other writers;

you probably can too. If nothing else, co-writing offers an on-site education in Songwriting 101, affording you the opportunity to watch and learn from another writer's approach to the craft.

Ultimately, every writer has to determine what their temperament can bear. Some writers are downright promiscuous, writing with any and all takers; others are married for life to one or two partners. When first starting out, be open to as many opportunities as you can find, at least until you've found a few partners with whom you consistently work well. Don't overthink the process. If it sounds like a somewhat interesting match up, give it a shot. Even a disastrous co-write is rarely life threatening. Check out the Rules of Collaboration on the next page for tips on developing your co-writer appeal.

And finally, a touching personal tale to close the chapter (which will also show you that not every co-write I did was a disaster).

When I was a writer, I was set up by my publisher to write with Steve Lunt, a writer with a number of hits to his credit (including "She Bop" for Cyndi Lauper). The day before the session, I called Steve to introduce myself and to see what time he wanted to start working. As we talked, we began to realize that neither of us had been given the right information about what the other did. He thought I played piano (I play guitar) and programmed tracks (I can arrange them, but I'm helpless when it comes to technology). We were both on the verge of canceling the session but finally decided to persevere and see what happened. As it turned out, we ended up working together as a writing/production team for two or three years. We've been friends for more than a decade, and now work together at Zomba Group, where Steve is the VP of A&R at Jive Records. He was the one who suggested I take the job at Zomba.

At worst, a co-write means staring at someone you barely know for a few hours, wondering how you ever got into this sorry situation. If moderately successful, it means writing a good song, possibly learning a little about a different way of working, adding to your network of contacts, and probably having a few laughs in the bargain. At best, collaboration can mean the creation of a hit song, along with an opportunity to make a good friend and ally in the industry. All in all, a chance worth taking.

The Rules of Collaboration

1. **Talk.**

   Mark D. Sanders, who wrote "I Hope You Dance" says, "If I can talk with someone and learn what is interesting or important to them, we can usually write a song together." Don't be afraid to open up.

2. **Listen.**

   The reason Mark can write a song from a conversation is that he listens to what's being said and draws an idea from that. The song is out there; you just have to hear it.

3. **Follow through.**

   Nothing is more frustrating to a co-writer than a demo that never gets recorded or a lyric that never gets written. Whatever your responsibility is, get it done.

4. **Experiment.**

   The whole point of a co-write is to try something new. Don't insist on doing what you've done before.

5. **Be humble.**

   Don't rub your credits, accomplishments, or current success in your co-writer's face. You will both have your ups and downs. Keep them to yourself.

6. **Be confident.**

   No matter how new to the game you are, you've somehow made it into the co-write session—so your opinion is worth something. Present it with confidence.

7. **Be honest.**

   If you don't like something, say so. If you don't want to finish the song, offer to let the co-writer take his or her part back or bring in a third writer to finish it.

8. **Be prepared.**

   If you're a lyricist, come to the session with some titles or concepts in mind. If you're a composer, have a musical progression started. At least it gets a conversation going.

9. **Be open.**

   If your co-writer doesn't like your idea, or has a different one, then try something else. The things you stumble on are usually the most interesting.

10. **Have fun.**

    Songs written in misery usually sound, well, miserable. If you're stuck on something, take five, go have a slice, tell a few stories, and come back to it. This ain't life or death.

    Oh yeah. I almost forgot. One more:

11. **Get a signed split letter at the end of your session!**

15

Do You Hear What I Hear?: Getting the Music Right (Means Getting the Demo Right)

I wish that getting the music right ended with getting the song right. That's hard enough. But getting the music right really ends with getting the demo right. As most working songwriters and Creative Directors will attest, that is sometimes even harder.

"Demo" is short for "demonstration record" (not "demolition," although sometimes it seems more like that). It is the recording of the song that will be used to "demonstrate" (and hopefully sell) the song to A&R people, artists, producers, and anyone else that might be buying. In the good old days of the somewhat mythical past, demos were usually rough tapes of the songwriter yodeling his way through the song, accompanied by a guitar or piano—the model of musical simplicity. Those days are gone. Demos today are more often full-fledged, almost record-quality recordings, many of which outshine the version of the song that actually finds its way onto the artist's album. The bar has been raised very high for the once-humble song demo, and while some writers are still able to deliver an effective piano/vocal performance, most Creative Directors will need something more impressive to grab the attention of the now-jaded weasel community.

Herein lies the difficulty. Clearly, there is no underestimating the importance of a great demo to the song pitching process. After all, it's the culmination of all the work you've put into getting the music right. Only you hear the song as it exists in your head. Everybody else hears the song as it's recorded on the demo. And that's what they're judging. If it's wrong on the demo, it's wrong. End of story.

Unfortunately, as crucial as the demo can be to selling the song, the financial realities of the publishing business dictate that demos are usually recorded on a shoestring budget (certainly in comparison to commercial records) and often without access to top-call studio musicians, programmers, singers, or recording equipment. At most major publishers, a full song demo is expected to cost somewhere between $500 and $1,000. On the other hand, the recording of a single song on a major album, produced by a big-name producer, can sometimes cost $50,000 to $100,000. You can see the challenge. It's a bit like being told you have to build something that isn't called a house, but looks and functions just like a house. And you only get $1,000 for supplies. Good luck.

Faced with this rather overwhelming proposition, let's ignore the practical aspects of the problem for the moment and delve into a bit of philosophy. After all, it's always safer in a theoretical world . . .

The Three Philosophies of Demos

Make It Sound Like a Record

This is an excellent theory. I don't know many Creative Directors that wouldn't prefer to go into a pitch meeting with a hot-sounding track that sounds like something straight off the radio. Who doesn't enjoy a good slam-dunk? Sure, it's obvious and requires little imagination—that's why it's so great. Songwriters are always complaining that A&R people lack imagination. ("Why can't they envision what the song would be like with strings and horns?") The truth is, imagination is unpredictable and you may not want A&R people using theirs. Sure, they might imagine the song better than it sounds on the demo. They might also imagine it worse. Better to remove the variables and give it to them exactly the way they want to hear it. An excellent theory, indeed.

It's just very tough to put into practice. For a producer/songwriter, particularly one who owns his or her studio, it should be possible to achieve something very close to a record-quality demo on a consistent basis. In fact, it's probably the only way you'll break into the production ranks. But many songwriters aren't producers, don't have their own studios, and can hardly afford to create a demo that rivals a Matt Serletic record. Which leads to theory #2 . . .

Don't Over-Demo

Not surprisingly, this theory has evolved from the frequent failure of theory #1. When songwriters who lack the production skill, the equipment, or the arranging know-how attempt to make a record-quality demo, the result is usually a complete mess. If it's unlikely that an A&R person can use their imagination to conceive of a production that *isn't* on tape, it's even more unlikely that they can use that same brainpower to listen through a bad production that *is* on tape. Clumsy drum programming, out-of-tune guitars, cheesy synth sounds, or a poor mix are almost impossible to ignore. They can do irreparable damage to a song's presentation.

Sometimes, even a well-done demo can be so precise in its production that it limits the song's appeal. A demo that sounds exactly like a Britney Spears record is unlikely to sell your song to Jessica Simpson. It may not even sell it to Britney, as it may remind her of something she's already done. A simpler, less stylized demo might allow the listener to hear the song's potential for a variety of artists or projects. Again, it's not easy for someone to imagine what something could be, but it's easier than trying to ignore what's already there. It's the KISS theory—"Keep It Simple, Stupid."

Sadly, most songwriters misinterpret the acronym. They "Keep It Stupid, Stupid." The theory of not over-demoing is usually just an excuse for a lazy, uninteresting demo that is neither simple enough to be powerfully intimate, nor strong enough to be exciting. Instead, you get a generic, personality-free vocal, or a dull, predictable arrangement, or a groove that doesn't really groove. This dreaded middle ground is the No Man's Land of songwriting. When A&R people hear these demos, they just say: "No, man." Whatever theory you choose to subscribe to, your demo must still be interesting and exciting in its own way. Remember, just because you are subscribing to theory #2 doesn't mean your competition is. Your demo is going to be heard right after something that sounds like a record. Somehow, your song still needs to stand out. Which brings us to what's behind door #3 . . .

Know Your Market

This is the "when in Rome . . . " philosophy. While it acknowledges that many in the industry expect demos to sound like finished masters, it also accepts the limitations of a songwriter's budget and production skills and suggests an eminently reasonable compromise. Do what is required to compete in your market, in a way that fits your individual capabilities. Hard to argue with that.

The art lies in the execution. Demos are judged slightly differently in every market, and it can be difficult to know what's important, or not important, to the professionals that will be listening to your CD. So here's a quick report from Weasel Land as to what the Romans like to hear:

Pop: By and large, this market demands demos that sound like records. However, be cautious about directly copying production styles, as pop fashions change so quickly that your song can become dated in six months. Try to think like a producer and anticipate the next trends. The production qualities of a pop song are almost inseparable from the song itself. Your demo is going to have to present a finished product.

The only exception to this might be adult contemporary-leaning ballads. On this sort of song, you may be able to deliver a piano/vocal or piano/string pad/vocal demo that sells the song effectively—maybe even more effectively than a more predictable, full production. It will still require top-level recording quality and a good mix, and a truly outstanding performance.

Rock: This market offers a little more flexibility, depending on the style and attitude of the music you do. Bands are usually expected to provide a demo that adequately represents their sound, but it's not expected that the recording will be on the same sonic level as a fully produced rock record. Of course, if you are the next Strokes or White Stripes, your demo can be pretty raw indeed. If you're trying to unseat U2, it's a little more challenging. Overall, the most important thing is to catch the spirit and energy of what the band is about and make sure that the group's strengths are highlighted.

Singer-songwriter types get a bit of a free pass. In most cases, this genre is well suited to a guitar/vocal or piano/vocal demo—just make sure it's recorded and mixed properly. In the event that you want to go a little beyond the minimum, my suggestion would be to keep it simple but interesting. A drum loop, a string quartet, or an interesting instrumental part can add to a demo without detracting from the focal point, which, in this case, should always be the singer and the lyric.

Urban: This is a producer-driven market, so the overall sonic standard is very, very high. The good news is that most urban styles, particularly r&b and hip-hop, are not overly difficult to produce adequately in a limited studio environment.

This is not to say that urban music is easy to create. The drums and bass need to create a groove so strong that it's a hook in and of itself; the keyboard parts and samples have to be unique and memorable; and the vocal has to be convincing. Sonically, a good mix is essential—bottom end booming, the snare up in your face. There's nothing simple about putting together an effectively simple track. I'm only suggesting that it doesn't require an SSL board and vast rack of outboard gear to do it. The key in this market is that the demo needs a certain raw, physical power. The A&R guy needs to feel the track, not just hear it.

Country: This market is its own special world. Most country demo sessions are done with a studio band, which will cut five or six songs in one three- or four-hour session. The band will learn the song on the spot, work out an arrangement, and then record a couple of takes. Given the talent of the Nashville studio musicians, that's usually about all they need to get it right. The vocals are then cut on a different day, usually at a less expensive studio.

I'll admit that I'm not a big fan of the Nashville demo tradition. To my New York pop ears, these demos usually sound perfunctory at best, with predictable arrangements, competent but uninspired musicianship, tempos that drag, and vocal-heavy mixes. If you have the necessary production skills and recording equipment, I would suggest that you break with tradition and develop your demos with more of a record-quality sensibility. Annie Roboff, the writer of hits like "This Kiss" and "If I Fall," is known for her fully produced demos—it's an important part of what sets her apart as a modern country writer.

On the other hand, if you're not production oriented, or you lack the equipment to do your own demos, the Nashville system is one that has worked for many successful writers over a good number of years. Who am I to argue with it? Try to focus on getting as much out of the studio musicians as you can in the time that you have—by preparing thoroughly, having some clear ideas about the arrangement and approach that you're looking for, and taking an active "producer" role at the session. Concentrate on getting a performance that is exciting, not just accurate. Don't let the musicians or the vocalists just "phone it in."

And don't discount the viability of a guitar/vocal or piano/vocal in this genre. The pure simplicity of this sort of demo can actually add impact to many country songs. And provided that the recording is clean and listenable, most A&R people are open to this stripped-down approach. If you go to clubs like the Bluebird Cafe or Douglas Corner, where songwriters perform their songs in a casual, intimate atmosphere, you will hear guitar/vocal performances that can rivet an audience. In my opinion, many songs sound better in this setting than they ever do on the commercial recording.

Know Yourself

I guess you've heard theory #4 before. Objectivity about your own material, knowing your strengths and weaknesses . . . hmm. There seems to a recurrent theme emerging in this book. Songwriter, know thyself. Creative Director, know thy writer. Even once you begin to understand the expectations that exist for demos in each market, you still have to consider what is within your capability, and how you can accommodate the needs of the marketplace. Whether it's a demo recording, a label showcase, or a guest spot on Letterman, one of the fundamental principles of any performance is: "Do what you do best." That means knowing what works for you.

Someone like Annie Roboff chooses to do fully produced demos in part because she is a very talented musician who has the production and arranging ability to pull off an elaborate recording. Her approach plays to her strength. At the same time, another successful country writer, Tom Douglas, comes from more of a singer/songwriter tradition—in my opinion, some of his piano/vocal performances are the definitive versions of his songs. They work for him. When David Frank, one of pop music's most successful writer/ producers ("Genie in a Bottle"; "He Loves Me, He Loves You Not") finishes a demo, it is 80 percent of the way toward being a finished record. And how could it not be? His writing is inextricably linked to his production style. It's all about maximizing your strengths and minimizing your weaknesses.

If you are a standout producer, then of course you should be doing record-quality demos. If you are a great singer, then by all means sing on your demos. If you're not, please (!) don't. Even in the urban market, you may be able to sell a guitar/vocal demo if it fits the song—"Words" by Tony Rich or "Seven Days" by Craig David could easily translate this way. I work with a writing team who is most effective when actually playing the song live or singing along with a rough track in an A&R person's office. They can do a great record-quality demo if necessary, but their personalities are such that they are even more effective in a casual, one-on-one setting. The job of the Creative Director is to find the most effective selling technique for each individual writer. To thine own self be true. You heard it here first—or at least most.

But enough philosophy. What about that $1,000 house we were supposed to build? No theory is going to manage that feat. The challenge is to create an effective demo within the constraints of a start-up company's budget, which is a thoroughly practical problem. So now that we've got our mind right, let's get down to it, and see what materials we have to work with . . .

Studio/Recording Equipment

Happily, there are more options in this particular area than ever before and there are more technological advances every day. We live in the era of the home recording studio, where a Pro Tools rig, a healthy set of plug-ins, some Acid loops, and a good microphone, is enough to compete sonically with almost any record on the market. Not that this stuff is cheap, but it's certainly inexpensive compared to a twenty-four hour lockout at a top-notch commercial studio. If the money is available and you have the audio engineering expertise, there is probably no better investment for your publishing company than to invest in building a studio. An investment of $15,000 could pay for itself after only ten or twenty demos, which should be less than one year's output of songs. And the studio could be rented to outside clients, as well, to actually generate income.

For those less technically inclined, the challenge is to find a programmer/producer/arranger with his or her own studio, who can be employed to do demos for a reasonable rate. In most cities that are music centers, this is not overly difficult. Ads in local music trade publications or word of mouth will often lead you to a songwriter/producer, studio keyboard player, or recording engineer that has carved out a viable business doing song demos. Of course, it helps to find a programmer/producer familiar with your particular genre of music, who can provide arranging ideas, musical parts, and the right sonic environment for that style. Ask to hear a reel of his or her work before you book the session.

If you're based outside a music center, or are extremely limited in the amount you can spend on demos, it may be more difficult to find a viable programmer or studio. A home recording environment alleviates much of the pressure, otherwise you may need to opt for periodic trips to a larger city, with the plan of demoing five or six songs in a week. Or make it a point to collaborate with a writer who has a studio facility at his or her disposal. You might even barter with a studio, or agree to book your sessions in the off-hours, in order to get the time that you need to finish your songs. What you cannot do is lower your standards based on the facilities or engineers available to you. The industry standard is what it is, no matter where you live, how much money you have, or what equipment you work on. After all, Brian Wilson made *Pet Sounds* on a four-track tape machine. No one's interested in hearing excuses for your demo.

Musicians and Vocalists

One of the tricky things about making music is that it requires musicians. For better or worse, with the rise of the keyboard player/programmer, it now requires a lot fewer of them than it used to, but it still helps to have someone around who can put a track together, play a bass part, add a percussion track, and make sure that the drums and bass are sitting in the pocket. If you're capable of programming or playing all the instruments on your demo, then you have this area covered—and you've just saved yourself a lot of money. If you're not that sort of multi-instrumentalist wunderkind, then it's time to start collecting some names for your Rolodex.

For most pop and urban demos, the primary challenge is finding one keyboard player/programmer who can do almost the entire track, which means programming drums, bass lines, percussion, loops, and samples, and adding keyboard parts, string pads, bell lines, and other ear candy. On certain songs, it may be necessary to call in someone who specializes in drum programming, or another musician to play guitar or bass. Any more than this, and you've likely exceeded your demo budget—unless of course you have friends. Friends are always good, particularly if they play instruments.

If your focus is more towards the rock or country market, you will likely be in the position of needing a whole band (this is assuming that you're not already in one). In most cases, this means finding one musician that you like and trust, and allowing him or her to act as the contractor for the session. The contractor is responsible for hiring the other musicians, negotiating the fees for each player, making sure that the session runs smoothly, and ensuring that all the musicians are paid properly. A good contractor will usually hire players who have worked together in the past, and can quickly find a comfortable blend and balance. If you are planning to cut several songs in a day, working out arrangements largely on the spot, this sort of seasoned camaraderie among the musicians is essential. Once you find a group you like, stick with 'em.

That sort of loyalty does not necessarily extend to singers. You'll eventually find those vocalists who consistently give you the performance you need, who intuitively understand your lyrics and phrasing. I have some singers that I've worked with for over fifteen years, who always seem to interpret the song perfectly. But every singer, no matter how versatile, has his or her own individual quality, and no one is right for every song. A professional songwriter that is also an effective Creative Director has a file of demo singers with a variety of different sounds, and is constantly seeking out new and unique voices. No single element in the demo is more important than getting a top-quality vocal performance from the right singer.

Even the best singers may not be convincing in certain styles or may at some point become overexposed. There's one session singer in Nashville (who shall remain nameless) who at one point seemed to do every pop demo done in that town. Although he was a fine singer, I had to start suggesting to our writers that they find someone new, simply because this singer had begun to be associated in A&R people's minds with all the mediocre songs that he had sung on. As soon as his voice came on, it just seemed to say "more of the same." A fresh, new voice always helps to set a demo apart from the pack.

Be aware that if you sing on your own demos and do it well, you will begin to receive requests from other songwriters and publishers to sing on their demos. This is a great opportunity, both to broaden your network of contacts, and to enjoy a nice income stream on the side. By all means, take advantage of it. But keep in mind that your voice can also become overexposed, just like every other demo vocalist in town. If your voice is part of what makes your own demos stand out, then each time you sing on another writer's track, your sound becomes just a little more familiar. This process is exacerbated further if the outside songs on which you're singing are mediocre, or worse. Try to exert some quality control, and be careful about taking too many jobs on demos aimed at the same market for which you generally write.

Arrangements and Rearrangements

We've already talked in some detail about the importance of an arrangement that both serves the song and adds to it with instrumental hooks and background lines. Most demo arrangements fail simply for lack of effort—they don't go far enough in trying to create a fully realized interpretation. If there's a string line, make it something melodic that elevates the track. If there's a guitar part, make sure the voicings add some sort of interest to the chord progression. Don't settle.

With that said, there are certain considerations that you need to keep in mind when working on a demo as opposed to a finished record. While it's always laudable to try to make your song demo sound just like something on the radio, you do have to remember that a song demo is created for a specific function, and ultimately should serve that purpose. Demos are made to be listened to by busy executives, as they make their way through a stack of similar recordings piled high on their desk. The ultimate function of the demo is to "demonstrate" the song to this harried, weary listener. With this in mind:

- **Keep intros short.**

A demo is not the place for a long, impressionistic intro. Start with a bang, but make it a short one—four bars is probably optimal. You've got eight bars maximum before the weasels are checking their watches.

- **Don't overdo instrumental solos, breakdowns, or outros.**

Unless the demo is intended primarily to show off the band, as opposed to the song, keep the musical virtuoso displays to a minimum. Extended guitar solos or vocal ad-libs that just won't fade out are self-indulgent in the context of a demo.

- **Make sure the vocals are audible.**

Personally, I'm pretty sensitive about vocals that are too loud, which has the effect of making the track sound wimpy—but it's usually better if the vocals are too loud rather than too soft. Try to get the balance right, but err on the side of caution. If the listener can't hear the melody and lyrics, I'm afraid the song "demonstration" has failed.

- **Hit 'em with your best shot. Fast.**

Demos are not the place for subtlety. There's a natural tendency for a producer to try to provide a dramatic build to the arrangement—so that the first chorus starts quietly, the second has a bit more force, and the final chorus is the big climax. But demo production is a slightly different animal—think of it as record production for an audience with severe attention deficit disorder. Most of the time, you've got no more than one verse and chorus to make your impression. So that first chorus had better come in loud and proud, with all guns blazing. You'll be judged by your first chorus, not your last.

As difficult as it can be to get your demo right, it's only just the beginning. To exploit a song to its full potential, it's often necessary to have several versions, with each of them tailored to a specific target market. After all, everyone has their prejudices—I've heard of female singers who can't stand to hear another female singing on the demo (for some reason, male vocals don't seem to bother women), or men that can't hear a female demo (life's rough for female demo singers), or pop producers that recoil at the sound of a pedal steel. If you want to sell someone a song, you've got to give it to the listener as they want to hear it. If that means a DAT full of different versions, vocals, and mixes, then so be it.

It's the job of the Creative Director to imagine all the possibilities for a song and to decide what sort of demos will be necessary to capitalize on the most viable exploitation opportunities. Certainly the success of songs like "Back At One," which had both urban and country versions, or "Heaven," a Bryan Adams rock classic that turned into a chart-topping Euro dance hit, has proven that songs can crossover in the most unlikely of ways. At the same time, many songs are limited to one specific genre by their lyric, subject matter, chord progression, or rhythmic structure. It's important that a Creative Director be both imaginative and realistic about what a song is capable of. And it's helpful if those decisions can be made while the recording is still in progress—the changes between versions may be as simple as adding or dropping a guitar from the mix or simply changing the vocal performance.

It's also possible that an older song may at some point need updating in order to be pitched effectively. In many cases, the more "fully produced" a demo is, the more likely it is to become dated. The drum sounds and rhythmic grooves always start to show their age. There's nothing less enticing to a Creative Manager than pitching an "old" sounding demo. Many A&R people take it as a bit of an insult, as if you're trying to sell them last year's fashions at this year's prices. If you believe in a song enough to feel that it's still worth shopping, then you should believe in it enough to pay for a new demo. Which reminds me . . .

Costs

I wouldn't be a real Creative Director if I didn't harp a bit about demo costs. After all, the challenge is to build something very like a house for only $1,000. If you spend $100,000 you might as well have built a real house. As the Creative Director, you are responsible for deciding on an appropriate budget for each song and then making sure that the costs stay within the guidelines. Unless you have a spectacularly high batting average of churning out hits, probably five out of every ten songs will never recoup the costs of their demos. Even if a song makes it onto an album, it will still have to sell almost 20,000 units just to make back a $1,000 demo bill.

It's easy to get obsessed when you're in the middle of the creative whirlwind. A budget is your not-so-friendly wake-up call from the outside world, reminding you of three important principles: spread your love around, put your money where your hits are, and know when to stop.

Spread Your Love Around

Sticking to your demo budget on any one song will help ensure that there is still some money left to demo other songs. It's not the most artistic way of looking at things, but one of the keys to developing a publishing catalog is simply increasing the amount of songs you have available to pitch. The truth is, things don't really start to happen until you get a fair number of songs in your drawer.

At the same time, it's only natural for songwriters to become overly excited about the song they've just completed, and consequently overspend on the demo. This means that by the time the next song comes in, which of course they're even more excited about, there's no money left to record it. It's the job of the Creative Director to make sure to manage the demo budgets, so that any song that needs a demo gets one . . .

Put Your Money Where Your Hits Are

Just because you want to spread the love does not mean that all songs are created equal. They're not. An essential part of the demo budgeting process is an assessment of a song's potential, a judgment that will most likely have to be made on the basis of a rough work tape or a quick performance by the writers. Even in that rough state, you should be able to discern which songs have hit potential, which are interesting ideas that might be viable, and which ones are better forgotten.

A Creative Director must consider the general quality of each song, the number of opportunities that exist for it in the market, its overall value to the catalog, and the sort of demo approach it requires. Then assign a dollar figure and stick to it. Out of ten songs, probably three or four should get a full demo, another three or four might warrant a good quality guitar or piano/vocal, and the remainder can remain as work tapes, at least until an opportunity for the song presents itself. You want to build up bulk, but at a reasonable cost.

Know When to Stop

Steve Lunt, whom I mentioned earlier, used to have a saying about producing records. He'd say, " A record is never done until you've run out of money." Part of the purpose of a budget is to tell you clearly and emphatically when you've reached that threshold. No songwriter ever feels that a song is perfect. Every producer hears a flaw in the recording. This is the sort of perfectionism that leads to artistic achievement. Unfortunately it also leads to a starving artist.

The truth about getting the music right is that it never really is. You've got to know when the music is right enough. Or when it won't get any righter. You can only invest so much in one song. At some point, you have to come out of the studio and start getting the music out there . . .

16

Songs for Sale: Understanding the Ancient Art of Song Plugging

It's very easy for a Creative Director to be so caught up in getting the music right, he or she never quite gets around to the second phase of the job. You're hanging out in the studio, checking out the new demos, putting together collaborations, listening to work tapes . . . it's all very . . . well, creative. Who has time to be sending out CDs or cold-calling artist managers? That sort of thing just feels like . . . like being a . . . a salesman or something.

The Facts of Life as a Creative Director

- You will not be successful sitting around listening to your catalog. You'll be successful by getting other people to sit around and listen to your catalog.

- Those who send out the most songs win.

- Every element in your day will conspire to prevent you from sending out songs.

News flash: You are a salesman. Get used to it. If there is one frustration that most writers have with their Creative Directors, and quite frankly, that most *companies* have with their Creative Directors, it is that nobody seems to want to sell songs. Everyone likes to listen to music, sign new music, or critique music, but no one seems to want to be bothered with actually sending the stuff out. The truth is that selling songs is the only part of music publishing that actually generates income. The whole company is reliant on someone going out and getting a song on a record, in a movie, or in an advertisement—and no one wants to do it. This is a jumbo-sized problem.

And you, Creative Director, are the solution. Getting the music right may be your first task, but getting the music out is your primary one. You must have the discipline to set aside a portion of your time everyday to devote to this particular part of your job. If you do it well, you will build a profitable enterprise and bring your writer fame and fortune in the bargain. If you don't, your publishing venture is kaput. How's that for a pep talk?

Beyond survival, there's one more important benefit to mastering the art of song plugging. If you succeed in building a track record of placing songs, you will likely find yourself well positioned for an executive position in the larger publishing industry, if at some point that's of interest to you. As I mentioned, there is a severe shortage of dedicated song pluggers in the music publishing industry—every company needs them and no one can find enough of them. Contact any major music publisher, tell them you are willing to focus solely on pitching songs, and offer a resume that gives some indication that you are effective at that task; I can almost assure you, someone will be interested in meeting with you. There's a certain job security in understanding the ancient art.

Of course, the first step in getting the music out is deciding just who to get it out to. Finding opportunities for songs is a bit like detective work. You check your sources, follow the leads, do your homework, round up the suspects, and try to figure out who's really running the game "behind the scenes." Three basic questions should give you a pretty substantial list of names to follow up on:

Who's Looking?

It's always easier to sell something if you can find someone who needs it. The point of determining "who's looking" is to focus your efforts on a buyer at the right moment.

Tip Sheets

One of the easiest ways of finding out who's looking for songs, and what they're looking for, is to check out those tip sheets that should be laying around your office. *New on the Charts* and *SongLink International* exist precisely for this purpose, and are updated regularly as some projects close and other new ones begin. This should be your first stop when in search of potential buyers.

But it's really just the tip of the iceberg. Most of the projects currently in development are never listed on a tip sheet, for any number of reasons. Many A&R types are skeptical of the quality of the material that a tip sheet listing brings in; others are hesitant to acknowledge publicly that an artist is having trouble writing the songs for a project. The dedicated Creative Director must dig deeper. Underneath that pile of tip sheets in your office, there should be some industry trade magazines. Let's move on to those.

Trade Magazines

While the major trade magazines will not necessarily publish precise information about who's looking for songs, they will provide you with a comprehensive overview of what's happening in the industry. This knowledge, combined with a little reading between the lines, should yield you a fair amount of names to add to your target list of customers. Here's what you're looking for:

1. Any mention of new signings, new projects in development, or artists switching record labels.

2. Information about newly created labels, production companies, or management firms.

3. Notices of executives moving into new positions or new companies.

4. Chart listings of artists who have a first single currently released, but no album out. If the single is doing well, you can be sure that the label is working on an album.

5. References to movies or television shows currently in development.

6. Information about new trends or upcoming companies in music-related businesses such as video games, advertising, or youth marketing.

Depending on the particular market that you are targeting, certain trade magazines will be more useful than others. If your primary focus is the record industry, *Billboard* should give you a good comprehensive overview. *The Hollywood Reporter* offers a helpful listing of almost all the current movies and television shows in production. Or if you are particularly focused on placing your songs in advertising, you may want to start picking up copies of *Ad Age*, or *Adweek*, which can provide the inside track on that complex world. Even Web sites can sometimes give you information as to what projects a company has in development. Leave no stone unturned . . .

Telephone Inquiries

And then there's the line of direct inquiry. If you want to know something, it's never a bad strategy to simply ask. Most major music publishers make up their own "tip sheet" or "who's looking" list several times a year—there's really not much to it. Each Creative Director gets on the phone, calls the various record labels, producers, and management companies, and asks what they're working on. Like I said before, this business isn't exactly rocket science.

Dig into that pile of paper on your desk. Under the tip sheets and next to the trade magazines, find your industry directories. You'll need to narrow down which companies are relevant for the sort of music you do, and try to identify one or two A&R contacts within the correct department. Then start dialing for dollars . . .

Obviously, the optimal result of each call is a direct conversation with the A&R person, which should get you a list of projects currently in need of material and a quick description of what each act is looking for. Without question, any time that you can have a dialogue with the person actually in charge of the project, you will not only get a clearer picture of what's needed, but also have a chance to establish that most valuable of all industry commodities, a relationship.

But unless you have something of a name in the industry, or someone else's name to drop, you will likely have a tough time making it past the wall of protection that shields most song buyers from the hundreds of sellers. Not to worry. In this information-gathering stage, it's not essential to have a one-on-one discussion with the name in the directory. In fact, when most major publishers put together their tip sheets, much of the information is gathered from A&R coordinators, assistants, and receptionists who have been briefed by their bosses as to what projects are in development. Here's how the conversation should go:

1. Identify yourself as the Creative Director of the publishing company. *Do not* indicate in any way that you are also a songwriter. This will set off a four-alarm weasel alert, and will probably end your phone call abruptly. You are from a publishing company, nothing more.

2. If there's an inquiry, or if you feel it is truly necessary (and only if), offer some description of your company, mentioning any noteworthy activity, success, or business partners. This is the time to drop that name if you've got one on you.

3. Explain that your company is in the process of updating their list of projects currently seeking material, and ask if you can speak to the A&R

person, manager, or music supervisor who is the object of your call. If the call is put through, then proceed again from Step 1. If the receptionist or assistant offers to provide the information, then proceed by inquiring as to what the company is working on at the moment.

4. Make sure you get the following information:

    - Name of artist or band
    - Type of material being sought
    - The appropriate A&R contact person
    - The current status of the project, and any deadline information

    If possible, try to find out:
    - What producers or other writers are involved in the project?
    - If the artist is involved in the writing, is he or she open to collaborations?
    - Is the company looking for finished songs or just tracks for others to write to?
    - Who's managing the act?

5. If, in your previous research, you've learned about projects that haven't been mentioned in the conversation, inquire about those. You'll earn extra points for having done your homework.

Then get off the phone. Unless you sincerely believe that the person on the other end is enjoying the conversation, or that you are developing an actual "relationship," there is no reason that this call should last longer than five minutes. In many cases it will be shorter than that—there may be few projects that the company is involved with, or the A&R person may simply offer to send you a prepared list of projects. Take whatever information you can get and move on. The point is not to see how long you can spend on the phone with some harried assistant, quizzing them on details that they either don't know or don't want to give you. Keep your phone calls brief and to the point. You've got a lot of companies to call.

Word of Mouth

And now I'm going to shock you with a startlingly generous suggestion, coming from a weasel like myself. Once you've begun to compile a useful list of projects seeking songs, call a few of the other songwriters and publishers in your musical community (you are part of a community, right?), and share some of the information you've gathered.

Huh? Share? After all your hard work finding out who needs songs, I'm telling you to give it away to other people? Your competitors?

Well, I'm not sure you should give it away, exactly. And I'm not telling you to share *all* of it. But throwing a little inside information into a conversation never hurts. Because it gets people talking. Before you know it, your Creative cronies, not to be outdone, are offering up a few of the projects they've heard about. Suddenly you are part of the proverbial grapevine, through which all essential information flows. Having a spot on that grapevine is far more valuable than any inside scoop you're giving away.

One final tip regarding the "who's looking?" method of song plugging:

This particular approach relies more than anything else on a quick response. A notice in a tip sheet is probably more than a month old by the time it reaches print and then finds its way to you. The same is probably true of anything you read in an industry trade magazine. A phone conversation with an A&R person is at best a snapshot of a single moment in a project's evolution—a song could show up tomorrow that changes the whole focus of the album.

If you are going to have success pitching songs to people that are looking, you are going to have to do it fast. Get the tip, enter it into a list on your computer, or write it on a whiteboard on your wall, then immediately start looking at your catalog for an appropriate pitch. If you don't have anything that works, see if your writers can come up with something that same week. As soon as you've got something to send, get the CD out of your office and into the hands of the A&R person. Correction to my Facts of Life item: Those who get the most songs out *fastest* win.

Who's the Song Right For?

This is the flip side to the first approach. The problem with the "who's looking" list is that inevitably there are many artists who are looking for something that you don't have. Likewise, there are a lot of songs gathering dust on your shelf, waiting for the right artist to show up one day on the tip sheet. You need a secondary plan of attack. By asking "who's the song right for?" you can take a more proactive approach to exploiting all, or at least the best, songs in your catalog.

So here we go—three easy steps to finding Mr. or Ms. Right for your song . . .

Know Your Audience

You must start with an understanding of the market in which your song will be pitched. I don't mean just having a general impression. I'm talking about having a real, in-depth knowledge of that particular world of music—who the top artists are, who the up-and-coming artists are, which artists are struggling, and why. You need to know what differentiates each artist from the other, in terms of production, lyrics, melody, rhythmic approach, and chord progression.

If you send songs out blindly, the problem is not so much that you fail—it's that you usually embarrass yourself in the process. You cannot pitch the same "pop" ballad to Christina Aguilera and Britney Spears. They are two completely different types of singers. A country song is unlikely to be perfect for both Tim McGraw and Mark Wills. Deborah Cox will not sing the same sort of song as Tweet. You must take into account the age of the artist, the image, the vocal range, and the musical history. Only after you've fully considered all of these factors, should you ever venture to suggest to a manager, artist, or A&R person that a song is "perfect" for their project. Remember, your credibility as a Creative Director hangs in the balance. You must do your homework before you make that call.

Keep It Real

You must also occasionally douse yourself with a quick splash of cold, bracing realism. There's nothing wrong with identifying one or two multi-platinum artists for whom the song would be a fit and working to get your CD into the right hands. But that's a wish list. It's not a strategy. In order to determine who the song is really right for, you've got to set your sights at a realistic level.

If you are just starting to build a name for yourself in this business, then you should be targeting artists that are accessible and open to new material, producers who are not also writers, and lower-level A&R people, who may not have a budget sufficient to hire the top-call writing and production teams for their new act. The idea is to avoid wasting your time and energy reaching for the stars. Instead, get in at the ground level and ride the elevator up . . .

I once had a meeting with a husband-and-wife writing team that wanted me to produce a demo of a song they had written. This was quite a few years ago—in fact, it goes back to when Kenny Rogers was the preeminent male solo artist in country music. (I know, I know—I'm really old.) I mention this because when I asked the writers for the name of the artist to whom they intended to shop their song, they bluntly informed me that it was "Kenny's song." Not quite getting their drift, I tried again—who else would they want to send the song to, in addition to Mr. Rogers? Silence. They looked at each other, exasperated, and then explained it again. This was Kenny's song. It was written for him. In fact, they'd waited outside the concert halls and hotels, and tried to hand him a cassette. (Scary, right?) Once, he'd even taken one. But of course he must not have listened to it, or he would have known it was his song. My job was to arrange the demo for Kenny Rogers and nobody else.

There are several words for writers like this—"obsessive" and "delusional" come to mind. But let's be kind and stick with "amateur." A professional understands what is comfortably within his or her capabilities, what is a bit of a stretch, and what is a long shot. If you're sure your song is a hit for Shania Twain, you're kidding yourself. Shania writes all her songs with Mutt Lange. That project is closed. If Aerosmith is the only group that can sing your song, all I can say is "dream on." Direct your efforts to developing artists, those in need of a hit to revitalize their career, or those trying to cross over from a small market to a larger one. In the early stages of your publishing company, you need to build up your track record. Take your shots at the ducks sitting in the pond. You can get to the big game hunting later.

Put on Your A&R Hat

The greatest difficulty that most Creative Directors have in figuring out who could perform their song is that they are thinking like Creative Directors. The mindset is that of a publisher, whose primary focus is finding high-quality, commercial songs and then sending them out to people who have done similar sorts of songs in the past. The problem is, this is not how most artists or their various handlers put together an album.

In order to pitch songs (or write them) effectively, it is sometimes important to slide over to the other side of your desk and put on your A&R hat. When you do, you begin to see that for most managers, record execs, and producers, an album is all about artist development. Most major record companies do not consider the making of hit records to be their ultimate goal. The ultimate goal is the creation of hit *artists*. Songs come and go; records last a year or two and then slide down the charts. A hit artist is where the real money is. If you're going to wear the A&R hat, you have to understand Artist Development.

- If the artist is your priority, it's not enough for a song to be catchy. It must also be appropriate to the artistic direction of the record.

- If the artist is to establish a public image, the lyrics the artist sings must reinforce that persona.

- If an artist wants credibility, he or she will have to show artistic growth. It's not enough to record songs that reconstruct past hits.

- If an artist wants to be perceived as a leader in the genre, it won't work to record songs that sound just like what's on the radio. That sound will be old by the time the album comes out.

Often a Creative Director will argue with an A&R person who's passing on a song, ". . . but it's a smash." The A&R person will respond, "Yeah, I know. But not for this artist on this album." When you go through the process of identifying the right artists for your song, you need to try to see things through the Artist Development prism. Think of each artist on your list, and put yourself in the position of his or her manager or A&R person. What new sounds should the act embrace? What aspects of their old sound should they avoid? What sort of image should they project? What markets do they need to capture to increase their sales? It's not enough to pitch songs that sound just like an artist's past work. You've got to anticipate where an artist is headed, and try to provide songs that will lead the way.

Remember, music publishers are all about the song. Everyone else in the record business is all about the artist.

Who's Listening?

Do you ever take the time to read the credits and "Thank You" sections in CD booklets? I worked on a soundtrack album recently (soundtracks are every record exec's worst nightmare)—there were close to fifty names listed in the credits and special thanks. At times in the project, it seemed like there were at least that many people involved in the decisionmaking process. If songwriting is often a lonely, isolated business, the rest of the modern entertainment business is the polar opposite. Most entertainment projects, whether they are records, movies, or television productions, are raging tempests of divergent opinions, political power plays, competing interests, and shifting alliances—out of which, somehow, an actual piece of product eventually emerges. Usually it's not a particularly good product, but by that point, everyone's just happy the thing got made at all.

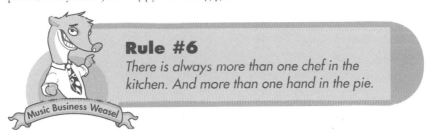

Rule #6
There is always more than one chef in the kitchen. And more than one hand in the pie.

Music Business Weasel

As a Creative Director, this committee approach to decisionmaking is both boon and bane. It's a boon because it allows you an endless array of ways to work a song into a particular project. If the producer doesn't like it, you can try getting it to the manager. If they say no, you can call the A&R

person. Hope springs eternal. The bane is the endless list of people who need to give a thumbs-up just to get your song recorded. Every approval is issued conditionally—"I like it, *but* I'll have to send it to so and so, and get their feedback . . . ." There's always one more hoop to jump through.

The key to success is to learn to take advantage of the chaos that surrounds most showbusiness endeavors. This means understanding who all, or at least most, of the players in any particular project are—and somehow deducing who has the power of the final decision. Of course, both the players and the power are constantly shifting, even within the course of one project, which is what makes the game so darn exasperating. Here's a quick breakdown of the usual suspects that show up on most projects:

Artists: Certainly if you can get your song directly to an artist, you've entered the inner circle. But don't assume that the artist calls all the shots. Superstars usually have the last word about what they're going to sing, but many new artists do not. Still, any time you can develop a relationship with the face on the album cover, you're in a good position.

Manager: Most Creative Directors don't spend enough time pitching the artist's manager. This is usually the most trusted figure in the artist's world, the one person with 24/7 access. Best of all, managers are the least likely to be inundated with a constant stream of demos. Their ears are somewhat fresh.

Label: It's important to try to decipher how the A&R process works at each different label. Some companies will assign a specific A&R person to each project; that person will generally be the only one listening to material for that album. Other companies use more of a team approach, with the whole A&R staff gathering songs and making a collective judgment as to what gets recorded. You can usually figure out each label's way of doing business by checking out the A&R credits on a few of the company's releases.

Producer: The role that a producer plays can vary widely from project to project. Producers that are active writers are unlikely to be open to songs from the outside, although many such producers also employ teams of writers (some credited, some not) who may be available for collaborations. Producers that are not writers are generally always on the hunt for "hits"—in many cases, their ability to land the production gig is dependent on them finding a song that everyone likes. Because most producers have a background as musicians, writers, or engineers, they are often more accessible than many of the executives in the business.

Film and television projects bring their own cast of characters. In the case of soundtrack projects, the Hollywood people are added to the list of players we've already discussed. You see why soundtracks are so much fun.

Director: Some directors have very distinct ideas about the music for their film, others less so. On smaller films, the director may be relatively accessible. On blockbusters, the director is usually far too busy trying to figure out how to blow up the car in mid-air or how to coax the stars out of their trailers, to be bothered listening to your song.

Music Supervisor: This is usually the person with the specific responsibility of finding songs for the movie or television show. Watch the end credits closely, and you'll see the same names show up again and again—these are the people you need to be pitching.

Studio: This is just as vague as it sounds. Most major motion picture studios are full of executives, lawyers, production coordinators, and assistants that spend much of their time trying to figure out what they're supposed to be doing and where they rank in the current corporate pecking order. Trying to determine who does what from the outside is almost impossible. Nevertheless, most studios do have someone for whom music is a focus, like Randy Spendlove, the President of Music at Miramax, or Burt Berman, in the same position at Paramount Pictures.

Production Company: Particularly on television projects, this is usually where the powers that be reside. The good news is that these companies are usually far less Byzantine than the major film studios, and if you can forge a relationship, they may come back to you for more than one project. *The Hollywood Reporter* and *Variety* are good sources for information about what various production companies are working on.

Soundtrack Label: For movies in which the soundtrack will play an important role in the marketing campaign, it can also be useful to attack the project on two fronts at once. I suggest pitching the music supervisor and production company, while simultaneously working the A&R department at the record label that will be doing the soundtrack. It's never easy to figure out who's calling the shots in these situations. All you can do is cover your bases. If you have a song that's a genuine hit, the record company can exert quite a bit of pressure to get the song in the movie.

And then there's the advertising and other "product"-related opportunities. Most of the decisionmakers in this process are associated with either the client (which is to say, the company that the campaign is promoting) or the advertising agency. If you've got a song you think is a perfect tie-in with a particular product, it's worth pitching both parties.

Have you ever played the game "Clue?" Then you know that it's not always the obvious suspects—Professor Plum, Colonel Mustard, or Mrs. Peacock—that wind up being the one who did the deed. Sometimes it's the butler or the maid. Never underestimate those in supporting roles. While it would be impossible to detail all of the assorted assistants and hangers-on that hover around every major artist, you should never count out the possibility of getting a song to someone's personal assistant, business manager, lawyer, personal trainer, or dog-walker, and having it wind up in the right hands. CDs are cheap. If someone says they can get your song to someone, give it to them. Opportunity in this business is not so much about aiming your dart at the bull's eye. It's more about throwing a lot of darts. The more people that are listening, the better . . .

17

And Here Comes the Pitch . . . : Making the Sales Call

Okay, the time has come. Time to make that big sales call. The pitch. Time to put the plug in song plugging. You've got the music right and ready to go. You've got your list of who's looking, who's right for the song, and who's listening. All you have to do is make that call . . .

So go ahead. What are you waiting for? Pick up the phone. C'mon . . .

Selling is hard. Maybe not for everyone. I suspect that just as there are some people who seem to have been born humming a melody, there are others who are just natural sellers. They love the challenge of it, and the occasional door slamming in their face just makes them that much more determined. Just for the record, I'm not one of those people.

I tell you this because I suspect that a fair number of readers are in the same boat—especially those who are combining the role of songwriter and Creative Director. There are a few songwriters who are natural sellers—and they are worth their weight in gold (records, that is). They are valuable in part because they are so rare. Most musicians and writers seem to naturally shy away from the selling process, which explains all the tapes gathering dust on the shelf. People that don't mind expressing their deepest feelings in a song that could be heard by millions are intimidated about making a simple phone call.

Fine. I long ago accepted the fact that the sales pitch is not my natural gift. I hereby grant you permission to accept your own shortcomings as well. But accepting our shortcomings doesn't mean we don't have to make the phone calls. There's no way around that. If you want to have a publishing company, then someone has to make the call. Unless there's another willing party hiding in your office, I think that someone is you. And while we may never become virtuosos at the craft, we can learn to be effective.

The goal of the next two chapters is to give you the information you need to be able to sell your songs in a competent, professional manner. Follow the guidelines, and you will be able to get past the awkwardness, the self-consciousness, and the fear of rejection. Don't be surprised if a few years from now, some colleague says to you, "Oh, but you're just a natural-born salesman. I could never do that . . . " You can fool a lot of the people, a lot of the time.

Step 1: The Approach

Now that you've got that list of potential buyers, the first element in your plan of attack is the approach. There are a number of ways to get to the people that you need—in some instances, it will be obvious which strategy to employ. In other cases, you'll need to try every possible maneuver in order to make contact. Consider the options:

The Referral

A name can mean so much. There is nothing that better paves the way for a sales call than the nice ker-plunk of the right name dropping on a weasel's desk. "Your friend _____ suggested I call . . . "; "Your colleague _____ thought you'd be interested . . . "; "I was given your name by _____." (Fill in the name of prominent weasel, or respected songwriter, or fellow publisher, or manager, or producer, or whatever you've got that will do the trick.) Needless to say, the right name in the right situation can be something of a free pass, getting you past the receptionists and the no "unsolicited material" policy, and onto someone's phone line or into their office. But where do you get that name?

By now, you should already have a couple of sources to draw upon. You are part of a community, after all. And that's what a community is—people who know other people. Your first source of referrals will likely be other writers and publishers who can open doors to some of their contacts—usually on the basis that you do the same for them. Of course, co-writing can accelerate this process by offering an obvious reason for all the publishers and writers involved in a song to pool resources. Other members of the community can also be helpful—for example, singers and musicians may have relationships at record companies for whom they do session work or with artists with whom they perform.

In addition to being part of a community, by now you should also have constructed a support team around your company. Your lawyer was selected in part because of who he or she has access to. While you may need to prove yourself a bit before a prominent attorney is willing to go to bat on your behalf, it is reasonable to expect that he or she can help provide an entree to at least a few of the people you need to know. Your contacts at the performance societies can also be useful. One of the nice things about BMI, ASCAP, and SESAC is that they work with almost every record company and publishing business, but do not actually compete with any of them. This makes the writer relations representatives extremely well connected and completely unthreatening to everyone in the industry (except each other). One of the factors that you will consider when choosing a performance society is their willingness to offer a reference when needed.

The more pitching you do, the deeper your pool of references will become. If someone reacts favorably to a song but feels it's not quite right for their act, inquire as to whether they know of anyone else that might be interested in it. If they offer a suggestion, ask if they would be comfortable with you using their name when following up on the tip. Even when a meeting doesn't result in someone wanting one of your songs, it has been successful if it leads to an introduction to one or two more industry contacts.

The art of name-dropping is a delicate one that requires a certain amount of finesse and good judgment to pull off safely. There are two inherent dangers to be avoided. The first risk is overdoing it and annoying the person with whom you are trying to establish contact. Writers or Creative Directors who offer an unsolicited litany of everyone in their Rolodex are unknowingly putting their own insecurity on public display, and are generally viewed as either desperate or silly. You should use a name only when necessary, which usually means when asked for one—then use the best one or two that you've got, and let it go at that. Constant reminders of who you know will not make the CD sound any better. It will just make you look worse.

The second risk in tossing names around is the danger of offending the person whose name you're throwing out there. This is a tough one to avoid. Generally speaking, I would not recommend that you use anyone's name without their permission, unless it's a simple case of mentioning some of the people with whom you've worked (that falls under the category of "just the facts, ma'am"). Particularly when it comes to A&R contacts, producers, or other publishers, you would be wise to ask them if it would be alright to mention their name as a reference. This may also help to ward off the possibility of using the wrong name with the wrong person. Casually dropping the name of someone's worst enemy can produce more of a thud, rather than the ker-plunk you were hoping for.

The Cold Call

Alright, let's make this a little harder. What if you don't have any sort of referral to pave the way? This is the toughest call to make, but probably the most necessary. The person who is entirely outside your sphere can remain that way indefinitely, unless you make a concerted effort to reach out. That means opening up your directory and taking the plunge.

Wait. Not so fast. Only fools rush in. The first key to successful cold calling is preparation. The call should be cold only in the sense that the object of the call doesn't know you—not because you don't know them. There is enough information available in the industry trade magazines and the Internet for you to know if the person you're about to call is in fact the person with whom you ought to speak. You should have done some research on his or her background and current role within the company. Know what successes he or she has had recently, who his or her biggest acts are, and what sort of material he or she gravitates toward. For a Creative Director, cold-calling should never be an attempt at telemarketing—phoning up perfect strangers because you found their number in a book and blindly attempting to see if there's something you can sell them. Do your research. You need to know who you're speaking with.

You also need to convey who you are. Quickly. Be prepared to identify yourself, give a one- or two-sentence description of your company (one of those sentences should highlight your biggest or most recent success), and then get straight to the point.

So what is the reason for your call? "I have some music I'd like you to hear" is not a reason. It may be to you, but it's not to the person on the other end of the line. "I have a song I think you need to hear for your new artist, and wanted to get permission to send it over." That's a reason. There has to be some impetus for the person who answers the phone not to hang up. A description of your background and career goals, along with a vague request to get some feedback on your material, is not enough. For the recipient of the call, this isn't about you. The question is: what's in it for the weasel?

The other thing to consider about a cold call is whether it needs to be a call at all. There are other means of communication. An e-mail with a quick introduction and a bio or discography will go directly to its target—and, even better, will allow the recipient to respond quickly and easily. From the weasel's side, it eliminates much of the nuisance factor in receiving cold calls. If one or two phone calls fail to break through to someone, try the e-mail option.

Face Time

There's always the opportunity for the chance personal encounter, although actually leaving it to chance is not much of a strategy. The trick is to find ways to be in the right place at the right time to actually meet the person you've been trying to reach on the phone or via e-mail. This is not necessarily as difficult as it sounds.

The music industry loves conventions. For weasels, a convention is an opportunity to escape from the office and to hang out with friends on the company's money, which pretty much ensures that everyone who's anyone will be there. At the same time, for a well-organized, aggressive Creative Director, a convention can provide a bounty of potential contacts—like fishing in an aquarium. You know the people for whom you're looking are somewhere in the vicinity; the challenge is just to find them.

Working a convention effectively is a matter of combining most of the same principles we've already discussed and altering them to fit this unique environment. Preparation is key. Try to get a list of attendees, panels and moderators, events, and exhibitors in advance. Utilize your community contacts and business team—find out what friends and associates will be there and who they'll be meeting with. At many of the larger conventions, there's usually a party sponsored by BMI or ASCAP; see if you can score an invitation. If the person you're trying to meet is on a panel of some kind then, by all means, attend. If the forum is open to questions from the audience, try to make an impression by asking an intelligent question.

This last strategy can also be used effectively at all the various industry educational and networking programs. ASCAP, BMI, SESAC, NARAS, and many other organizations sponsor frequent panel discussions on a wide range industry topics. Speakers on these panels are exactly the sort of insiders that you need to meet. The inevitable question-and-answer period is an opportunity for you to have a one-on-one dialogue, even if it is in front of a crowd of people. Having spoken on many such panels, I will tell you that most people who come forward with a question completely squander what should be a golden opportunity. Whoever said there are no stupid questions has never spoken on a music industry panel. When the meeting is over, there will likely be some opportunity to approach the panelists. I guarantee that if you've asked a "good" question, everyone on the panel will remember you and will probably be willing to have a quick conversation.

Beyond the conventions and educational panels, there are a myriad of opportunities to get some "face-time." Industry parties, awards events, fundraisers, and showcases can all offer a chance for an "accidental" meeting. It's up to you to make an impression. Two quick bits of advice in that respect:

Keep it casual and quick. This is not a meeting; it's an introduction. Plan on getting out three sentences, which should include who you are, who you know, and something noteworthy that you've done. The last sentence is reserved for, "Is it okay if I call you at the office next week, or would you prefer an e-mail?" In between, it's always nice to work in a little humor.

Keep it to a conversation. Leave your CDs at home. These sort of face-to-face meetings are not the right moment to be digging a CD out of your bag and thrusting it on your quarry. God forbid you should try to play the person something on your Walkman or sing them an idea (yes, I really have seen people do this). The point here is not just to make an impression; the point is to make a *good* impression. This is the wind-up. The actual pitch is still to come . . .

Step 2: The Pitch

You did it. Whatever method you used, you've managed to sneak past the fire-wall of protection, past the receptionists and assistants, and get your songs a chance to be heard. These days, that is no small feat. The truth is, most of the actual pitch is out of your hands—it's now up to the music to speak for itself. Nevertheless, it's important to understand the pitching process, and to understand the Creative Director's role in presenting the songs in the best possible light. There are really only two basic methods of getting your songs out there:

"Send It Right Over . . . "

Whether you get it there in the mail, via messenger, or on an MP3 file, the fundamental nature of this type of pitch remains the same. Your music is in the weasel's office, but you're not. This freaks a lot of people out. Days go by, no response is heard, and pretty soon you're convinced that the CD has been lost on the island of misfit demos, never getting even a cursory listen. Aargh!

Relax. Songs are sold everyday without Creative Directors being right there in the room. Many A&R people, myself included, prefer to listen to songs in privacy, rather than in a face-to-face encounter. It may not happen as quickly as you would like or with the thoroughness that you would wish for, but most A&R people will listen to the CDs that they receive. Like it or not, it is their job.

This process starts with obtaining permission to send the material, which as we've already said, can be done over the phone or through an e-mail exchange. When you send the material, make sure that the envelope is marked "REQUESTED MATERIAL." And once you've obtained permission, send the material immediately. If you're in the same city, you should messenger the material to the office that same day. If you're out of town, send the song for a next-day delivery. If you are sending the package outside your own country, you really have no choice but to use some sort of express mail service. Remember, the weasel has a very limited memory capacity. Your name and the conversation you both had regarding the song will only be retained for a day or two. After that, you're back in cold-calling territory.

The package you send should be professional but need not be elaborate. It should include:

- A brief cover letter on your company's letterhead, recalling your phone conversation, highlighting your company's recent activity, and providing any pertinent information about the material. (Be sure to include the name of the project for which it's being submitted.)

- The CD itself, with a label that includes your company's logo, the song titles, writer information, and contact information (include your e-mail address). Remember, **no cassettes**.

- Lyrics. This is somewhat important when pitching in the pop and country markets, essential when pitching for film, television, and advertising projects, and less important when working in the urban or rock markets.

- Bios, discographies, or press clippings can be helpful, particularly if this is the first contact you've had with this A&R person. These should be on the company letterhead, and probably packaged in some sort of folder.

Of course, if you are sending MP3 files, you will need to adapt your approach. You should still include some sort of cover letter, lyrics, and background information, all of which can be sent as e-mail attachments.

Most importantly, you need to consider how much music to send. If you are pitching songs for a specific project, there is no question that the strongest pitch is usually one song—the one you believe is a "perfect fit" for the artist. One song on a CD implies a certain level of confidence on the part of the sender and imparts a degree of importance to the song itself. It is an unequivocal statement: "This is the song you need." Period.

However, if you're pitching for several projects, or if you simply can't decide which songs are the most appropriate, you can probably get away with three songs on a CD. But that's the limit. Unless you receive a specific request from the recipient, *never* send more than three songs on one CD. Better to be able to follow up with a few new songs three weeks later than to barrage a listener with your entire catalog in the first pitch. It's the oldest rule in showbiz: Leave 'em wanting more.

Let's Take a Meeting

This is your big chance. Not only are you there to make sure your music really does get a fair listen, but you've got an opportunity to watch the reaction, to see how the song and the demo stand up under fire, and to make on-the-spot choices about which songs to pitch based on the listener's feedback. Even better, you have a chance to establish a relationship with this new contact—to send more material in the future, to find out about upcoming projects, and perhaps to gather a few suggestions about potential co-writers or other places to send your songs. This is your shot at putting yourself on this particular person's radar screen. You need to be at the top of your game.

Most likely, you will have somewhere between twenty and thirty minutes to make your case. Here's how that breaks down:

00:00:00—00:05:00: Small Talk

00:05:00—00:15:00 The Pitch Session

00:15:00—00:20:00 Summary and Send Off

Don't underestimate the first five minutes, and the last five. Just because you're not playing music doesn't mean that nothing is happening. These are your moments to make a personal connection. The rest of the time, you're just sitting there listening to a CD.

Small talk should probably start with congratulations to the A&R person for their most recent success, a quick description of your own background, and a mention of all the exciting things happening with your company. You can follow that with an inquiry as to whether there's anything specific that the A&R person needs, or if there has been any change in what he or she is looking for since your last phone call. If you can do it naturally, an attempt at a personal connection is worth the effort. Take a look around the office. Anything that might suggest a shared interest in sports, art, travel, children, or hobbies can serve as a conversation starter. Even the weaseliest weasel has a human side (I think).

The last five minutes is the final impression, which is usually the one that endures. The summary should include:

- a review of the songs that you've played, and the A&R person's reaction to them

- a confirmation of which songs the A&R person would like to receive copies of (if you don't have a CD you can leave at the office)

- a reiteration of what the A&R person is currently looking for

- a clarification of the time frame for the project

That leaves about two and half minutes for the send-off. That should include an expression of thanks for the meeting, a promise to stay in touch, and a friendly goodbye. Then you should get out of the office. Overstaying your welcome will negate all the positive work you've done up to that point. By getting in and out of the office quickly, you establish yourself as a busy professional who appreciates the value of time management. You also make it that much more likely that you will be invited to have another meeting in the future. Which is the ultimate goal.

And then there's the pitch session itself. Prior to the meeting, I suggest you select four songs to put forward. Burn them to a CD, which you can then leave with the A&R person. Out of these four selections, I suggest that three be aimed directly at whatever project you are pitching toward; the other should simply be your best song, regardless of style. Also bring with you a DAT or CD of additional songs from your catalog, so that if you find you are way off the mark with your preselected choices, you can make adjustments on the spot. If the A&R person responds to one of these alternate songs, you can send a copy as soon as you get back to the office. A hint: be sure to check your CDs before going to the meeting.

When you are pitching songs, put your confidence in the music itself. It's acceptable to preface a song with a mention of the writers or the artists who have recorded the song in the past, or projects that it's currently being considered for. That should be all that's necessary. No sales pitch and no excuses. You've already done your work getting the music right. Just hit Play.

Don't be surprised if the A&R person listens to only a verse and a chorus. Time is of the essence in a pitch meeting. If a song isn't what he or she is looking for, the A&R person is actually doing you a favor by stopping it quickly and giving you a chance to take another shot. Don't be offended if nothing you play quite hits the mark. It's understood by everyone that there are always many more misses than hits. The important thing is to demonstrate a high level of quality in the material. That should be enough to make a favorable impression.

So which is preferable—sending a package to the office, or a face-to-face meeting? Most song pluggers will come down firmly in favor of the personal meeting, whenever and wherever possible. I tend to agree, although I think the healthiest approach is a reasonable balance between the two. Most A&R people are hesitant to schedule a meeting until they've heard something that they like—you'll probably need to send something over once or twice before someone's willing to have a sit-down chat. Once you've established a relationship, one or two meetings a year should be enough to keep up the contact. The rest of the time, you can just send the song.

With that said, be aware that some people simply refuse to listen to songs in a meeting. If that's the case, don't push it. Every Creative Director has relationships in which he or she has never met the contact in person. I once wrote a song with Jermaine Jackson and never even spoke with him. It's perfectly plausible to do business solely through the telephone, FedEx, and e-mail. If a contact is uncomfortable about scheduling a meeting, don't force the issue.

There's one delicate issue that may come up in the course of the pitching process. Having initially approached the A&R person as the Creative Director of a publishing company, it may be a bit awkward when you explain that you are also a songwriter. This requires some finesse. As I said, when first speaking to an industry contact, you should usually identify yourself as a Creative Director, not a songwriter. But never try to hide the fact that you are one of the writers represented by your company. If you are one of several writers signed to your publishing company, you can acknowledge your own creative contribution, while also emphasizing that the company has a varied roster of talent. If you are the sole writer for your company, then acknowledge that fact, but emphasize that your publishing entity is a full-service music publisher and that your role as Creative Director is separate from your work as a writer. The most important element in making this distinction will be your conduct. If you are well prepared, organized, and businesslike, you will easily be accepted as a Creative Director. If you are anything less than that, you will be seen as having used the title to fake your way in the door. And you will probably be shown out through that same door.

Step 3: The Follow-Through

It's always important to finish strong. I'm amazed at how often writers and publishers fail to follow through after making their initial pitch for a project. The real art of selling lies much more in the follow-through than in the pitch itself. Once you've identified an opportunity and gone after it, the key is to seize whatever openings you've been given and make the most of them. That's the art of the follow-through.

If you've sent a package to someone's office, the follow-through should probably begin about two weeks later. At that point, call to ensure that the package was received, and see if there's been any reaction to the material. You may be told, "Yeah, I received it, but I haven't had a chance to check it out," This buys one more week before you call again. If the material has been reviewed, then the goal is to get as much feedback as possible. Positive beats negative, but sometimes negative is even more useful. Try to speak directly with the A&R person and find out specifically what he or she liked or disliked. Then lay the groundwork to try again. "I've just gotten a new song in that I think you might like. May I send that one over?" "I really appreciate the feedback. I'll see if I can come up with something closer to what you're looking for. Can I touch base with you in a two or three weeks to get an update on the project?" If you've missed the mark, then you need to try again. If you've hit the mark, then there's even more reason to try again. If you pitch people once and never send them anything else, you've failed on your follow-up.

The post-meeting follow-through should be considerably quicker. Anything that was requested from the meeting should be sent over the next day. An e-mail should go out immediately, thanking the A&R person for his or her time and reminding them of the songs they liked. After that, you should plan on touching base in some manner every six to eight weeks. That can mean sending a new song, an e-mail message regarding some recent success of your company, a congratulatory note for a recent success at the A&R person's company, or a phone call to see what other projects are in development. The goal is an ongoing dialogue.

Keep in mind that no one expects you to show up with a smash hit in your first pitch meeting. Overnight success is a myth that is bought into largely by those outside of the industry—those on the inside have long given up on such fantasies. We have signed many writers at Zomba before they were capable of writing genuine "hit" songs. We signed them because we saw consistent productivity, and we noticed that each song seemed to be a little better than the last. As long as you're moving in the right direction, you can stay in the game.

The message sent by a good follow-up is that you are in this business for the long haul. It tells the A&R community that yours is not a one-shot effort at hitting the mark, but that you intend to keep working until you can deliver what's needed. Doing so lays the groundwork for the most important element in the entire selling process:

The Relationship. More on that next . . .

18

Smooth Operator:
Song Plugging Master Class

One of the best song salesmen that I've ever seen is not a publisher. He's a songwriter—and a very good one, which of course makes selling his songs considerably easier. Gary Baker is one of Nashville's most successful songwriters, having penned with partner Frank Myers crossover classics like "I Swear," recorded by both John Michael Montgomery and All 4 One, and "I'm Already There," recorded by Lonestar. Both songs were named "Song of the Year" by the Country Music Association (in 1994 and 2002, respectively). In addition to his numerous Top-10 country hits, he has also written songs for pop superstars like the Backstreet Boys, 98°, and Ronan Keating. No question, this guy can write.

But he can also sell. The strangest thing is, if you spend time with Gary, you hardly ever notice him doing it. At least not with the methods that we just discussed. That's because he's busy with something more important. He's building relationships. Tip sheets, cold calls, and pitch meetings will get you started, but relationships are what you build a career on.

Relationship Selling

The first thing to notice about relationship selling is that it's largely invisible. When it's done well, not only is the buyer unaware that he's being sold, but the seller is hardly even aware that he's selling. Most expert practitioners of relationship selling never seem to be doing all that much. They just seem to have an uncanny ability to turn up at just the right moment or to happen to be buddies with exactly the right person. That's precisely the point.

The truth is, the usual selling process is something of an uphill battle. The seller feels self-conscious delivering his or her pitch, and the buyer is suspicious that he or she is being "hustled." If selling is not something to which you look forward, think of your buyers. Being sold is probably not the high point of their days, either. Relationship selling aims to take the pain out of the procedure.

This is hardly a new technique and certainly not one unique to the entertainment industry. Most companies long ago recognized the value of building relationships with their customers. This would explain the corporate season tickets to the local sports teams, the lunches, dinners, and the rest of the expense account largesse doled out in the interests of entertaining clients. The basic theory behind relationship selling is this: Let the seller and buyer develop a personal bond, let them discover shared interests and begin to consider each other friends, and they will find a way to do business together in a way that is mutually beneficial.

"Oh, I get it," you say. "He's telling me to be phony and pretend to be someone's friend just so they'll do me a favor and cut my song." No. In fact, being phony is probably the worst thing you can possibly do, in part because it's always more transparent than you think and also because it's inherently short-term. Relationship selling is not geared toward quick results. A faked friendship will not survive the inevitable give and take that is part of any business relationship. Phony will not work.

Relationship selling is not about "favors" either. You don't build a business on the hope that someone will put your substandard song on an album as a "favor." The idea of building a personal relationship is that it will afford you not just opportunities, but a deeper understanding of the buyer's needs and preferences. Gary Baker's involvement in writing "I'm Already There" grew in part out of a long relationship with Lonestar lead singer and fellow writer Richie McDonald. But Lonestar wasn't doing anyone a "favor" by recording the song. The power of that song spoke for itself.

So if phony and self-serving doesn't work, what does? What will it take to advance to the level of "relationship" selling? Three things: concern for others, selectivity, and patience. The best part is, they are the same sort of values that your mother said would make you a better, happier person. Relationship selling is one of the few times in the music business that nice guys can actually finish near the top of the heap.

Concern for Others

The real key to relationship selling is changing your point of view. No longer is your focus centered on you and your need to make the sale. Instead, your interest is in the people with whom you are doing business. The idea is to get to know them, their likes and dislikes, their goals for the project, their hobbies, you name it. It's all about them and what you can do for them—not because of what's in it for you but because of a friendly desire to help.

Ever see "Miracle on 34ᵗʰ Street?" The part where Macy's Santa refers the customers to Gimbels if Macy's doesn't have what they want—that's relationship selling. If you remember the movie, you know that Macy's business skyrockets as a result. All the happy customers write to Mr. Macy, complimenting him on the store's new, altruistic holiday spirit. As you make the transition from salesman to friend, you'll begin to see the difference. Your phone calls get answered quicker. Someone calls with a hot tip every now and then. A meeting turns into dinner. Suddenly, you're an insider rather than an outsider—and opportunities just start to come your way.

Selectivity

Make lots of friends, but choose them wisely. Some people, quite a few actually, are simply not interested in developing a relationship. They're wary of ulterior motives. Maybe they're just not very nice. Don't waste your time. You can't force a relationship on someone—either it clicks or it doesn't. If it doesn't, continue to pitch your songs as one professional to another, and leave it at that.

Here's another concept. When you're picking your friends, pick people that you like. Or admire. Or can learn from. Avoid deadbeats, losers, users, liars, and anyone who's generally bitter and angry. Building relationships is an investment of time and energy, and successful people learn to invest wisely. Avoid the temptation to always surround yourself with friends that are less successful than you. Usually the motive in this is not to generously pull your friends up, but to make yourself feel better by comparison. Build relationships with people who challenge and inspire you to do more than what you're doing.

Patience

And then, wait. Relationship selling is not like planting a flower; it's more like planting a tree. You've got to hang on quite a while to see results. It's perfectly possible that you may develop a relationship with someone for five years before anything much comes of it. Like I said, it's an investment and it doesn't come with a guarantee. If you've picked your friends wisely and nurtured the relationship diligently, more often than not, something good will happen.

The difficulty here is that nurturing a relationship is no easy task. That is particularly true of relationships that span decades, surviving business ups and downs, disputes, misunderstandings, conflicts of interest, changes in lifestyles and position, and all the other factors that enter into friendships. It takes a consistent effort to stay in touch, to make the small friendly gesture (a note of congratulations or a call of sympathy), to return calls promptly, or do the odd favor. It also takes a willingness to understand that business is business (and to keep disputes from getting personal), to assume the best of intentions, to accept mistakes, and to understand that changes in status, attitudes, lifestyles, or social circles is an inevitable part of everyone's life. This is indeed an investment—a long-term one—and you can't allow short-term fluctuations to make you give up on it too soon.

If there's a flip side to the theory of relationship selling, it is probably the advice that seems to be dispensed more often than any other to aspiring writers, publishers, and artists . . . .

Be Aggressive

More dangerous words were never spoken. They're dangerous not because they're false, but because they're both true and false at the same time. In a world in which "aggressive" can mean anything from sending a follow-up e-mail to storming the office with an attack mob, the words are just too open to misunderstanding.

In fact, much of the time that you spend trying to navigate past overly vigilant receptionists and "no outside material" policies is a result of the efforts of "aggressive" songwriters who simply wore out their own welcome and yours as well. My colleague David Gray makes the distinction between "assertive" and "aggressive," and I think it's an apt point. Relationships are built by assertive people. They are usually destroyed by aggressive people. Anyone who plans to sell anything—but particularly music—needs to understand the difference.

Being assertive means:

- doing your homework before you cold-call anyone

- developing a rapport with the receptionist and assistant, with the hopes that they get their boss to call you back

- making sure to convey the exciting things that are happening with your company

- responding to requests for changes by immediately getting the A&R person a new version that incorporates their feedback

- following up a meeting or song submission with a phone call, and if that gets no response, an e-mail

- submitting a steady flow of material that demonstrates continued creative growth

- sending out requested music immediately

- making sure that you've gotten your song to everyone who's involved with a project, including the artist, management, and label

- following up regularly about songs that are "on hold," and keeping your options open if the recording process should begin to stall

- finding every opportunity to make the professional contacts you need, and, whenever possible, to develop those contacts into long-term relationships

Being assertive does not mean:

- calling every name in the A&R directory until somebody takes your call

- berating or demeaning a receptionist or assistant because your call hasn't been returned

- rubbing your success in the face of someone who has turned down your material in the past

- arguing with someone who feels that your song could be improved or isn't right for their particular project

- trying to persuade the listener why the song is better without the changes they've asked for

- calling a dozen times a day to see if the song has been listened to

- vowing to call the office a hundred times a day until you get a response

- putting all your efforts behind one song and refusing to take no for an answer

- demanding a meeting so that you can play the song in person

- going back to the same person more than twice with the same song

- issuing empty threats about pulling your song from a project if your timeframe is not met

- waiting night after night outside Kenny Rogers' hotel with a cassette tape of "his" song

In short, being assertive should be almost synonymous with being a solid professional. Responsive, organized, well prepared, confident but realistic—this is the image that any Creative Director should strive to present. It is as aggressive as you should ever need to be. What some writers call aggressive is more like amateurish and naïve, or desperate and delusional. You cannot build "relationships" with that sort of aggression.

Before I close this "master class" of selling, I want to touch on another one of those things I only learned once I got on the publisher's side of the desk:

The Rules of Office Etiquette

It never occurred to me until my first day at Zomba Music Publishing—up to that point, I had never spent a single day in an office. I worked a few odd jobs in high school (not very well) but they were never office gigs. Then I went to college. Then I started writing. Sure, I'd visit my publisher every now and then—"work" the office a bit, say hello to everyone, drop off some tapes. Then I'd leave. When I started my current gig, I had no idea how to even transfer a call or file a check request. I knew nothing of Office Etiquette.

Most writers don't. Most writers have very little sense of the rhythms of office life, or the demands of a 9-to-5 gig (well, okay . . . more like 10:30 to 6:30). As a Creative Manager, you will be spending much of your day working with people who are not rolling out of bed at 1 P.M., or going off to work at 8 P.M. at night. This is not to say they work harder than most writers (I don't think I've ever worked harder than when I was a writer), but it does mean that they work differently. The more you can adjust your way of doing business to accommodate the unique pressures of office life, the more work you'll be able to get out of your office-bound colleagues.

- Never call someone at 10 o'clock on a Monday morning. Never call someone at 6:30 on Friday night. Never ever call someone on Tuesday morning after a three-day weekend.

- Don't call more than necessary. It is not necessary to call to request permission to submit material, then call again to let the A&R person know that you've sent the song, then call again to see if it was received, and yet again to see if it was listened to. Request permission, then send the CD. Call in two weeks to see about the reaction.

- Don't call to request permission to send the song until it is written, recorded, and ready to be mailed. Then send it immediately after the call.

- Don't expect things to happen overnight. Checks cannot be cut, contracts cannot be sent, reservations cannot be made, and demos cannot be received in an office without some sort of process. Things take time in an office.

- Do not ask more than one person in an office for the same thing. In doing so, you are not "working" the office. You're working people's nerves.

- Understand that it really is possible to spend an entire day in a meeting. I never thought it was. Unfortunately, it is.

- In an office, 2 P.M. means 2 P.M. Harsh, I know. But be on time. Not early, not late.

- Do not drop by without an appointment, or at least a call before you arrive. In an office, surprises are only good when it's a birthday party.

- Develop relationships with people's assistants or staff. If someone suggests that you speak to his or her assistant, you are not being foisted off on an underling. You are being referred to the person who actually does stuff. Make friends.

- When someone looks at his or her watch, it's time to go.

Another songwriter who is an excellent Creative Director and very effective song plugger is my old writing buddy Jeff Franzel, who I mentioned earlier. Like Gary Baker, Jeff's approach is based on the building of relationships, on being "assertive" but not "aggressive," and on having sensitivity to the demands of an office environment. He is the consummate professional. He always stays in contact but never barrages anyone with calls or material. He responds immediately to any request for a change or alteration in a song. He is confident (and properly so) but always understanding if a song doesn't work for a specific project. And he's pleasant to everyone—not just the person he's selling to but to each individual in the office.

In fact, the nice thing about joining the song plugger's Master Class is that most of the people in it are . . . well, nice. There's a lesson in there somewhere. On some days, you will sell a song. On most days, you will experience rejection. But everyday you have the opportunity to build two things that will endure and will eventually become the foundation of your business: your reputation and your relationships. If you're going to be in it—be in it for the long run.

19

The Rules of the Game: Getting the Music Out

For what should be a relatively straightforward process—you like the song, you take the song, you record the song, and we'll all meet up at the Grammys—the song pitching game can get pretty complex. Like every other game, it has its own vocabulary, constructed primarily to imply that there is a set of rules for what in reality is a lawless free-for-all. Like having a referee in rugby. But in the interests of enabling you to toss legal-sounding phrases around with the best of them, and to possibly even understand the underlying issues behind those phrases, I give you:

The Song Plugger's Glossary

The Pass

Let's start with the bad news first. "Passing" is the politically correct way of conveying that your song has not found a home in this particular place. It's a shorter way of saying, "Thank you for your submission, but it does not meet our needs at this time," and a slightly kinder method than the very succinct "No." It can be delivered verbally, via e-mail, or by form letter. (No one likes getting a standard-issue rejection letter, but some companies simply require that the A&R department provide a written record of response.) The thundering silence of no response at all is also assumed to be a pass.

However it may be delivered, don't be offended by a pass—there's really no great method of delivering bad news, and delivering bad news is about 75 percent of an A&R weasel's job. Another Creative Manager once told me, "You could pass on 100 percent of the things that come across your desk, and statistically, you would only be wrong 5 percent of the time." It's true. "No" is not rude; it's just "no." Don't argue with it, try to change it, or be emotionally crushed by it. Move on. There's always someone else to pitch to.

The Hold

This is the good news and the bad news delivered simultaneously. When executives put a song on hold, they are saying, "I like this, but I need some time to make a decision." This is the good news. They are telling you they like it, after all. The not-so-good news is that they are asking you to temporarily refrain from committing the song to another project until they can make up their mind and review the song with the artist, manager, producer, or other decision-maker. The problem is, they're not telling you how long all this could take.

I think most publishers would say that eight to ten weeks is probably a reasonable amount of time for a hold to last. If that seems long, remember the number of cooks in the kitchen. Try to comprehend the difficulties of decisionmaking when an artist is on the road, filming a movie, renegotiating a contract, or doing all three at the same time. In fact, most publishers would admit that on superstar projects, holds invariably last much, much longer. The hold situation on the recent Faith Hill album *Cry* reached epic proportions in Nashville. There were at least a hundred songs on hold at various times for that project, and a good number of them were on hold for over a year.

It doesn't take a great deal of foresight to anticipate the way holds can affect your song pitching efforts. Particularly with a small catalog, you can quickly wind up with your three or four best songs caught in limbo—waiting on a thumbs-up from one project and subsequently not available to be placed on more immediate or possibly more lucrative records. Navigating your way through the hold process is probably the most sensitive, difficult part of the song plugging game. A few guidelines:

Holds are about relationships, not rules. The principle of granting holds is a courtesy extended by publishers to their customers—it's not a law. If someone wants to put a song on hold, you have every right to say no. You can simply say, "If you decide to cut the song, I'm happy to let you know if it's available, but I can't take the song off the market at this point." Or you can say, "I can give you three weeks, and then I'll pay you the courtesy of letting you know if someone else is interested in recording the song." You won't make many friends in A&R this way (as most weasels consider the granting of holds a God-given right), but you will keep your options open.

You have to decide what you are comfortable with as far as the granting of holds, based on the value of the relationship and the project, the timing, and the importance of the song in your catalog. The same is true when it comes to your respect for holds. If someone believes they have a song on hold, and you give the song to a more lucrative project, you haven't broken any laws but you've probably made an enemy. Sometimes it's worth it. Sometimes it's not. Personally, I will usually keep a song on hold for eight to ten weeks. After that, I will grant the A&R person "right of first refusal." If someone else expresses interest, then the person holding the song gets one last chance to give a commitment. Otherwise, all holds are off. Superstar projects are another matter. On those, you just have to find a new level of forbearance.

Granting a hold does not mean that you can't pitch the song. Some A&R people would argue this—they feel that putting a song on hold should take it off the market entirely. I don't buy it. I think it's perfectly appropriate to pitch the song, so long as you preface the pitch by letting the listener know that the song is currently on hold. The message here is, "If you like the song and are prepared to give me a commitment, I will go back to the party holding the song and ask them to make a decision as to whether they are ready to move forward." It is understood that whoever has the song on hold has the right of first refusal.

Never issue empty threats. As the hold process drags on, it can be very tempting to try to force an A&R person's hand. There's nothing inherently wrong with saying, "I have someone else who wants the song, so you have three days to give me a date that this is going to be recorded." As long as you really do have someone else interested. If you don't have somewhere else to take the song, be very careful about calling someone's bluff. A&R people don't appreciate being pressured by publishers. This tactic is the equivalent of threatening to leave your job if you don't get a raise. Definitely an option of last resort.

A better strategy for an appropriately assertive Creative Manager is to focus your efforts toward consistently following up with an A&R person (every four to six weeks) as to a song's current status. Don't assume that you would have been told if it was being dropped from the list of potential songs, or if it was already recorded. You could easily find out that you've been holding something that has long since become available or pitching something that's already cut.

Recording Commitment

This is a vague concept that is really little more than an indication from the project's A&R staff that your song is, in fact, scheduled to be recorded. Sometimes it's the selection of a producer or a statement regarding the anticipated recording schedule. If you are a writer/producer, it might be the initial discussions regarding your production agreement. Or it could be as simple as a request for lyrics and a lead sheet. The idea here is to get some sort of indication as to the company's intention to record the song—which will then require you to take the song off the market.

This sort of commitment is not a contract. At best, it would be an e-mail exchange, to provide some written confirmation of the discussion. In many instances, it will be a phone call or a casual conversation. Understand that a commitment to record your song is no guarantee of anything. Sessions get postponed or cancelled, artists change their minds, and everything always takes longer than anticipated. Sometimes songs are recorded and simply don't turn out as well as everyone hoped. A commitment to record is a statement that the process is moving forward, and most importantly, that money is about to be spent.

Not surprisingly, this last bit is the real crux of the issue. Once the recording process is set in motion—studios booked, producers hired, musicians scheduled—money is being spent. At this point, you have an obligation to take the song off the market. You can play it for people as a demonstration of what you do; you can even pitch it with the proviso that the song would only become available if something falls apart in the recording process. But unless you hear otherwise from the A&R person, you really have no right to pull the song away from the artist who is planning to record it. This is not to say that it's never been done, but it's definitely a "you'll never work in this town again" move. Once an A&R person expresses an intention to record the song, the song is officially sold.

First Use

Of course, just because it's sold once doesn't mean it can't be sold again. Later. The concept of first use is an acknowledgement that the first recording of a song is usually the one that defines the song in the mind of the public and therefore has a greater significance than subsequent performances.

Once a song has been released commercially, it is fair game for everyone and anyone—from cover bands at weddings to other major label artists. So long as they pay the appropriate royalties to the publishers and writers, anyone can record and release the song. If a song has never been released previously, then the publisher must grant a first license to the record company. As the term "first use" would imply, this is an exclusive license granted to only one artist. Obviously, the intent is to avoid a situation in which an artist records a song and is beaten to the punch by another artist who gets his or her version out at the same time.

The importance attached to the first use of a song also affects the publishers and their right to grant the mechanical license. The law provides that on a song with multiple writers and publishers, any one party can grant a mechanical license, even over the objections of all the other parties. At the same time, the law also recognizes that a substandard first use can degrade the value of a song in the marketplace. If a writer or publisher can legitimately claim that a potential recording will damage the song's value, they may be able to prevent the issue of a license. When a song is exploited for the first time, you will probably need the consent of all the writers and publishers involved.

Different Markets

It is possible to sell a song in more than one place at the same time. The idea of placing a song in two different markets by two different artists has a long history—think "Tutti Frutti" by Pat Boone (for the white pop audience) and Little Richard (for the r&b market—and all others with good musical taste). While it might be less common now than in the 1950s, it still happens. Country artist John Michael Montgomery and pop vocal group All 4 One worked the trick twice, with "I Swear" and "I Can Love You Like That." The idea here is that the two markets are different enough that one artist's version will not detract from the other's.

Contemporary Christian music publishers will refer to this concept as a basis for shopping a song to a pop project, even though a Christian artist is already recording the song. Country publishers will do the same if they feel something could work in the pop market. Urban publishers might consider gospel a substantially different market. A rock-oriented publisher would feel that a song's presence on a predominantly urban-oriented soundtrack would not interfere with a rock act's recording of the same song. All of the publishers would probably agree that an international release is unlikely to interfere with anything happening with the song in the US.

In order to preserve the relationship between your company and those who are recording your song, it's best to try to be as open as possible about any intentions you have to place the song in a "different market." If there are objections that one release will detract from the other, even if it is in a "different market," you need to try to answer those objections. Point out the difference in the target audiences, the radio formats, the marketing approaches, and the timing of the projects. If that's not persuasive, then you may have to make a choice as to which market is more valuable and which relationship is more important.

So long as you are open and honest, even in disagreement, you should be able to survive these sorts of disputes without any lasting damage to your reputation. On the other hand, if you choose to conceal the fact that you are placing the song with another artist in a "different market" (under the theory that what a weasel doesn't know won't hurt it), you could find yourself in some very uncomfortably hot water. Try to get the blessings of all parties involved; if you can't, then you may need to make a choice. Don't try to keep it a secret. A&R guys hate surprises.

Recording Restrictions

This is applicable only if the writer will also be producing the song. In most producers' agreements, there is a clause placing them under a re-recording restriction. This stipulates that they cannot produce the same song for someone else within a set amount of time (usually somewhere from three to five years). It's easy to understand the thinking behind this. The record company and artist are trying to make sure that you don't record the same song with someone else and put it out in competition with their version.

There's not much you can do about a "re-record" restriction—it is a relatively standard part of a production agreement. If possible, try to insert very specific guidelines as to what sort of re-recordings would be restricted, taking into account different markets and the differences in record life-spans. There is always the danger that you could produce a song only to find out that the record is not being released. Under most contracts, you would still be restricted from recording it with anyone else. Try to build into the production agreement a stipulation that the record must be released by a certain date or the re-record restriction is lifted.

When it comes to the Herculean task of getting the music out, there's one more thing I have to mention. It won't keep you from having your heart broken (that's as inevitable in song plugging as it is in love), but it might keep you from doing any financial damage to yourself or your business.

Rule #7

A song is never on a record until you buy it in the store.

Music Business Weasel

No matter what assurances you've received from the A&R person, manager, artist, or producer; no matter how great the song sounds with the artist's vocal on it; no matter what you hear through the grapevine; no matter where you've seen it advertised: nothing is definite until the day the CD shows up at your local record store. Believe it when you see it.

I heard recently of a Nashville writer who, upon learning that his song was being cut by a major country/pop artist, immediately ran out and bought a boat, largely on credit. It was not until the day the album was released and he went into the store to buy the record that he realized his song had been dropped from the project at the last minute. He spent the next year living on his boat—as most everything else he had was gone.

When I was a writer, I tried to avoid mentioning any song of mine that was being cut until I knew the album had been released. Call it superstition, but I just felt that talking about it would jinx the whole thing. Other writers are less reticent but still prone to add caveats like, "It's supposed to be on . . ." or "They're telling me it's on . . ." when discussing upcoming releases.

Despite all the high-minded discussions of holds and recording commitments and re-record restrictions, the making of a record (or even worse, a movie or television show) is really not a particularly thoughtful, well-organized endeavor. The last few days of putting together the final sequence of an album are incredibly frenetic, filled with eleventh-hour histrionics, power plays, disputes, horse-trading, and compromises. Anything can happen—and often does. No writer or publisher should ever spend money on something that is going to happen. Sit tight, stay quiet, and wait till you're sure it has happened.

Unwrap the CD first. Then you can crack open the champagne . . .

20

Keep Rising to the Top: Moving the Writer Up

Oops. Not so fast. Put the champagne bottle down. You're not done yet. Remember, there are three primary functions that make up the Creative Director's job. You've still got one to go. Just as an A&R person understands that the real job of making records is not just to make hit records, but to develop hit artists—a savvy Creative Director realizes that the work is not done when a song is at the top of the charts. The publishing business is not just about hit songs. It's also about developing hit songwriters.

Of course, nothing helps in that quest more than having hits. By getting the music right and getting it out, you've laid the groundwork for any writer's career. The music always comes first, and if it's done well enough, it may be all that's necessary to lift a writer into the big leagues. Mutt Lange has had more hits than almost anyone can count, and has won more than a dozen ASCAP awards for his work, but he's never shown up for a single awards ceremony. You'll almost never see his picture in a magazine. You don't need to. Everybody who needs to know, knows exactly who he is. Hit songs will do that.

At the same time, there are other writers whose presence and stature in the industry seems to far exceed their actual commercial success. It can be baffling at times to watch a writer move up the industry ladder to a position of prominence when no one seems to be able to pinpoint any particular hit song that he or she has written. It's the Zsa Zsa Gabor phenomenon—famous for being famous. How does it happen?

It happens largely because someone is thinking strategically. Whether it's the writer, the Creative Director, a manager, or a publicist, somebody is making a deliberate effort to raise the writer's profile, to place him or her in the right situations, to receive the right sort of attention from the media, and to build a powerful network of supporters within the creative community. A plan has been developed that is certainly aided by having a hit record, but is not reliant upon one. The strategies we will discuss in this chapter are not song-focused; they are writer-focused. For the next few pages, it's all about the writer, not the song.

Before we proceed, it's worth asking a simple question: why? Why should a publisher care about how a writer is perceived? After all, a publisher represents the catalog, which is to say the songs, not the writer. A publisher is not a manager or agent who receives a percentage of everything the writer earns. A publisher receives a portion of what a specific song earns. If a writer becomes a celebrity, the publisher will not necessarily benefit. So why should a publisher invest effort in raising a writer to prominence? What's in it for the weasel?

You do it because you have to. Song plugging is an ancient art, but in many ways, it's also a vanishing one. It's being replaced by what we might call writer plugging (if that weren't such a nasty little phrase). Rather than finding individual songs to make up an album, most A&R people are now oriented toward a sort of "package deal"—finding writers and producers who (hopefully) can be employed to come up with several songs. Writer/producers are engaged to provide three or four songs for an album; writers are asked to co-write with the artist; or writers are put together in specific combinations to try to provide the sound that the A&R people are seeking. The goal is to find a creative "nucleus" for the project—the person who can generate all or most of the material that will make up the album. The challenge is this: how do you get your writer into those exclusive settings?

Everybody Make Some Noise!

Hype. It is up to the Creative Director to help create around a writer the sort of energy and heat that attracts A&R people, managers, producers, and executives, and convinces them that this hot new writer can bring something exciting to their project. Certainly, a resume of hit records helps provide that aura, but when it comes to hype, quite a bit can be done with smoke and mirrors. A Creative Director must find a way to create a "story" for a writer—a blend of past successes, exciting current activity, name recognition and reputation, and general industry buzz. While it may not benefit the publisher directly, that "story" will help to get the writer in the optimum situations. You can't hit a grand slam with no one on base. A Creative Director's job is to get his or her writer a chance to go to bat with the bases loaded. Given enough opportunities, a writer is bound to get a hit.

Remember, this is show business. Everything is a blend of fact, fiction, and a little razzle-dazzle. Forget about the music for a second. The goal is to get the weasels weaseling. Don't believe Chuck D. Believe the hype.

Publicity

This is an obvious place to start. There are a already a myriad of books on the market that can offer you the specifics of preparing press releases, planting stories, and generating media exposure—I'd recommend Peter Spellman's *The Self-Promoting Musician* (Boston: Berklee Press, 2000). I'm going to simply suggest a few of the best opportunities out there to get people reading and talking about your writer. I'll leave it to you to work out the logistics . . .

Trade Publications

Keep in mind that when it comes to publicizing a writer, the purpose is to increase visibility among those in the industry, not among the general public. You're hoping to have ten A&R people calling on the phone to try to set up meetings, not ten thousand screaming teenagers looking for autographs. Consequently, it makes sense to target your efforts at publications directed toward weasels, rather than music fans. An article in *Billboard* will do a lot more for you than one in *Spin*. And it will be a lot easier to pull off.

If you read the bylines in most trade publications, you will notice that there is a relatively small staff of writers and reviewers. It should not take a great deal of effort to cultivate relationships with the people who might have an interest in your writer. A feature article, a positive review, or a favorable mention or picture in the pages of *Billboard*, *Hits*, *The Hollywood Reporter*, *Music Row*, or *The Source* will be seen by everyone in the industry. The performing rights societies also have regular publications, BMI's *MusicWorld* and ASCAP's *Playback*, that regularly highlight new writers who are starting to make waves. So do trade groups like NARAS. The good news is, trade publications exist for the purpose of spreading industry hype. In fact, they rely on it to fill their pages. If approached properly, they are likely to be happy to help you tell your story—considerably more so than the *New York Times* or *Rolling Stone*. It's all about targeting the segment of the industry that you are trying to reach, and building relationships with the appropriate editors and writers.

Awards

The record industry loves to give awards. It's a bit of no-brainer, of course. Everyone likes to get them (except Mutt Lange, apparently) and even for those who don't win, it's still a night of free publicity. Which is my point.

Of course, it's not just the Grammys, the American Music Awards, and other high-profile, nationally televised awards shows. There are awards shows sponsored by ASCAP, BMI, SESAC, and NAIRD (National Association of Independent Record Distributors). There are the CMAs (Country Music Awards), the Dove Awards, The Source Awards, and on and on and on. Then of course there are also regional awards shows sponsored by local music papers and music associations—Best Local Band, Most Likely to Succeed, etc. Everyone's a winner baby, that's no lie . . .

A word to the wise. As you may have expected when watching some of these ego-fests on television, not all awards are presented on merit alone. If you want to win an award, or even be nominated for one, you are going to have to campaign. Now I'm not suggesting that you should take on Miramax in competition for an Academy Award. But if you set your sights on regional or local awards, or even a competition sponsored by an industry trade organization, you can certainly take steps to improve your chances. Join the organization, donate time and energy serving on committees, buy ad space in the trade group's publication or the awards show program, and network with the organization's hierarchy. Gee, I can feel your chances improving already. I know, I know—I'm a hopeless cynic. Comes with the territory.

One more bit of advice. If you win an award, or even if you're just nominated, the important thing is that everyone knows it. You're not collecting these things to decorate your walls. Make sure that you send out press releases, e-mails, and call all your friends to bask in your glory. This is not the time for quiet humility.

Showcases

If your writer is an artist or part of a band, showcase performances are inevitable. Of course, showcases go on every night of the week in the major music centers—most come and go with little notice. But every now and then, there are performances so strong that the repercussions reverberate around the industry and careers are established. Elton John made his first impression in the US playing at the Troubadour in LA. More recently, Alicia Keys generated an overwhelming pre-release buzz on her debut album by performing a series of industry-only showcases hosted by Clive Davis. The Strokes' live performances helped to fuel their reputation as the most talked about new rock act of this decade. If you've got the goods, there is no question that a well-attended industry showcase can still spark a fire in the A&R community. At different stages in a career, a great showcase can say, "I'm here—put me on the map," "I'm back—put me on the map again," or "I'm still here—don't even think about taking me off the map."

Even if your writer is not normally a performer, showcases can be an effective means of attracting industry attention. Clubs like the Bluebird Cafe in Nashville or the Bitter End in New York often feature songwriters performing their own material. Although the writers are not always polished performers, audiences are attracted to the intimacy of hearing a writer deliver his or her songs directly in a more casual atmosphere. Many of these shows will include several writers, each performing four or five songs—so it's not necessary for a writer to have mastered a huge repertoire. Obviously, if you can get your writer on the bill with one or two more prominent writers, you've already accomplished something. Your writer's stature increases just by being on the same stage as the others.

The most important considerations in scheduling a showcase are the timing and the guest list. For a showcase to have maximum impact, it should be scheduled at an optimal moment in the writer's career (we'll discuss this more in a second) and also at a time when it will have the most impact on the industry. At a most basic level, that means avoiding weekends, holidays, and the month of December. On a more sophisticated level, it means trying to tie in with any appropriate music conventions or events (when every A&R person will be in town).

Without question, the most difficult part of putting together a showcase is getting the right people to come out. Studies show that the average weasel spends a third of his or her time at any showcase actually watching the show; a third noting what other weasels are in attendance; and the final third watching the other weasels' reactions to the show. If you can get enough high-ranking A&R people in one room to make each other nervous ("Is he going after this?"; "Do you think they've made an offer yet?"), your showcase is a success. If you can get one or two A&R people to actually appear excited or interested (this is almost impossible), you are sure to generate some major buzz. It is as much about who's there as what actually happens there.

It will likely take the combined efforts of everyone on your team to fill the seats with those who matter. Your lawyer should be able to help in this regard. This is his or her moment to pull the big names out of the Rolodex and start twisting some arms. Your performance society can also be useful; in some cases, BMI or ASCAP will even sponsor the showcase or put you on the bill of one of their own events. The other writers and artists in your musical community can also lend their star-power. If there's a major star, or even a budding star, that is a fan of your writer, try to get him or her to come to the show or maybe even do a guest spot. That one's a double pay-off—you get the glitter of a celebrity and the credibility boost of an endorsement from a respected peer.

Another tip: the more exclusive an event appears to be, the more everyone wants in. Choose a small club and try to fill it with top industry people. As soon as you know a few people that are committed to attending, start to let people know who else will be there. Nothing is more motivating to a weasel than simple jealousy.

Conventions

By holding a multitude of industry types captive in one place for three or four days, these events offer maximum impact publicity opportunities. Of course, most industry conventions are centered around showcases, which are usually plentiful and relatively well attended. The great part of a convention is that word of a strong performance will spread like wildfire. The downside is that it can be easy to get lost among the vast array of featured acts. If you're going to perform at a convention, you'd better be prepared to do something that can cut through the clutter.

Another convention staple is the industry panel, in which a variety of insiders discuss topics of interest. "The Ins and Outs of Music Publishing"; "A&R—Looking for the Next Big Thing"—I've spoken on dozens of these panels and they always seem to have the same subjects. With a few well-placed phone calls to the organizers of the convention, you may be able to place you or your writer on one of these panels. That means a chance to be seen with others who are more established in the industry, to talk about all of the exciting things happening in the writer's career, to make personal contact with the other people on the panel, and in many cases, to get in free to the rest of the convention.

And of course, what's a convention without a party? Or parties. Anytime there are weasels gathered together, there will be companies throwing parties—which can range from a room service order of cheese and crackers in a hotel suite to a gala event. If you're looking for a way of attracting attention, it may be worth having your publishing company consider hosting some sort of get-together. The key here is that the party itself must enhance the image of the company. The space, the food, and every other element need to be carefully thought out for maximum effect. If you're baffled by this sort of thing, use a party planner. Also consider featuring your writers at some point in the evening, whether it's a possible live performance, an award presentation, or a "listening" session for an upcoming release.

A few more ideas for publicity opportunities:

Samplers: Never underestimate the power of free stuff. Sure, the idea of sending out three- or four-song CDs as a publicity gimmick could be a little cheesy. But if the packaging is done well and the songs are hot, it doesn't hurt to get some product in the A&R community's hands. Just make sure you don't put too much on the sampler—fifteen minutes of music, tops.

Web Sites: You never know who may drop by. In light of that, it's wise for your publishing company to maintain an up-to-date Web site, which can act as both a publicity forum and an information center. It should include discographies of the writers, mentions of current activity or achievements, and if possible, a selection of songs or snippets that can be downloaded.

Planning the Attack: Timing Is Everything

One fundamental principle of publicity is the importance of grouping events together, in the same two- to four-week span, for maximum impact. This way, events are part of a strategic campaign, rather than just isolated attempts to grab the public eye. Like advertising, publicity works largely by repeated exposure—an A&R guy gets your sampler in the mail, then he sees your name in *Billboard*, then a colleague mentions that he went to your party last night. None of those things would be enough to make an impression on their own, but the cumulative effect can get the whole industry talking.

For example, when you have a major release coming out, that's the time to try to place a feature story in *Billboard*. Then, during the same week, schedule your writer to appear on a panel at an industry convention. At the end of the week, host a party to preview the upcoming record. If you organize the events strategically, your campaign will give the impression of your company and your writer being everywhere at once. It's that repeated exposure that builds industry buzz. To see this theory in action, simply watch the promotional campaign that precedes any major motion picture release. There will be a cover story on one of the stars in a national magazine, followed by a premier party covered by *Entertainment Tonight*, followed by a guest spot with Letterman or Leno—all happening in the same week that the movie is released. Coincidence? I think not.

A&R Meetings

Timing also applies to A&R meetings. The month prior to a big upcoming release, or the week of an awards show in which your writer is nominated, or the week that your writer happens to be in town working with a major artist, are all opportune moments to schedule a round of A&R meetings. Yes, I do mean a *round* of meetings. If one A&R person meets you or your writer, then talks to another A&R person who's just met you, and then runs into yet another A&R person who just happens to be seeing you tomorrow, you will have made an impact far greater than could be achieved in any one individual meeting. For that reason, try to schedule A&R meetings in chunks. Do five or six within a week, rather than one every two weeks.

Don't forget that there are weasels all over the world. If you've got an upcoming release, or a hit in a foreign territory, it may be the time to send you or your writer across the ocean to meet a whole new cast of characters. If your New York–based writer will be in LA to work with an artist or to accept an award—now you have a story to tell. Make sure you set up meetings with all the relevant power figures in Hollywood.

It's interesting how much easier it can be to set up meetings with people when you are coming in from out of town. I'm not sure if it's some surprising residue of hospitality that infects the locals, or just a certain exoticism that is conferred on the visitor ("Oh, he's from Sweden, ooh . . . "). But A&R people just seem to go for the old "we're in from the coast for a week" routine. Prior to setting up the meetings, try sending a fax to the A&R people, updating them on your writer's current activity, and indicating that you will be calling to set up an appointment.

A&R meetings themselves come in two varieties. There is the "pitch" meeting, which we've already discussed. The focus of this sort of meeting is to play songs for whatever project the A&R person is engaged in at the moment. There is also the "meet and greet," which is really just a chance to get acquainted. Some music may get listened to (or not), but the A&R person is likely to prefer songs that simply give a representative sampling of the writer's work, rather than anything specifically targeted to a project. As the name would imply, the "meet and greet" is relationship-focused rather than song-focused.

Be prepared at any time for either sort of meeting, or for a combination of both, and then try to read the vibe once you get in the room. The important thing is to go with the flow. Don't try to force song pitching into a "meet and greet," which will make you seem like an overzealous huckster. Likewise, too much conversation in a "pitch" meeting will give the impression that you don't have any songs to play. Your goal is to raise the visibility of your writer and establish a positive image. That means getting in the weasel's office and keeping him or her amused and happy while you're there. Selling songs is a secondary concern.

As you can see from the past ten chapters, the Creative Director's role in the publishing company is a constant balancing act between the creative demands of getting the music right, the practical business challenges of getting the music out, and the public relations aspect of moving the writer up. It's a balance between listening and selling, between being the critic and being the "hype" man. You wear a lot of hats in one day, and juggle a lot of balls in the air. Sort of like a circus clown. Like a clown, you usually drop more balls than you catch. I suspect you may have already seen how often the day-to-day demands of the paperwork, business affairs issues, and licensing questions can sidetrack your efforts as a Creative Director.

Our next section will deal primarily with the administrative aspects of music publishing, which are substantial, complex, and extremely important in their own right. But they are not the priority. To be successful in the music publishing business, you must do first things first. That means:

Getting the music right.

Getting the music out.

Moving the writer up.

Then, and only then, are you ready to proceed to part III of this book. Subject: Getting the money in. And keeping it in.

PART III
TAKING CARE OF BUSINESS

21

License to Fill (Your Coffers, That Is): Fun with Administration and Licensing

I suppose I've made it fairly obvious that when it comes to the various aspects of music publishing, my bias lies on the side of the Creative Department. Over on the Administration side, it always seems like the offices are a little too quiet, and there's too many piles of paper (which in my mind always seems to translate as real work), and someone arguing about numbers (which is a fight I know I'll lose). It just seems a little . . . well . . . okay, I'll say it . . . boring. Let's just admit it, when up against getting the music right, or getting the music out, or moving a writer up—the nuances of getting the money in are just not that interesting.

Until it's your money. Wow, that focuses the mind, doesn't it? All of a sudden, the world of administration becomes a most interesting place indeed—as you try to figure out why your song is on the radio but you don't seem to be making any money, or why that platinum album in France hasn't seemed to ever bring in any actual American currency. Or why the royalties always seem to be in the proverbial music industry "pipeline" but never seem to get to the desired destination. I once found out that I had several years' worth of performance payments that had been held up by BMI because they didn't have a correct address for me (you see how competent a publisher I was at the time). Yes, the world of administration can be much more exciting than you might think.

With newfound enthusiasm, then, let's get down to the business of music publishing . . .

Administration is something of an umbrella term, encompassing three of the five functions of a music publisher—administration, collection, and protection. Each of these jobs is fundamental to music publishing, and all of them overlap and impact each other. If you fail to fill out a license, you may not be able to collect the money later on. If you're not clear about what percentage of the copyright you own, you could find yourself unable to protect your interests if they're infringed upon. If you don't give BMI your correct address, you won't get your check. Two out of three won't do the job here. You've got to administer, collect, and protect.

Having acknowledged the difficulty of isolating one of these functions from another, let's make an attempt to break the "administration" of a copyright into manageable pieces. We'll begin with what we already know—always a very good place to start. Ladies and gentlemen, get out those split letters . . .

Knowing What You Have

Oh no, not this again. Yup. The first role of the administrator is to know exactly what you're administering and what rights you have to give away. The good news is, you should already have most of this work done. For each copyright, you should have a signed split letter that will identify what portion of the song is owned by your writer, what portion you publish (remember, this may not necessarily equal the writer's share), and the necessary information about the co-writers and co-publishers. You should also have a Copyright Administration Checklist in your files. That "Notes" section should tell you if there are any limitations to your control of the copyright.

If you are the only writer for your publishing company, you can assume that you publish each of your songs for the lifespan of the copyright. A copyright's lifespan begins on the date the song is written down or recorded and extends for the lifetime of the composer, plus seventy years. (By the way, this means that if your publishing firm is a solo venture, it's invariably going to outlast you—either you sell out in your golden years or give it to the grandkids.) You can also take for granted that you have a right to make any administration decisions without obtaining approval from an obstinate writer.

On the other hand, if you publish writers other than yourself, that "Notes" section can make for interesting reading. Depending on the agreements that you've made with your writers, there could be any number of restrictions on your ownership of the copyright and your right to exploit or administer it. As I mentioned before, the more of these restrictions you agree to when trying to sign a writer, the harder you make your life later. It's not enough to know that you publish the song. You've also got to know the details:

Duration

Some writer deals provide that the copyrights will "revert" back to the writer after a certain period of time. If the copyrights have been recorded and released during the term of the agreement, that reversion would probably occur fifteen to twenty years after the deal ends. Often the reversion may be based upon the status of a writer's account, with copyrights reverting only if the writer has "recouped," which is to say, earned back his or her advances. Another variation on this idea provides for the reversion of all unexploited copyrights—those are the ones still sitting in the drawer that have never been released. Unexploited copyrights commonly revert to the writer after three to seven years.

While my soft and fuzzy songwriter side empathizes with a writer's desire to limit the length of time a publisher can hang on to the copyrights, the weasel in me screams, "No, no, NO!" Publishing empires like Jobete, Almo Irving, and Zomba are built on obtaining songs for the lifetime of the copyright, with no reversions.

A publishing deal in which a songwriter's catalog reverts a few years after the conclusion of the term may be good for the writer, but it doesn't do much at all to build your publishing company. It means that you don't really own your catalog at all. You're just renting it for a set period of time. It takes a great deal of work and an even greater amount of luck to create one classic copyright. You can't afford to allow your company's greatest assets to slip away before you have reaped all the benefits. A huge corporation, with deep pockets and an equally deep catalog, can be more flexible. But a small, independent publisher should insist on contracts that provide ownership for the lifetime of the copyright.

Even the lifetime of copyright isn't as long as it would seem to be. While the copyright extends for the life of the composer plus seventy years, the law provides a window of time during which a songwriter can reclaim a copyright from a publisher. This window is a five-year period, beginning either thirty-five years from the date of publication, or forty years from the date the song was assigned to the publisher. The writer or heir is required to notify the publisher of the intent to reclaim the song; that notification must be made at least two years prior to the date the writer wishes to take back the copyright.

There's not much you can do about this, except to hope your hard work and diligence as a publisher persuades the writer to let you continue to publish the song. Or you can rely on the premise that writers being what they are, will likely forget to file the necessary paperwork. If the five-year window passes without notice, the song remains with the publisher for the rest of the copyright's lifespan.

First Use

There are some instances in which a publisher will also give the composer the right to approve a first-use license. This is most common with singer/ songwriters or band members, in situations where most of the material is intended for the writer's own project. To keep the publisher from giving material away to another artist, a writer/performer will sometimes insist on a first-use approval.

Territory

Before you start sending those songs overseas for projects you saw listed in *SongLink International*, you'd better be sure you have worldwide rights. Especially in light of the current state of the American record business, a publisher would be foolish to sign a song or writer for the US only. There are too few opportunities in this country at the moment, and too many lucrative opportunities in the rest of the world, to limit the scope of your ownership based on territory.

Unless you absolutely have to. There may be instances in which a top writer is only available for certain territories, or may be hesitant to sign a worldwide deal to a small publisher that doesn't have offices around the globe. In these cases, you'll have to weigh the advantages against the drawbacks. Keep in mind, if you succeed in developing a hit song in America, you've created something that has immense value all over the world. In most cases, it's not cost effective to invest in a song for the domestic market without the potential payoff of worldwide success.

Alterations and Adaptations

When writers start referring to songs as their "babies," get nervous. Very nervous. Because when you sign up to publish those songs, it means that you're adopting their babies. They're now yours to care for as you see fit. Or at least that's what it should mean.

Some writers will require approval over edits, lyric changes, restructurings, or translations—in other words, you can't touch your adopted baby without Mom or Dad's approval. You can imagine what fun that is. Film placements and advertisements will often require small changes in the lyric or song structure. Pitching a song overseas will likely lead to the need for a translation. To clear such decisions with a writer can be both a logistical and creative nightmare.

Similarly, beware of contract restrictions that grant the writer first opportunity to make the requested changes. Opportunities come and go very quickly. You don't want to miss the chance for a lucrative exploitation because of an overly precious writer. If you have to give writers these sorts of approvals, make sure that they understand the need to deal with issues quickly and reasonably.

Specific Uses

Many publishing contracts will require the writer to approve the placement of their baby in certain types of films, advertisements for certain products, or use in political campaigns. Make sure you know what these restrictions are before you pitch the song for this sort of placement.

Reduced Royalty Rates

More about this in a second. Suffice to say, the music industry has devised a number of different ways to get songs at a discount—forcing publishers to accept less than the full statutory mechanical royalty rate of 8 cents. A writer's primary concern is usually to prevent a publisher who is also affiliated with a record company from licensing a song to the associated record label for less than the full rate. To guard against this, a writer will sometimes demand approval over any licensing at a reduced rate, or at least over any such licenses granted to a company in which the publisher has an interest. Fair enough.

If you've done your work correctly up to this point, your split letter and Copyright Administration Checklist should give you a pretty clear idea as to exactly what you own and what you are allowed to do with it. In addition, the latter should be an early warning system for any limitations that you may have in exploiting or collecting on a song. The first function of Administration is to know what restrictions are in each writer's contract and to understand how they will impact the collection process.

Ironically, once you've figured out what you've got, the most important thing you can do is give it away. For a price. The very phrase "copyright" means, quite literally, the right to copy. Owning a copyright only has value if there's someone else that wants a copy. The issuing of licenses is the process by which a publisher grants the right to use a song, most often in exchange for a fee or royalty payment (we hope). Copyright licenses are like love—the more you give away, the more you get back . . .

Knowing What You're Giving Away

Mechanical Licenses

Covers: "Mechanical reproductions" of sound recordings, including vinyl records, CDs, tapes, and videocassettes.

Rates: The current full statutory rate for a song of average length (you're not writing anything over five minutes, are you?) is 8 cents. Recordings over five minutes in length receive an additional 1.55 cents per minute or fraction thereof.

Who Sets the Rates: The federal government—through the Copyright Arbitration Royalty Panel (CARP). (Great acronym, right?) The Librarian of Congress appoints the members of CARP.

Who Issues the License: The Harry Fox Agency or other licensing organization. We'll discuss our friend Harry Fox in the next chapter. It's also possible for publishers to issue mechanical licenses on their own.

What the License Contains:

- song information

- record label information (including record, disc, or tape number and configuration)

- representation of ownership by publisher

- accounting requirements for record company

- statement of rate

- acknowledgement by record company that the license is limited to specific artist and recording.

- remedy if record company fails to account as required by license

Things to Argue About: Oh boy. This could take a while . . .

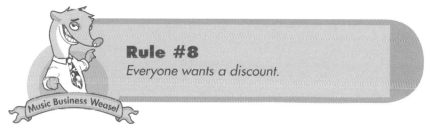

Rule #8
Everyone wants a discount.

Music Business Weasel

If it seems like the mechanical license process should be relatively straight-forward—after all, it's a set royalty rate—you are in for a quick education in the ways of weaseldom. Much to the dismay of music publishers large and small, the record industry has invested more creativity in figuring out how to avoid paying the statutory rate than it has in actually making good commercial records. Inventions like the controlled composition clause and the three-quarter rate are little more than straight-faced attempts at paying less than the amount written on the price tag. It's the record company's way of saying, "We don't like this price. We'd prefer to pay less." A nice trick if you can pull it off—try it on your landlord or your local grocer and let me know if it works. All I can tell you is, in the record biz, it works a lot more often than it should.

Controlled Composition Clause

This is a killer. Originally aimed primarily at artist/writers, it extends to producer/writers as well. The controlled composition clause states that the mechanical rate for songs that are written or "controlled" by the artist will be 75 percent of the statutory rate (reducing 8 cents down to 6 cents). Then to add insult to injury, it usually sets a total mechanical royalty "cap" of ten times the three-quarter rate for the entire album. That multiple of ten comes from the days when albums were generally made up of ten songs—of course, many CDs now have twelve to fifteen tracks. If a controlled composition is on an album with twelve songs, then the rate is further reduced to 5 cents.

And I'm not done yet. If some of the songs on the album are by writers who are not controlled (which is to say that they are not the artist or the producer, and are therefore not forced to accept anything less than full stat), the rate for the controlled parties drops even further, in light of that mechanical royalty "cap." If there are samples on the album, which of course require payments of mechanical royalties to the artists and writers whose work is being borrowed, that rate goes down yet again. It is quite possible to receive a rate that is 2 cents or less for each unit sold. Great system, right?

The most frustrating aspect of all is that there is little a publisher or writer can do to avoid this pinch. If the writer is also the artist, he or she will almost inevitably be subject to the controlled composition clause as part of the recording contract. Likewise, all but the most powerful producers will also find themselves forced to acquiesce to what has now become an industry standard. The correct way to fight this would be for a unified action by the music publishing community—but that sort of solidarity is elusive in an industry where everyone has a lot more songs than there are albums to put them on. My advice? Suck it up, and go on. Change those things that are within your power and accept those things that aren't.

Reduced Rates

The one way to avoid being caught in the "controlled composition" trap is to be neither the artist nor the producer. A writer who simply submits a song to an outside artist and doesn't produce the record is not obligated to accept less than the full stat rate. But that doesn't mean the weasels can't ask. Forcefully.

Record companies will frequently ask for a reduced rate (usually 75 percent of full stat) from outside writers, under the guise of trying to be fair to the parties who are "controlled." Remember, the controlled parties will have to make up the difference for every writer and publisher that receives the full rate. This can often put a songwriter and publisher in a very uncomfortable position, as they are pressed to make concessions not only by the label, but also by the artist and other writers. Of course, the implied threat is that your song will be dropped off the album and your relationship with the artist or producer irreparably damaged, if you won't agree to the reduced rate. And that could very well happen.

Negotiating reduced rates is one big poker game. Everyone's bluffing and posturing, and your only hope of winning lies in knowing who's holding the strongest hand. If your song is just an album track on a major release, the label will probably drop it from the album if you insist on a full rate. If your song was recorded with a full symphony orchestra, is said to be the title track of the album, and is the artist's favorite song—you'll probably get your full rate. If your song falls somewhere between those extremes, then your guess is as good as mine. When you're starting out, you'll probably need to be somewhat agreeable. Ultimately, it's more important to make something happen than to grab an extra couple of pennies on the rate.

In such negotiations, the greatest factor in favor of the writer and publisher is the general ineptitude of most record companies. Much of the time, record releases will outpace a label's licensing department, which can mean that requests for reduced rates will go out to publishers when the finished record is already sitting on the shelves in the stores. Now the balance of power shifts drastically, and for once, the publisher is in the driver's seat. Enjoy it. There is very little reason for a publisher to agree to a rate reduction in such situations, unless you have a great deal of future business at stake with the record label or artist. The best strategy in rate negotiations is for the publisher to do as little as possible and hope that the record comes out before an agreement is reached. Never call a record company to ask about a rate. Let them come to you.

Record Clubs and Special Products

Remember when you got twelve records for a penny just for joining the mail-order record club? Well, it's payback time. Most of the time, you're looking at a 25 percent reduction in the mechanical rate (that's on top of the already reduced, or "controlled," rate) for product sold through the record clubs. Other products, like special compilation albums, theme albums, or CDs in cereal boxes, will require reduced or even gratis rates. On these sorts of promotional projects, try to get some sort of advance based on guaranteed sales, in exchange for the lower royalty.

Performing Rights

Covers: Any commercial performance of the song on the radio and television, or in nightclubs, concert venues, restaurants, elevators, and almost anywhere else in the world, other than the comfort of your own home or car.

Rates: It's a little complex to break down exact rates for the myriad of different performance situations. Suffice to say that while rates per performance are usually only a few pennies, a hit record can generate a very substantial income. A chart-topping pop hit could easily bring in more than $100,000 in performance income over two or three accounting periods.

Who Sets the Rates: Rates are negotiated by the performing rights societies (ASCAP, BMI, and SESAC), with the broadcasters, and other licensees. When you join a society, you are authorizing them to grant the performing right on your behalf.

Who Issues the License: BMI, ASCAP, and SESAC issue what are called "blanket" licenses to music users. This allows the licensee to use any songs in the societies' catalogs, rather than apply for individual licenses on a song-by-song basis.

Things to Argue About: In general, this is a much more agreeable process. Still, there are always disputes about the relative merits of ASCAP, BMI, and SESAC, as well as confusion over exactly how much airplay or use a song may have had. In chapter 22, we'll talk more about the relative merits of each society, and how they go about collecting your money.

Synchronization Rights

Covers: Just about any situation in which music is "synced" to visual images, to create an audiovisual work. This includes movies for theatrical release, television shows, videos, commercial advertising, and nontheatrical or noncommercial works (like instructional videos or corporate presentations).

Rates: Whatever you can get. Sync licenses are negotiated between the publisher and the producer, studio, or whoever wishes to use the song.

Who Sets the Rates: The rates are determined solely by what the market will bear. However, there are limits. If you ask for too much, you can be assured that the production company or studio will find another song to fill the slot—no piece of music is indispensable to a motion picture. Rates are largely determined by the following:

> **The Use:** Title and end credits and on-screen performances are considerably more valuable than nonfeatured uses like background instrumental spots, or incidental music.

> **The Duration:** A use that extends over a minute in length is considerably more valuable than a quick 10- or 20-second snippet. Full-length

uses in movies are relatively rare, but certainly anything approaching two or three minutes is significant and worth a pretty hefty fee. It's also possible that a song could receive multiple uses—again, this ups the ante.

The Artist: If your song is performed by a superstar artist, its value increases substantially.

The Soundtrack Opportunity: If a movie studio can guarantee a placement of the song on a soundtrack album, it may be worth taking a small reduction in the sync fee. Obviously, a soundtrack can bring in mechanical royalties that will compensate for the reduction in sync money.

The Budget: This is always a tricky one, as even the richest producer will cry poverty when negotiating fees. The general ranking, from deepest pockets to no pockets at all, is as follows: major motion pictures and advertisements, then network and cable television, then independently produced movies or television shows.

If a producer insists that he or she is giving you all that is available in the budget, you could try requesting a "favored nation" clause. This provides that you will receive no less than the highest fee granted for any other song (in a similar placement). These clauses are not too popular with producers or studios, but are relatively common in licenses for major "hit" songs. No one will give you "favored nation" status for an unknown song in a background use.

Who Issues the License: In most instances, the movie studio or production company will submit the license to the publisher for approval. But if a movie appears on television, it will be covered by ASCAP or BMI's blanket performance license. If it appears on a commercial video, the "mechanical" right will be licensed separately, either by the publisher, or an organization like Harry Fox.

What It Contains: These sorts of licenses vary depending on the type of usage, but most will include:

- song information

- administrative share (this is the percentage of the song controlled by the publisher)

- duration of license (motion pictures will generally require a license in perpetuity—and that's a long, long time—while television and other uses tend to be for five years or less)

- limitation to specific motion picture

- the amount of the sync fee)

- the granting of non-exclusive rights to the song (some producers will want exclusive rights, which means more money for you)

- the nature and number of uses, including timings

- the territories (for most motion pictures, the license will be for worldwide rights; television, commercials, and other uses may be more limited)

- requirement for producer to provide cue sheets, usually within thirty days of release

Things to Argue About: Because of the wide variety of sync uses, these agreements can get somewhat complex. For instance, the licensing of a song for a motion picture does not automatically grant to the studio the right to create a commercial home video version, or to make that video available for rental. The use of the song in a movie trailer (I mean in previews, not in the star's dressing room) may also require a separate fee. In some instances, these contingencies will all be part of the original sync fee negotiation. In other instances, such contingencies will be dealt with only as the situation arises. Make sure you understand exactly what rights you are granting in the license and that you are receiving fair compensation for each type of use.

There are two other issues that need to be mentioned in relation to sync fees. Let's take the good news first. It's important to understand that the publishing sync license applies only to the copyright, that is, the song that is being used in the movie. It does not cover the actual recording of the song that appears on film. The licensing of the "master recording" is a separate issue, to be negotiated between the owner of the master (usually the record company) and the producer of the movie. In most cases, this "master" license involves a fee roughly equal to that of the publishing sync license. (Most publishers will request "favored nation" status in relation to the licensing of the master recording.)

So the record company gets paid, too. What's so good about that? Well, what if the publisher is also the owner of the master? Particularly in low-budget movies or television shows, it may be possible to place the demo version of a song directly into the film. In this instance, the publisher, who most likely paid for the demo, is the owner of both the master recording and the copyright. You've just doubled your money. To this end, many publishers of important copyrights are now producing their own recordings of them, which can be licensed directly to film and television producers, usually for considerably less than the more famous hit recordings. It's a good argument for making sure you get your demos right . . .

Now the bad news. Not to be outdone by the Music Business Weasels, the Movie Business Weasels (same animal, nicer suits) have come up with their own method of siphoning off a portion of your money. In Hollywood, everyone wants a piece of the action. Almost all of the major motion picture studios are also in the music publishing business, and will likely try to grab a portion of the publisher's share of the song.

If the song was written specifically for the movie or television show, is a recurrent theme song, or was previously unexploited, you will most likely wind up giving up at least a third, and possibly half, of the song's income. You might even be forced to deem the song a "work for hire" and give up all ownership and control in exchange for a flat fee. On the other hand, if the song was already a hit before the license was requested, then you should resist any attempt to dip into your money.

Generally, the best compromise in these situations is to give the studio a portion of the income generated by the copyright as a result of the movie, rather than an actual share of the copyright. This means that if you place the song somewhere else two years from now, you won't have some money-grubbing movie studio benefiting from your efforts. Like I said, change what you can, accept what you can't . . .

Foreign Rights

Covers: All uses of the song outside of the US. This means mechanical, performance, sync, and other income.

Rates: These can vary significantly depending on the territory, and the deals you are able to negotiate with subpublishers.

Who Sets the Rates: Depends on which ones we're talking about. Mechanical rates for recordings are usually set by some sort of government-approved formula in each territory—for the most part they are based on the RSP (retail selling price) or PPD (published price to dealers) of the album. The royalty rate is determined for the album as a whole, regardless of the number of songs, and then pro-rated (divided up) by the number of songs. Performing right rates are determined by the performance societies within that particular territory.

Who Issues the License: Could be a number of different parties. There are several ways of dealing with foreign licensing, the most straightforward of which is to engage a subpublisher, or several subpublishers, for various territories. We'll deal with that subject in chapter 22. In many instances, it is possible to issue licenses directly, and to collect the money through the reciprocal arrangements that ASCAP, BMI, SESAC, and the Harry Fox Agency maintain in foreign territories.

Things to Argue About: Weasels are weasels the world over—so there are always disputes between publishers and subpublishers. These can range from shady accounting practices, currency exchange rates, splits, and foreign taxes, all the way down to failure to provide the foreign publisher with adequate demos, writer information, and release notices. In the interest of international brotherhood, unity, and greater earnings for all, it's best to have your subpublishing agreements negotiated by your lawyer, to do business with companies of good reputation, and to get as much money as possible up front.

Advertising

Covers: Use of the song in a promotional or advertising campaign for a consumer product or service company. As most songs written specifically for ad campaigns are done on a work-for-hire basis (meaning the agency or client maintains full ownership of the copyright), we'll limit our discussion to the use of a pre-existing song in an advertisement.

Rates: Subject to negotiation. There is no standard here—numbers can run from a few thousand dollars for a local advertisement, to the mid six figures for a major hit placed in a national spot.

Who Sets the Rates: The rates are ultimately negotiated between the client (that is, the subject of the ad campaign) and the publisher, usually with the advertising agency running interference between the two.

Who Issues the License: This is issued by the publisher directly, though it may require the writer's approval, particularly for certain types of products.

What It Contains:

- **Use:** Clarify whether the campaign is for television or radio, or both. Obviously, television warrants a higher price than radio.

- **Territory:** Will the song receive local, regional, or national exposure? I would recommend you resist anything involving worldwide or foreign rights, and make those part of an option discussion.

- **Duration of playing time, and license:** Most commercials will be 30, 45, or 60 seconds. Needless to say, the more they play, the more they pay. At the same time, you should clarify the duration of the ad campaign itself, and limit the license to that time period. Generally speaking, a year is as much as you should grant at one time. Any more than that can be offered as an option.

- **Options:** Alright, so let's talk options. The need for extended license periods, rights outside the US, or increased exclusivity should be accommodated by the granting of options, which can be exercised as necessary, with additional compensation to the publisher.

- **Alterations or adaptations:** So they wanna change the lyric, eh? Anything for a price. Ad campaigns will often require some altering of the original song; the publisher should be compensated for what could be the devaluation of the copyright. Remember, this may also require the writer's permission.

- **Exclusivity:** Most clients will seek to prevent the publisher from licensing the songs to similar or competitive products. The more zealous marketers will seek total exclusivity, which, not surprisingly, is considerably more expensive.

Things to Argue About: You could argue with your writer about whether or not an advertising placement degrades the copyright. Or you could argue with the agency about a license for a regional or off-air test. Or you could argue with the client about why the artist and record company that controls the master recording should have received more than you and your writer. Or you could just take the money and run. You can probably guess which option I would choose. If you get a song in an advertisement, just smile, smile, smile . . .

Other Rights

Oh there's more. There are licenses for print rights, which apply primarily to the sale of sheet music, but can also include reprints of lyrics in magazines or books, or references to lyrics in greeting cards, board games, or advertisements. There are grand rights and dramatic rights that apply to the use of a song in the context of live theater. And happily, there are licenses for special uses that grow more diverse daily—this includes everything from karaoke, to video games, to in-flight programming, to the much-loved Billy Bass, the singing fish. All of these licenses can provide significant income, and all raise certain issues that must be resolved. When in doubt, consult your lawyer to find out what limitations you should insist on and what compensation

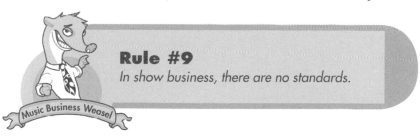

Rule #9

In show business, there are no standards.

Music Business Weasel

is appropriate. But remember, licenses are only good if you give 'em away. Don't be too careful. You only get what you give . . .

In case you haven't noticed, most licensing agreements are not locked into set rates (with the exception of performance payments). Even though there are thousands of such licenses issued every day, there are no set standards that apply uniformly. Everyone's making a deal—some good, some not so good. In the interests of trying to get more of your deals to fall into the "good" category, we'll close this chapter with a few quick negotiating tips . . .

- **Information is power.** The more you know about the people and project that you're involved with, and the importance of your song to the project, the stronger your position is. Prepare for battle.

- **Start with the easy stuff.** Resolve the simple issues first, and then go on to the tougher points. A little positive momentum is always helpful.

- **Use your lawyer for advice, but not for the initial negotiations.** In most instances, bringing your lawyer in will send the weasels scurrying for cover. Unless it's a big deal, try to keep things on a personal basis.

- **Give with one hand and take with the other.** If you make a concession, try to extract some small concession in return.

- **Don't play hardball if you can't afford to lose.** Most negotiating simply comes down to who needs the deal more. If you're the needy party, then avoid threats, nitpicking, and ultimatums.

- **Get it in writing.** After a negotiation, follow up with an e-mail or memo outlining the discussion and the deal points agreed upon.

- **Leave your principles at home.** In any licensing discussion, the only thing you're arguing about is money. So abandon your moral crusades—don't fight for anything on the basis of "principle." Get the best financial deal you can and don't get your feelings hurt.

If all of this feels a little overwhelming, don't give up yet. In chapter 22, help is on the way . . .

22

Ooh, You're My Best Friend: The Collection Crew

There's a scene in the original *Rocky*—it's before Rocky Balboa gets his big break, and he's out collecting debts for the local mob chief. He's sent out to find some guy who's late on paying back his loan; Rocky's supposed to break the man's thumbs. You need a few guys like Rocky on your team.

I'm joking. Sort of. As we learned from Music Business Weasel Rule #1: *It's never easy getting paid.* When I tell you that you need some allies that will help to collect the money, you know I'm talking about teammates that are aggressive, thorough, and connected. I've already mentioned these names to you in previous chapters, but now we'll look a little harder at the role each one plays in the collection process. Publishers, meet your new best friends . . .

Harry Fox—Hungry Like the Wolf . . .

Good ol' Harry. Operated by the National Music Publisher's Association, the Harry Fox Agency is the primary mechanical rights society in the US. They handle over 200,000 licenses every year and represent more than 27,000 publishers, both large and small. They collect more than $400 million in revenue annually. These guys know where the money is and how to get it.

When publishers affiliate with the Harry Fox Agency, they are authorizing HFA to issue mechanical licenses on their behalf, and to collect and distribute the mechanical royalties generated from those licenses. For doing so, HFA charges publishers a stated rate of 6 percent of the gross mechanicals collected.

While HFA collects only in the US, the society has reciprocal agreements with corresponding organizations in almost every overseas territory. This allows Harry Fox to collect royalties on foreign releases, through the local licensing society. While such an arrangement results in a slightly inflated commission charge (the foreign society deducts its share, then pays Fox, who in turn deducts its administration fee), it may eliminate the need for a subpublisher in that territory, which can save a lot of time, effort, and money.

Here's the best part. Harry Fox doesn't just take the royalties the record labels dish out. They go in and take a look at the books. As you may have heard from that angry mob of recording artists who recently marched into a California Senate committee hearing to demand industry reform, record company accounting practices are sometimes . . . well . . . confusing. Somehow, records that are certified as selling 500,000 units always show up in statements as having sold less than 250,000. Or money seems to get stuck in that infernal pipeline. It's hard enough to get paid at all. But to get paid correctly . . .

The difficulty in getting to the bottom of this confusion is that few individual writers and publishers can afford the expense involved in auditing a record company. By representing hundreds of publishers, Harry Fox can make the auditing process cost-effective for its members. Using both an in-house staff and outside audit firms, Fox audits every major record label every two years and smaller labels every three years as necessary. Needless to say, they uncover more than a little in the way of under-payments. These audits have captured as much as $22 million in additional royalties in one year.

Joining Harry Fox is relatively easy. It's just a matter of filling out a publisher-client membership package, which can be obtained directly from HFA, or online. You will need to show that you have at least one commercial recording that needs to be licensed—this does not need to be on a major record label, but it can't be on your own independent label. There is no upfront cost for signing up—everything comes out of the money HFA collects. While you're at it, you may also want to consider joining the National Music Publisher's Association. NMPA is an effective and important trade organization, and it can be an effective forum to network with more established, experienced music publishers.

In the interests of fairness, I should mention that Harry Fox is not the only game in town. While considerably smaller, there are other organizations offering similar services, the most established of which is the American Mechanical Rights Agency (AMRA). AMRA will issue licenses and collect mechanical royalties, and will also handle sync licenses (which Harry Fox no longer does). AMRA's fee is 10 percent of the gross income collected.

I understand that there are advantages to being a large fish in a relatively small pond—if you feel that an organization like AMRA will make your company a priority, that could be a persuasive reason to opt for a smaller environment. On the other hand, there is often strength in numbers, and the

Harry Fox Agency provides the combined clout of a vast array of prominent publishing companies. Personally, I like the guys on my collection crew to be as big and strong as possible. I'd go with Harry Fox.

What I can't understand is trying to collect mechanicals on your own. There are too many record companies, the accounting process is too complex, and the whole endeavor is too time consuming for a small independent publisher to try to go solo. Choose whichever organization suits you, but choose one. If someone wants to go to battle on your behalf, by all means give them a uniform and tell 'em to suit up. You can't do this alone.

ASCAP/BMI/SESAC—They Said It on the Air, on the Radio...

We've already discussed the support that ASCAP, BMI, and SESAC can offer to writers and publishers by providing networking and educational opportunities. Now let's talk about their real job.

The idea of monitoring the amount of airplay and other performances any one song receives is a bit mind-boggling—particularly when one considers the thousands of radio and television stations across the US, not to mention dance clubs, aerobic studios, lounges, concert halls, and restaurants with stereo systems or a jukebox in the corner. Needless to say, it's something less than an exact science. But the systems devised by ASCAP, BMI, and SESAC have been enormously effective in compensating copyright owners for the use of their product, while continuing to encourage the public performance of music in an ever-increasing array of venues. In the United States, ASCAP and BMI collect over $1 billion annually in performance income—worldwide, that number is closer to $3 billion. For most publishers, performance payments constitute a little less than half of their annual income.

How do they do it?

While the organizations differ somewhat in their approaches, the fundamental system is relatively straightforward. All three societies issue blanket licenses (at a variety of different cost structures) to companies that use music in a public way. If you check closely, you may even see the ASCAP or BMI sticker in the window of your local restaurant or bar. As we said before, these licenses allow music users to use any song from the society's catalog without having to request thousands of individual licenses. The revenues from these blanket licenses are then distributed among the thousands of writer and publisher affiliates on a song-by-song basis—depending upon how many public performances each work has received. This is the tricky part . . .

ASCAP and BMI both carefully monitor their licensees to find out what songs they are playing, though they go about it in slightly different ways.

BMI tracks radio airplay primarily by reviewing programming logs, provided by the stations, on a rotating basis. Every station is monitored for at least three days out of each year to verify the accuracy of their reporting. ASCAP, on the other hand, uses a three-pronged approach—reviewing playlists provided by the broadcasters; taping radio stations around the country and utilizing musical experts to identify the music being played during the sample period; and employing digital tracking systems like Broadcast Data System (BDS), which continually monitors most of the largest radio stations across the country.

For most mainstream commercial singles, this system works pretty well. If a song is a "hit," it will likely go into regular or heavy rotation on similarly formatted stations all over the country for a period of three to six months. After that, it will receive fewer spins but may remain in steady rotation for some time, possibly even one or two years. It's not too difficult then to look at a number of playlists, see what level of rotation a song is in, and deduce approximately how many plays the song is receiving each week across the country. For television performances, most of the necessary data is compiled from cue sheets, which all stations are required to submit to BMI and ASCAP.

For non-commercial music, which might only receive eight or ten plays on small local stations, tracking becomes a greater challenge. In many instances, ASCAP and BMI have tried to make adjustments to compensate for this. Certainly, both organizations make every effort to track college radio stations and other non-commercial broadcasters; they have also created payment systems to reflect the differences in the quantity of uses for music outside the mainstream. Concert music pieces, for instance, which might receive only two or three performances in a year, are monitored in a different manner and paid at a much higher rate than three-minute pop songs. Performance royalty rates are based on:

- the nature of the performance (feature, background, theme, live)

- the duration of the performance

- the size and nature of the venue or broadcasting network (concert hall, restaurant, network television, syndicated radio)

The number of performances can figure into the rate structure, as well— both BMI and ASCAP have bonus plans that reward songs receiving a certain amount of airplay. These bonuses can substantially increase the earnings of a major radio hit.

ASCAP and BMI distribute royalties quarterly; these include foreign distributions, which are collected through the societies' reciprocal organizations all over the world. It's important to understand that the payments to writers and publishers are made by divvying up the big pie, which is the amount received by BMI and ASCAP from their blanket licenses, minus the societies' administration charge to cover their own costs. These costs are approximately 15 percent of the gross income for both organizations. All those helpful services and great parties that BMI and ASCAP offer their members don't come for free.

SESAC is considerably smaller than either ASCAP or BMI, and over the past ten years has systematically revamped its approach to monitoring performances. SESAC is perhaps the most technologically progressive of the societies—it was the first to fully embrace the BDS system and now tracks all "popular music" airplay through that technology. It has also partnered with Verance Technologies, utilizing Confirmedia watermarking technology for the identification and tracking of performances in other formats. For music outside the commercial mainstream, SESAC relies on a program called Audible Magic, which provides more precise information for stations specializing in markets like jazz or Americana.

Unlike ASCAP and BMI, SESAC does not present itself as being open to all interested writers or publishers. In order to become a member, you will have to obtain an invitation from the Writer/Publisher Relations Department. At the same time, as a means of competing with ASCAP and BMI, SESAC is also sometimes willing to offer advances to attract important new members. If you bring a catalog of established hits, SESAC may be willing to offer a recoupable advance to entice you to join. But remember, this is for publishers with an established catalog—you'll need some big hits before you can cash in.

So, armed with that wealth of information, let's get down to the big question. Which one do you join?

I don't know. ASCAP is older and very much a society of writers, both in spirit and in fact. It is essentially run by writers, with past presidents like Hal David, and current leader Marilyn Bergman. The Board of Directors includes writers John Bettis, Jimmy Jam, Jimmy Webb, Paul Williams, and Cy Coleman. BMI is a bit larger and more corporate—it was founded in part by the broadcasting industry that it now negotiates with. However, it has its own historical importance, particularly as the first society to open up to black American writers and the early rock and roll community. Unlike the other two, SESAC is a for-profit organization—but it is small enough that a new company might expect more attention than it would receive at BMI or ASCAP.

As a writer, I've been affiliated with both ASCAP and BMI at different times, and I've written many songs with co-writers from either society. To tell you the truth, I've never noticed a significant difference in what each society paid in royalties for the same song. Both organizations can make very persuasive cases as to why they pay better—but they can't both be right. Like I said, I've never seen it. I don't know. You can consider history, size, the character of each organization, the monitoring system, the payment system—if that stuff matters to you.

Or you could take my advice, and take a good long look at the relationships you've developed at each organization. By now, you should have at least a passing familiarity with the writer/publisher relations reps at each society. Make an in-depth assessment of who has been the most helpful, the most willing to answer questions or offer references, the fastest to return a phone call, and the one you most enjoy working with. That's your winner.

The truth is that both BMI and ASCAP, and even SESAC, are large bureaucracies. On a bad day, dealing with any of them can be like trying to work out a problem with the IRS. At times like those, the most important thing is not the history of the organization or the percentage of income that each spends on administration. The important thing is to have a human being that you can call—someone who has a genuine interest in you and your company. At the end of the day, the people make the difference.

Or you could join all of them. As I mentioned earlier, a publisher may find it necessary to affiliate with all three organizations. While a writer can be a part of only one performing rights society at a time, a publisher is not similarly restricted. If you represent an ASCAP writer and a BMI writer, you have no choice but to be associated with both societies. If you subsequently take on a SESAC writer, then you'll need to join there as well. An ASCAP writer must be represented by an ASCAP publisher; a BMI writer by a BMI company. As a publisher, your writers will ultimately determine what societies you will be associated with.

Foreign Subpublishers—My Money Lies Over the Ocean, My Money Lies Over the Sea . . .

So if Harry Fox collects mechanical royalties outside of the US through its international reciprocal organizations, and BMI, ASCAP, and SESAC do the same for performance monies, what's left for a foreign subpublisher to do? Why do you need one anyway?

Answer: You might not. If your catalog is small (less then thirty songs), contains few commercial releases and no hits, or is in a style with a limited appeal outside the US (traditional country or underground rap, for example), it is probably not necessary to think about a foreign subpublishing deal. Not yet, anyway. The team you already have in place should be able to collect whatever foreign income your songs generate.

But if you represent a sizeable catalog, or have a couple of hits under your belt, or are working in a genre that is particularly viable overseas (pop and dance music, for instance), you may find that a foreign subpublisher can provide a presence for your company internationally that Harry Fox or ASCAP cannot. A good foreign subpublisher provides you with an actual business partner on the other side of the ocean, who will not just collect your money, but will help to find local exploitation opportunities, set up collaborations and writing trips, and aggressively promote your company in territories outside the US. Just as importantly, advances for subpublishing deals can often provide quick working capital for your business while you're waiting for those royalty checks to arrive. A foreign subpublisher's primary role may be that of collection, but many subpublishers go far beyond that. Like I said before, if you go into the jungle, it's good to have a friend out there. Preferably one who speaks the language.

Your lawyer will likely be the best resource when seeking a subpublishing deal. A well-established music business attorney in the US will almost surely have done subpublishing deals for other clients, and will likely have a sizeable network of international contacts to draw upon, along with strong opinions as to who the reputable players are in each territory.

Many American lawyers attend MIDEM, the international music conference held in Cannes, France each January. This is the true music business melting pot—and an ideal spot for networking with publishers and record labels from all over the world. Licensing and subpublishing deals are the focal point of business at MIDEM. If you're looking to do a deal, this would be an excellent place to test the waters. Your lawyer can also give you some idea as to the most suitable type of deal for your company in its present situation. There's more than one way to handle your international licensing opportunities, and different approaches may make sense for different territories.

The Standard Subpublishing Deal

A typical subpublishing deal involves the full passing of the baton—you license exclusive publishing rights to a subpublisher for a certain territory for a set period of time. The subpublisher then assumes all rights to the song or catalog in that territory. This means that a subpublisher can license the mechanical, performance, sync, and print rights within the prescribed territory, collect the proceeds, and then account to you, the original publisher.

Most full sub-pub deals are based on a 75/25 split of the income, which is to say that the original publisher receives 75 percent of the income.

This 75 percent is made up of the writer's share (50 percent) and half of the publisher's share (25 percent). In other words, a subpublishing deal is essentially a co-publishing deal with the subpublisher. Out of every dollar received by the subpublisher, 25 cents stays with the foreign company, and 75 cents goes to you, the original publisher. From this 75 cents, 37.5 cents is owed to the writer, the other 37.5 is retained as the publisher's share. Note that the subpublisher does not receive a portion of actual ownership in the copyright. This 75/25 split is, like everything else in this business, entirely negotiable. In many cases the percentages can shift to as much as 60/40, particularly if the income is related directly to exploitations obtained by the subpublisher.

It's probably worth incentivizing a subpublisher in this way, as the primary goal of doing a subpub deal is to find opportunities for your copyrights or writers in territories outside of the US. A good subpublishing deal should lead to:

- covers of your songs in the local market

- placements of your songs in local television and radio programs

- promotion of your releases in the international territories

- tips on local projects seeking material

- publicity and marketing for your company and catalog

For instance, you may be able to work with your subpublisher in setting up a trip for your writers to collaborate with foreign artists or producers. It's well worth giving up a larger percentage of the income if it encourages your subpublisher to take an aggressive approach to exploiting your catalog.

The other trick to motivating subpublishers is making them fork over some money as an advance. If you have one or two songs in your catalog that have generated some heat in the US, it is perfectly reasonable to expect an advance from a subpublisher. The amount will depend on just how big your hits were, the viability of your genre in the foreign territory, and the size of the split the subpublisher will receive.

As I mentioned before, these advances can be very helpful quick money when cashflow problems arise. For that reason, I would be hesitant to enter into a subpublishing deal without something up front. If you don't have any hits to raise a foreign publisher's interest, you should probably wait until you develop a stronger catalog. In the meantime, you can always rely on the Harry Fox Agency, and ASCAP, BMI, or SESAC.

We're not through yet. Once you've decided what sort of subpublishing deal makes sense for your company, there are a number of important decisions left to make. The subpub deal can be applied territory by territory, song by song, or for an entire catalog. It is quite possible that you will have deals structured in different ways for different territories. Again, your attorney should be able to help guide you to the most practical and profitable option.

Territory by Territory vs. Ex-US

The question here is whether it makes more sense to have a lot of little deals with local publishers, or one big deal with a large international publisher. There are persuasive arguments on either side of the equation.

The strategy of making separate subpublishing deals for each distinct territory has a number of clear advantages. With some savvy negotiating, you may be able to get advances for each small territory that in total far exceed what you could get from one large deal for the whole world/ex-US (i.e., excepting the United States). Further, you may find that these smaller local publishers are more accessible, better connected, and much more aggressive in their market than the regional office of a large international corporation. And finally, even if a few of the deals go sour, they may be balanced out by exceptional performances in other territories. At least you haven't put all your eggs in one big multinational basket.

On the other hand, a dozen subpublishing deals around the world can be an awful lot to keep track of. It's far easier to have one contact person at EMI or BMG that can deal with any problem worldwide than it is to run down an errant subpublisher in Singapore. If your company is having some success, there's something to be said for a coordinated effort to establish your company as a worldwide presence, rather than a piecemeal approach among a dozen different entities in a dozen different locales. Don't discount the inherent advantages of some real corporate muscle to settle local disputes over infringement, administration, and accounting issues.

Song by Song vs. Exclusive Catalog

There is a decision to be made as to whether you want to make subpublishing agreements for individual songs or if you want to grant to the subpublisher the exclusive rights for your whole catalog. Again, each approach has its benefits and drawbacks.

Like weasels in our own country, subpublishers like to bet on a sure thing. If you have one song in your catalog that has had substantial success, you may be able to get an advance for that one song that is almost equal to what you would receive for exclusive rights to your entire catalog. This is especially true if none of the other songs in the catalog have had major releases. In such a situation, it may be more lucrative to license only the one song, take the advance money, and wait until you have another hit. Then you can work the same exercise all over again, for another advance check.

Needless to say, this beats giving up your whole catalog for what amounts to a one-song advance. It also allows you to get a sense of a subpublisher's performance before you get in too deep. There is a certain hard-boiled realism in the idea of the single-song publishing deal. Catalogs don't get exploited as a whole—they get worked song by song. To that end, it may be better to simply sell them the songs they want, rather than the whole inventory.

The disadvantage of the song-by-song deal is pretty obvious. You thought a dozen different subpublishing deals were tough to keep tabs on? Multiply that by five or ten songs, all with different subpublishers in different territories, most likely for different periods of time and under different contractual terms. Confused? I thought so.

In my experience, these song-by-song deals amount to taking whatever advance money you can grab and going home. Monitoring what each subpublisher is doing with each song, checking the accounting, and making sure that the contract is being abided by, is almost impossible. This approach is all about getting the upfront money.

If a subpublishing deal is really about trying to build a presence for your company internationally—to develop relationships overseas and find all avenues of exploitation for your catalog—then you should probably opt for the exclusive catalog deal. You will never be the top priority of a publisher who controls only one or two of your songs. Nor will there be any chance that your subpublisher finds an obscure song in your catalog and turn it into a "hit" in a foreign territory. (Of course, this sort of thing doesn't happen often, but when it does, it's like hitting the lottery. You get a call one day and find out you have the No. 1 record in Finland). And you certainly can't expect a subpublisher of a single song to invest a great deal of effort in developing your writers or raising your company's profile. Relationships involve commitment. (I feel like a marriage counselor again.) If you want an ally in a foreign land, you're going to have to make him or her a real member of the team.

If you want my advice as to what sort of subpublishing deal is right for your company, I'm afraid I don't have any. There are simply too many variables to consider. Just for starters, I'd have to know your company's track record, the genre in which you specialize, your financial needs, and the foreign opportunities that are available.

In fact, you don't need my advice. Because as complex as these deals sound, as soon as you move from the hypothetical to the actual, things get much more clear. Once you have some offers on the table and you're building relationships with actual people whom you either trust or don't, and you've gotten a sense from others in your musical community as to what sorts of deals have worked for them, the decision will be much easier. And hey, when people are offering to give you money, you can't go that far wrong.

By the way, if your relationships with your collection crew do go wrong, you may want to take a look at your own operation before you start pointing fingers. As I mentioned at the beginning of the previous chapter, lax administration on your part will invariably impact your business partners as they try to collect and distribute your money. No split letter means no license. No license means no royalties. No address means no royalty check. It all starts at home.

When you begin taking on business partners, you must make sure that your paperwork is thorough and accurate. Songs should be registered with mechanical rights and performance societies prior to release, with full information as to splits, co-writers and co-publishers, release dates, record numbers, and other necessary information. Subpublishers should receive copyright notice information, detailed release information including sync uses in the US and other territories, promotional materials, and a steady stream of new demos, with lyrics and split information. Maintain copies in your "Song File" of registration filings and any other relevant correspondence. Check up regularly with everyone collecting on your behalf to make sure that all of their song and contact information for you remains accurate.

That includes getting your address right.

23

Can't Touch This: Protecting Your Copyrights

Collection, protection . . . This business is starting to sound more like a Mob racket with every chapter. As any small business owner can tell you, it's not enough to get the money into the cash register. You also have to protect your income from those who would seek to grab a piece for themselves. Getting the money in and keeping it in—you have to do both to survive and thrive. As a publisher, you are entrusted with protecting the family jewels (that would be those songs in the drawer) and making sure they stay in the family, untarnished, for the next generation.

Understanding the Threat

The problem is that most songwriters and publishers are worrying about the wrong things. Because it's so dramatic, the risk of someone "stealing" a song is the threat that seems to occupy the minds of most fledgling writers: "Imagine my surprise when I turned on the radio and there was *my* melody!"

I'm not going to tell you that it can't happen. But I can tell you that given the amount of money invested in producing and marketing a record, very few companies would knowingly release a song they thought had the potential to generate a lawsuit. In fact, of all the possible threats to your copyrights, outright song theft is probably the least likely. By focusing protection efforts on such a farfetched scenario, publishers waste money and energy that could be put to better use. If you live in the middle of a secluded forest, it's probably more important to own a fire extinguisher than a burglar alarm. Protect against the greatest threats first—worry about the other stuff later.

Split Disputes: Smiling Faces Sometimes . . .

You know where I'm going with this, don't you? The sad truth is that the greatest danger to your copyrights is not from a stranger or a sleazy Music Business Weasel to whom you once submitted a song. The real threat is from people you know. Most copyright battles are fought between friends. They are disputes between people who worked together in some capacity and who now can't quite agree on exactly who did what. A musician who came up with the bass line, a singer who added something to the melody, an engineer who suggested an edit, or another writer who just tossed in a word or two while he was hanging out—now that the song is on the radio, they're all sure that they should own at least some small portion. If only someone had some sort of document, maybe a letter, that listed the names of the writers and their respective shares, and had their signatures on it . . .

As you probably suspected, split letters are your first line of defense against the vast majority of copyright claims. While such a letter may not entirely disprove someone's claim to a portion of the song, it will certainly raise the question as to why the newly announced writer never asserted the claim earlier. In addition, the split letter can provide you with an ally: if other writers or publishers are co-signers, they are essentially confirming your version of the songwriting process.

The Song Submittal Form can also help provide a record of how a song came to be. By listing the dates the song was written and recorded and by keeping notes as to the engineer and studio, you can begin to reconstruct exactly who was involved in each step of the process. It's wise to hold onto work tapes and other records of the writing session itself. Often, these sorts of disputes boil down to one person's version of events versus another's. It goes without saying that whoever has kept the most accurate and detailed records will likely prevail.

Many publishers require any demo vocalists, engineers, musicians, or arrangers who are paid for their work to sign a letter confirming that their contribution to the demo was made on a "work-for-hire" basis. The phrase "work for hire" indicates that the signer has no ownership in the copyright— the fee received for the work itself is the sole compensation. Of course, this sort of paperwork can be extremely helpful if singers or arrangers later decide their work was really a songwriting contribution. I find it a bit heavy-handed to ask every person involved in a demo to sign such a letter, although it's probably a wise policy. But you should certainly consider such a letter if someone's behavior indicates a potential problem—a general shiftiness of the eyes for instance, or a tendency to refer to the recording as "our song."

Split Adjustments: Got to Give It Up

When I said that the scenario of outright song theft was relatively unlikely, I was referring to the idea of people simply taking your idea and calling it their own. What is much more likely and much harder to defend against is what I call the shakedown scenario—and I'm not talking about a dance step. Again, this sort of fleecing is usually done between friends. In fact, it almost invariably comes from the same people with whom you've been cultivating relationships as you scramble to get your tune cut: "The good news is (artist, producer, manager, A&R guy) loves the song. But we feel it may need a few changes before we record it. We're looking for (blank) percentage of the song . . . " Hey, everybody do the Shakedown.

This move has a long history (Elvis was well known for grabbing a percentage of any song he recorded) and it appears to have a solid future. If anything, it becomes more prevalent each year. Producers ask for a piece of the publishing; artists insist on a piece of the writing; movie studios want a cut for putting the song in a movie; labels want you to give your share to their related publishing company; even individual A&R people are now showing up on the copyrights.

Sometimes the threat is explicit: "Give me a piece or the song doesn't go on the album." Sometimes the coercion is more subtle: "There are just a few lines that the artist had some concerns about . . . " Sometimes it means an artist showing up for a co-write, spending fifteen minutes in the room (on the phone the whole time), and expecting a third of the song. This joker has a thousand faces—but it all amounts to someone trying to grab a piece of your song in exchange for an exploitation opportunity.

Sadly, there's almost nothing you can do. After all, you need to get the song on the album or in the movie. Sure, whoever is twisting your arm might be bluffing. Then again, they might not be. Copious record keeping will not do much for you on this one, because no one is claiming that they were legitimately a part of the writing process. This is a power play, pure and simple. More often than not, the publisher is not the one holding the heavy weapons. The best protection you can muster in this situation is to try to limit the damage.

Strategy #1: Stall

But don't let them know you're stalling. Give the impression of being responsive (so no one gets nervous), but just don't move too fast. Return calls in a day, rather than an hour, and call after you know the office has closed. Drag things out.

The point here is to buy some time, and see whether someone is really prepared to pull your song from the project. In the meantime, try to use whatever contacts you have to find out:

- if the artwork is done (if it is, and your song is listed, it's unlikely that the song would be removed from the record)

- if your song has already been recorded

- if the album's single has been selected (if you're it, you've got a little more power, but also a lot more at stake)

As I mentioned before, your primary advantage is the weasel's natural tendency toward disorganization. Sometimes, you can wait it out and hope the balance of power changes.

Strategy #2: Draw Some Lines

If you have to give something away, and chances are you will, then at least try to establish some limits. Offer to give up a share of the income from the project but not a share of the copyright. This requires you to share any money generated by the release in question, but still allows you to place the song in other venues without giving up a portion. If that doesn't work and you have to give up a percentage of ownership, try asking for a reversion. This would mean that the percentage you give up would revert back to you after a set period of time, should the song never be released as a single or the album never achieve a minimum level of sales. If all that fails, try to at least hang on to the administration rights for your portion.

Strategy #3: Take the Credit

Sometimes you just can't win. Should you have no other choice but to give away your entire publishing share, try to at least hold onto your credit, so that your company's name appears on the publishing line of the song. Even if you never see any publishing money, you should see your company's name on the record, in the movie, or on the *Billboard* charts. This is not an exercise in vanity. People in the music industry actually read liner notes and end credits, and this is an important opportunity to promote your company. Sometimes perception beats reality—if your name is on the record, no one will know how much of the song you do or don't own.

Strategy #4: Keep Shopping

One of the problems with placing a song "on hold" is that it leaves a publisher vulnerable to the old weasel shakedown. By continuing to play the song for other executives and projects, even with the proviso that it's currently committed to another artist, you can at least be aware of whether there are other places to take the song. Needless to say, if you have two artists of roughly equal stature ready to cut the song, you can turn that shakedown around—and start asking what the weasels will do for you . . .

Strategy #5: If You Lose, Do It Gracefully

If you're in a losing battle, the worst result is not surrender. The worst result is that you continue to fight until you lose not just the battle, but the whole war. No one enjoys being coerced into giving money away, and no one in the industry expects you to be happy about it. But if you let the negotiations become acrimonious and ugly, you will have only increased the damage. You'll still lose a piece of the song, and you'll also lose the relationship with the artist, label, producer, or manager. Keep your exchanges on a friendly, businesslike level. Get the best deal you can and then put on a happy face. If you're in the ring with a bigger, stronger, faster opponent, it's best to just get knocked out quickly and get it over with. Don't get him mad at you.

Unauthorized Use: That Dirty Little Secret

At least in the shakedown scenario, they ask your permission before they rip you off. As you move a little outside of the mainstream music industry, you will also find plenty of characters operating on the theory of "what the publishers don't know won't hurt them." Be assured, if you have a significant hit, soon enough you will find your copyright turning up in unlikely places, usually being used without a license, without proper compensation, permission, or credit. At least, you hope you find it . . .

The difficulty in combating this sort of infringement is that you have to catch someone at it. With some exceptions, copyright infringement happens most often on the margins of the industry—a song shows up in a foreign television production or an independent film, is used repeatedly as a parody on a local morning radio show, or gets sampled for an underground hip-hop record or club track. Unless you spend your days scanning the airwaves and your nights hitting the clubs, it's unlikely you'll manage to find everyone who's "borrowing" your song. At the very least, you'll need some help from your team.

Given that your greatest vulnerability is outside of the US, the benefits of an active and vigilant foreign subpublisher are obvious. Subpublishers can be your eyes and ears in their individual territories; it is an important part of their role to uncover and pursue cases in which your song is being improperly exploited.

At the same time, within this country, you need to rely on your network of industry contacts to help uncover what may be happening right under your nose. In my experience, most of the time you find out about this sort of thing from an excited friend or collaborator calling to congratulate you after he or she just heard your song in a local advertisement, or at a dance club, or in some straight-to-cable movie. "Wow, you must be really excited. Why didn't you tell anyone you had a song in that movie?" they ask innocently . . .

Time to call your lawyer. Once you've uncovered an unlicensed exploitation of the song, you would be wise to get your attorney's feedback on the most effective way to take advantage of the situation. Note my words. I did not suggest that you try to stop the use of the song. Certainly there is the option of sending a letter or threatening a lawsuit to prevent someone from continuing to use your song—and in the case of certain parodies or other uses damaging to the copyright, that may be the best response. But in many instances, you may not want to stop the use of your song at all, at least not right away.

In fact, you may have unwittingly hit the mother lode.

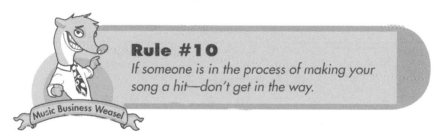

Rule #10

If someone is in the process of making your song a hit—don't get in the way.

Music Business Weasel

Now that you are aware of the infringement, in many cases your best strategy will be to wait until the unlawful user has maximized his or her ill-gotten gains before you swoop in for the kill. There is no profit in taking legal action against a small company with no money. Wait until the violators have made some money —then go claim your share, plus some.

About ten years ago, a friend of mine wrote and recorded a dance record that he released on an independent label. The song was a minor underground success, but as is usually the case, did not generate any serious royalty income. However, one of the mixes on the original 12" record was an a capella mix, which is the key to the next part of this story.

Several years later, that a capella mix was uncovered by a couple of Italian dance producers on what was now a fairly obscure 12" record—they borrowed one or two lines from a tag section just after the final chorus and used that vocal part as the basis for a whole new record. When the new record proved to be quite popular, the producers took the next step and found a new vocalist to re-sing the original lines, which eliminated the master recording infringement.

But the melody and lyrics were still directly lifted from the original composition, which meant that it remained a potential copyright infringement.

The story doesn't stop in Italy. As you might have guessed, the song became a huge hit and soon crossed over to other territories around Europe. By the time it reached the UK, the song had become a club staple and had sold over a million units. It also spawned an album by the Italian group; the album subsequently became one of the biggest dance albums in Europe. It was at this point, just before the song began to cross over to American shores, that my friend learned what had happened. What should he do?

Exactly what he had done up until that point. Absolutely nothing. It was only when the song had been released in America and peaked at the top of the dance charts here that he launched what was virtually an open-and-shut copyright infringement claim. This entitled him to a huge portion of the profits of both the single and the album worldwide—and left the label and the Italian producers with virtually no choice but to pay up. Like I said, if someone's making a hit out of your song, let 'em. Someone using your song without permission is not necessarily bad news.

Copyright Infringement: You Turned the Tables on Me . . .

Conversely, being accused by someone else of infringing on their song is never fun. The unfortunate reality is that when it comes to outright theft of a song, you are much more likely to be the accused than the accuser. Perhaps it's a reflection of the increasingly litigious nature of our society, or maybe it's just an indication that there are fewer and fewer lyrical and melodic ideas that haven't been used, but these sorts of cases seem to proliferate every year. Should you have a big worldwide hit, it's quite likely that someone will show up with an infringement claim.

Of course, some of these claims are disputes between established industry professionals—as in Michael Bolton versus The Isley Bros., over "Love Is a Wonderful Thing," or Ray Parker Jr. and Huey Lewis arguing over the theme song to *Ghostbusters*. Not surprisingly, these cases are well publicized when they reach the point of actually going to court. The majority of such claims are settled quietly between publishing companies before they ever go to trial.

More often, infringement claims come from unknown (and usually unsuccessful) writers and are directed toward writers and artists whose track record alone would indicate that they are unlikely to pilfer songs from amateurs. To be kind, most of these cases are dubious at best and would hardly withstand the scrutiny of musicologists or a competent jury. I'm convinced that there are a good number of opportunists who have made vocations out of filing spurious copyright claims and collecting payouts from large publishers who figure it's easier to pay than to fight. In case you haven't noticed, there are a lot of crazy people on the fringes of show business.

These sorts of battles take quite a bit of effort to fight. You'll need:

- work tapes from the writing sessions, to show the process of creation

- testimony from co-writers, engineers, musicians, or singers that were in the room while the song was written

- records of when the song was completed, demoed, and where it was pitched

- possible testimony from others in the industry who may have heard the song in pitch meetings or other venues

- supporting analysis and testimony from expert "musicologists" explaining the similarities and differences between the songs in question

You also need a good lawyer, which is never cheap. While the publisher is responsible for protecting the copyright, the costs of fighting such a case are recoupable from the writer's share of income. In fact, as soon as such a claim is filed, the publisher will begin to place the writer's royalties into an escrow account, pending resolution of the case. The publisher reserves the right to settle the claim, without the approval of the writer.

Of course, if you're the writer as well, none of that is particularly helpful. Should you find yourself in this exasperating predicament, the best advice I can offer is to make sure you're wearing your publisher hat and not your writer one. There is nothing more upsetting to a writer than the implication (legitimate or not) that he or she has lifted someone else's work. In order to maintain a positive and productive mental state, you must learn to deal with these issues as business arguments, rather than creative ones. Try to take the emotion out of it. If your lawyer tells you to settle, then settle—no matter how convinced you are of your innocence. It's just business.

One key issue in this sort of infringement claim is that of access. It is not copyright infringement if, purely by chance, you happen to write a song strikingly similar to another song written by someone else. In order to prove that you purposely copied his or her work, the plaintiff must show that you had access to his or her song at some point prior to completing your composition. Could you have heard it on the radio or on a commercially available album? Was a band in a live venue actively performing it? Or did you at some point receive a demo of the song? If the plaintiff can show that you received a demo of his or her song prior to writing yours, your case just got a whole lot more difficult. If you're wondering about the origin of the "no unsolicited material" policy that most record and publishing companies have adopted, there it is. It can be very dangerous to accept demos from people you don't know.

I'm not suggesting that you draw the shades, lock the doors, and quit going out to pick up your mail. I am counseling you be careful about taking CDs from obviously amateurish writers or people that appear to be mentally unstable. If you receive something that makes you uncomfortable, return it immediately. I would suggest that you avoid accepting unsolicited packages in which a proof of receipt will be provided (return-receipt requested, Fed Ex, Express Mail). Finally, make sure that your record keeping is accurate and comprehensive. Try to keep a list of all incoming material, and if possible, your response to it.

Copyright Infringement: There Goes My Baby . . .

Only now do we come to the subject that seems to be the greatest fear of most new writers and publishers. What if someone takes your song? What if you send your song off to Joe Superstar, and six months later, you realize you know all the words to his new single the very first time you hear it? What should you do?

First, be sure you're right. A song with the same title does not equal copyright infringement, nor does a song with the same chord progression. (You didn't invent A minor to G major to F major.) A similar shape to the melody will not usually constitute infringement (although it could, if that shape is so unique, or combined with the same lyric, or if that shape is the only melody in the song). A similar lyrical subject matter is certainly not enough to justify a claim.

There is no set rule here—because of the nature of music, it remains a subjective judgment. For instance, it is generally not possible to claim an infringement for a similar drum pattern. But in the case of a rap record, in which the drum pattern might be the sole distinguishing musical element, it may be possible to claim ownership of a drum part in the same way that Joe Perry can own the riff in "Walk This Way." Ultimately, musical experts will make the call. Use your common sense, listen to the advice of your lawyer, and don't waste your time and energy on pointless claims. More importantly, don't make all the rest of us waste our time and energy on pointless claims.

If you really do have a legitimate infringement case, then gather all your paperwork and lay it quietly in the hands of your attorney. If your attorney is wise, he or she may quietly contact the publishers of the song in question, quietly present your evidence, and quietly negotiate an appropriate settlement.

If that sounds like a rather unsatisfying response to such a dastardly deed, remember, this is not about punishment or revenge. It's about getting what's yours, nothing more. The last thing you want to do is go public with this in any way, least of all in court. That's not because you might lose (which is always possible). It's because the last thing you need is the publicity of leveling a copyright infringement claim, especially if the accused is a well-known figure. One front-page article in *Billboard,* and you'll never get any weasel in town to accept your demos again.

Or your lawyer may choose to wait a while. As we discussed, sometimes you're better off letting the record have its run—you don't want to strangle the goose before it lays the golden egg. If the song is shaping up as a hit, just sit tight and wait 'til it peaks. Then you can speak up. Quietly.

Registering Your Claim for Copyright

If it seems strange that we're this far into a chapter on protecting copyrights, and we're just now taking a look at the actual copyright process itself—there's a reason for that. It's not that I feel that copyrighting your material is unimportant. It is an essential role of the publisher to register the copyrights in a timely manner. But you should be aware of two things:

An original song is protected as a copyright as soon as it is fixed, which is to say, written down or recorded in some manner. Your rough work-tape version of the song is, for all intents and purposes, copyrighted. In the eyes of the law, you already own your song. What most people are referring to when they discuss the copyright process is the act of registration. Registration is simply the submission of your claim to copyright with the Copyright Office at the Library of Congress. It's a public record of your statement of ownership.

Registration does not mean your statement of ownership is valid. It does not stop anyone from disputing your claim. The point is, copyright registration alone will not protect you from any of the threats we've discussed in this chapter. It will not stop a collaborator from wanting a bigger share, it will not protect you from a greedy artist's shakedown, and it will not prevent someone from using the song without your permission. It won't even definitively establish your ownership of the song. All it will do is indicate that on a certain date, you claimed to own a particular song.

Why bother, then? There's a $30 fee (if you write ten songs annually, that's $300 every year) and forms to fill out. Why not just use the old-school method of mailing a copy of the song to yourself and keeping the unopened, postmarked envelope as proof of the song's existence? Or couldn't you just put a © on the demo and the lyric sheet? Well, okay. Those methods are not perfect, but they do work to some extent. The first option is not terribly necessary, particularly if you keep accurate records and hold on to your work tapes. The latter is a good practice under any circumstances.

But neither can replace the formal process of registering a copyright. This is especially true when things get ugly. You cannot take action against an infringement of your copyright until the song has been registered, and you could lose your claim to any monies earned by that unauthorized use prior to the date your claim was filed. If there is a dispute as to who actually owns a song, the party who first registered the copyright claim will likely carry the day. The question then is not whether or not to register your songs with the Copyright Office. The question is, how and when.

The process of registering copyrights is straightforward. You'll need a Form PA—you can obtain this form from the Copyright Office. Once you've completed the form, you simply return it, along with a check for $30, and two copies of the "best edition" of the song. In most cases, this will be either a demo or master recording, although it could also be printed sheet music, or a homemade lead sheet if you prefer.

Some time later, you should receive a copy of the form back from the Register of Copyrights, which will include an official copyright number. This form should go in the song file, along with the validated registration forms from your performing rights society and your mechanical licensing organization. That's it. You're now in the Library of Congress.

The real question is how to go about registering your work in the most cost-effective manner. That answer is only slightly more involved. Certainly, you can register each song, one by one, as it is completed—but at $30 a song, it violates the fundamental principle of frugality that should be part of your company culture. A better solution would be to register a group of songs as one collection. This means putting all your new, unreleased, and unregistered songs on one CD, and registering the whole thing as a collection.

This can be done any time you've accumulated enough material to make it cost-effective. I'd suggest that you do it upon accumulating ten or fifteen new copyrights. If one of the songs is cut and released, you should register it again individually, using the commercial recording as the "best edition."

Feel safer now? I've noticed that one can often proceed through life feeling relatively secure (probably falsely so) until an event or warning triggers panic. Then, as efforts are made to increase safety, threats seem to multiply, popping up everywhere until one despairs of ever feeling secure again. Don't get paranoid. Yes, there are many threats to your copyrights—evildoers really do lurk out there in the shadows, ready to make a quick buck off of your creativity, talent, and hard work. But there is also a danger in being overprotective. For instance, being sampled could be the best thing that ever happens to you. If you take the necessary precautions, stay on top of your paperwork, and keep your eyes and ears open, you can sleep comfortably at night, knowing your songs are as safe as possible.

Here's a shortlist of protection fundamentals:

DO:

- Include a © notice, the year, and your name on any demos and lyric sheets. You can write either © 2003 Ima Weasel, or Copyright 2003 Ima Weasel.

- Keep all work tapes, studio records, and invoices relating to any original compositions.

- Have a standard work-for-hire acknowledgement letter to be signed as necessary by musicians, singers, engineers, and others who may have worked on the song, but will not receive a portion of the copyright.

- Keep records of all incoming and outgoing material, as well as notes as to where a song has been pitched.

- Find vigilant subpublishers to protect your copyrights outside of the US.

- Listen to your lawyer. Avoid wasting time on infringements that are frivolous, or on matters in which little money is at stake. If your lawyer says it's time to settle a dispute, do it.

- Get signed split letters after every writing session. There—you knew I had to say it.

DON'T:

- Have large groups of people hanging out at a writing session. More people, more problems. Keep it private.

- Ask someone to sing, play, or engineer on a demo with a vague promise of "taking care of them" if and when something happens with a song. Make your promises clear and specific.

- Send out music without adequate contact information on both the cover and the CD itself.

- Assume that a musical idea that you "borrowed" is so small or obscure that no one will know or care. Somebody cares.

- Personalize copyright disputes. This isn't about anything except money. Save your moral crusades for things like world peace.

24

You're the One That I Want: The Final Frontier (The Art of Acquisition)

For any business built on the unique talents of one person, there is an inevitable moment of truth. Whether you are a musician, an actor, a songwriter, a business consultant, architect, or hairstylist, sooner or later you will hit a wall—one that can't be broken through just by fortitude and a few sleepless nights. It's a simple fact of life: a business built around one unique individual can only get so big. If your publishing company is built around your work as a songwriter, you may already be seeing the wall looming in the distance.

Businesses built around systems of mass production don't have this problem. If you own a widget factory and demand begins to outpace supply, you can buy more machines, build more factories, and make more widgets. It's a little tougher if you're a songwriter. Sure, you can try to write faster and step up the production line of songs. You can co-write and hope the division of labor frees up a few more hours every day. You can become choosier about the projects you work on to get the maximum value out of each song you write. But still, one day . . . BAM! You hit the wall, head-on. Written on that wall is a message:

There's only so much one person can do.

We all have our human limits. Since a music publishing business is inevitably built around the creative contributions of human beings, there comes a time when the only way to grow your business is to add some new faces to the line-up. It's time to sign some new writers and songs. This is at once the greatest opportunity and the greatest risk your enterprise will face.

In a simpler world, adding songwriters would be like buying more machines or building more factories. Let's paint a very rosy picture, and imagine that your efforts as a publisher are showing some big results for you as writer. You've got a hit record climbing the charts and the calls are starting to come in. Artists want to write with you; weasels want to take meetings; Hollywood wants you to write the theme song for *Men in Black VI*. It's good, but it's too much of a good thing. You need another you.

Adding another songwriter is not adding another you. The new writer can't necessarily write the hits that you're writing. He or she certainly can't write the same hit that you would write. This addition to the factory doesn't really get you more widgets—it gets you a new line of widgets. That is both a benefit, and a risk.

In addition to simply providing an extra set of hands to share the workload, one of the greatest benefits of expanding your roster is the chance to diversify. No matter how hot you may be as a writer at any given moment, there will be times when you are equally cold. Whatever is in fashion must eventually be out—if only so it can be brought back in again. Part of the value of having several writers on the roster is that when one's sound is fading in popularity, another's may be ascending. Diversity is an insurance policy against the fickle nature of the music industry's tastes. If you want to have the flavor of the month, you need more than chocolate and vanilla in your fridge.

Diversity can also help to counter the natural creative ups and downs that are part of any writer's career cycle. Most songwriters will struggle at times, often for a year or two, searching for a direction or a sound. Then suddenly they'll hit their stride and get on a bit of a roll. Then, just as quickly, they get distracted, or overly self-conscious, or just plain bored, and start the whole process over again. Needless to say, if you only have one writer in your publishing company, those struggling and searching periods can be pretty tough to weather. Ideally, different writers will peak at different times and in different market environments. There is indeed some safety in numbers.

But there's some risk too. Here's the most obvious one:

Picking hits, whether it's hit songs or hit songwriters, is the single hardest thing to do in the entire music industry. No one, and I do mean no one, can do it consistently. Certainly there are a good number of executives that have built a reputation on discovering talent, and deservedly so. But if you looked at all of their signings, you would still find more misses than hits.

I've always thought that other writers, musicians, and artists should make the best judges of talent. But judging by the lackluster performance of most artists' record label imprints, I'm not sure that stands up, either. No matter how convinced you are about the merits of a song or songwriter, you are much more likely to be wrong than right. Over 90 percent of the acts signed to major labels lose money. I suspect the statistics of songwriters signed to publishing companies is slightly better, but not by much. If you're a betting person (and if you're paying advances to sign writers, that's exactly what you are), you can't like the odds.

There are risks beyond just betting on the wrong horse. While additional writers may carry some of the workload on the creative side, they may create additional work on the publishing side. Many successful writers and producers have attempted to increase their career longevity by signing a staff of writers to their publishing company, only to find their own creative energy sapped by the pressures of managing three or four other writers.

Diversity can easily lead to a loss of focus, pulling you away from what you excel at into an area in which you're less effective. If it's your strength as a writer that's driving the publishing company, you've got to keep writing. Your company can't afford for you to sacrifice your own writing time in the interests of developing the other writers on your roster.

My suggestion? When checking out the pool of talent, don't dive in. Test the waters first. Stick one foot in, then another, moving a little deeper all the time. I admit it lacks the drama and bravado of a big belly flop off the diving board—but it stings a lot less too.

Unless your company has extensive funding, you need a cautious growth strategy, starting with a few sure things (or as close as you can get in this business) that can provide a steady income stream, then moving on to one or two low-risk, short-term ventures. Only when you have had some success with these initial signings should you consider gambling on the more high-risk, long-term deals. This will reduce your financial risk, and it will allow you to see how much you can handle as a writer/creative director/administrator.

The Sure Thing: The Single-Song Deal

Pretty sure, anyway. These are the sorts of deals that involve very little risk or effort. While they won't make you millions, they can provide some additional income. Surprisingly, there are more of these opportunities out there than you might think. It's all about knowing where to look.

Collaborators

I tipped you off on this one way back at the beginning of the book. This strategy is not so much about creating additional catalog as it is about increasing your share of those songs in which you already have an interest. Here's the way it can work:

Let's say that your writer (that is, you, or someone else that you represent) collaborates with a writer who is not affiliated with another publisher—the song is a 50/50 split between the two writers. And let's suppose too that the unaffiliated collaborator has not yet read this invaluable guide and is not actively engaged in being his or her own publisher. Why not make a simple proposal?

Try this one: If the song is commercially released as a result of your publishing efforts, the collaborator agrees to sign all or part of his or her publishing share (for this one song) to you.

From your standpoint, it's something of a no-brainer. After all, you're the one who's going to be shopping the song anyway. If you get it cut, you'll already be administering part of it as well. This deal could allow you to double your income without doing substantially more work than you were already committed to. In fact, your job actually becomes easier when you control 100 percent of the publishing, as you no longer have to obtain approvals from another publisher, should you want to license the song in a movie, television show, or other venue.

At the same time, it's not a bad deal for the collaborator either. If the song is released, he or she would have to go to someone to administer his or her publishing share—most large publishers wouldn't be interested in handling a single song and would be unlikely to offer much of an advance. Better, then, to offer you an incentive to try to get the song placed and be administered by a company for whom this song is an important copyright.

In most instances, I don't think it's necessary to offer an up-front advance for this sort of deal. As I said, advances for single-song deals are generally minimal, even from large publishers, unless the song is placed on a multi-platinum artist. Since you're only taking the publishing share if you manage to place the song, there is almost no up-front risk for the writer. If the song is placed on a major artist, you could consider offering an advance of $1,000 to $2,500, just as a gesture of good faith.

Foreign Publishers

If you or your writers regularly collaborate with those outside the US, there may be other opportunities to increase your share of the copyright. Even if a foreign writer is actively involved in operating his or her own publishing company, he or she may not yet have established a subpublishing deal in the US. If you are able to place a song in which you share an interest, it may be worth suggesting that you subpublish that song in the US. This would allow you to administer the song in this country and keep a portion of the income collected here. Again, you're going to be administering the song anyway on behalf of your own writer.

These types of single-song, no advance, "spec" deals are a simple and relatively safe way of developing relationships with new writers. By structuring deals on a song-by-song basis, you remove much of the risk for both parties. The writer is not forced to make an exclusive commitment to a still-unfamiliar publisher, and you are not saddled with a writer's entire catalog, only to find that there's just one marketable song. By predicating the agreement on the placement of the song on a commercial release, the writer asks you to "prove yourself" before he or she assigns the publishing share to your company. At the same time, you don't waste time and money negotiating a publishing agreement for a song that never gets recorded.

Of course, this type of agreement can present problems as well. The most obvious one is that a handshake deal based on "if you get it cut, you can take the publishing" can be conveniently forgotten once the song is slated for release. If possible, it's probably best to have all parties execute a letter outlining the general understanding before you begin to shop the song.

The other drawback is that this approach doesn't really do much to diversify your catalog. You simply own more of something that you already had. Still, it allows you to begin working with new writers in a structure that involves very little risk—which makes it an excellent starting point.

Outside Songs

The next logical step in developing your catalog is to consider publishing outside songs in which you don't already have a collaborative interest. Again, I recommend that you approach this on a single-song basis, with the agreement that you will pitch the song and if you place it, will receive in return all, or a portion of, the publisher's share. If you hear a song that you feel would be right for a specific project, you can simply gain the writer's approval to the general terms of the deal, and put the song forward for consideration. Only when there is a commitment to record the song do you need to execute a single-song contract.

A few precautions:

Be careful about telling the writer where you intend to send the song. It's just a little too easy for a writer to take your suggestion and get the song there before you do—and then decline to cut you in. Likewise, don't give out too much information about the unsigned writer to the weasel you're pitching to. You may later see the song on the record, with the publishing share going to the weasel instead. Finally, make sure that you get a healthy portion of the pie for all your efforts. Don't waste time on songs where the writers are willing to give up less than 50 percent of the publisher's share.

By proceeding on a single-song basis, you're able to watch a writer develop, see how their work is received in the marketplace, and get a glimpse as to how they might fit into your company—all without putting any money at risk. It's a nice arrangement, but it's a little like a courtship. It can only last so long.

The Not-So-Sure Thing: The Writer Deal

Let's say you first meet New Kid in Town through a collaboration; the two of you write a song that you subsequently manage to place in a movie and on the related soundtrack album. Being the new kid, NKIT is thrilled by this first taste of success and agrees to give you his share of the publishing. Next week, he brings you a song he's written all on his own. Again, he offers to give up his publishing share if you can get the song recorded. Voilá, soon enough you've placed this new song as well. So you execute a second single-song agreement.

Now you're approaching a crossroads. New Kid is eventually going to resent giving up the publisher's share of all his most successful songs to a publisher who has made no financial investment in his long-term career. With a couple of cuts under his belt (thanks to you, of course), New Kid has some choices to make. He might be able to go to a larger publisher, do a co-publishing deal (which means he could keep half of the publishing), and probably collect some advance money on top of it all. But if he continues to give away his publishing to you each time a song is placed, he'll never own enough catalog to interest another publisher.

You're in a bit of predicament as well. Sure, you've made out okay so far—but not without a fair amount of effort. You've invested time in New Kid's career, and helped him make a name for himself. (He's now known as "Hot New Kid in Town.") But if other people are talking about him, you run the risk that another publisher will step in and capitalize on the groundwork you've laid. What if some other company throws him an advance check and takes him away, just when he's on the verge of big success?

This is when it gets interesting. The primary thing to keep in mind is that there are a wide variety of options open to you. It's easy to feel trapped in such a situation, especially if your company is low on cash and larger companies are offering New Kid some big money. Never let another company force you into making an offer that doesn't make sense for your company. It's all good to be creative in your deal-making and to find ways to structure proposals that are competitive with those from more cash-rich publishers. But it should never be done at the risk of your company's financial future. Consider a few possible responses to the NKIT scenario:

You could walk away. This is sometimes the best possible strategy. You have to ask:

- Is New Kid's success a product of his skill as a writer or a result of your connections as a publisher?

- Is New Kid's work improving or do you have a sense he may have peaked creatively?

- Is there a specific market in which New Kid has had his success? Is that market growing or shrinking?

Small publishers have survived for years by discovering talented young writers, grabbing their early and best work, and then letting a large Johnny Come Lately corporation overpay for what turns out to be a quickly fading career. In the proverbial pool of talent, it's just as important to know when to get out as to know when to get in. If you've made good money and acquired some solid copyrights, you could walk away with no hard feelings.

Or you could find a way to share. If New Kid were to sign a co-publishing deal with another publisher, he would be giving up half of his publishing share. But that still leaves the other half available. You could suggest that you continue doing what you've been doing for him, with the agreement that he will give you his half of the publishing, or perhaps a portion of his half, for any song that you place on a commercial release. Remember too, you already own two of New Kid's presumably valuable copyrights. If you would be willing to share those with the other prospective publisher, both New Kid and the other publisher might be willing to give you a small piece in future copyrights.

Or you could sell. Those two copyrights might be worth a lot more to NKIT's new suitor than they are to you. Your advantage here is access to the books. You know how much the songs are earning and should have some sense as to whether the bulk of the income has been collected. If you believe that the pipeline is running dry for these two copyrights, or that the musical style of the songs is sliding out of fashion, it may be more lucrative to contact your competitor and offer to sell them your publishing share. This gives them ownership of New Kid's entire catalog, including his two commercially released songs—and gives you some quick cash to invest in some other younger, fresher New Kid.

Or you could compete. If you really believe that New Kid is an exciting talent on his way up, then it's time to fight for your man. You will most likely want to counter by offering some type of exclusive songwriter contract. There are countless ways in which these contracts can be structured, but most fall into three basic types:

- **Full Publishing:** This requires New Kid to assign 100 percent of his publishing share to you for any songs written during the contract term. (NKIT of course retains his full writer's share of the song.) You have full control over licensing and administration and, unless you agree otherwise, retain your share for the life of the copyright.

- **Co-publishing:** This allows New Kid to keep a portion (usually 50 percent) of his publishing share, while you take the other 50 percent. In most instances, you should insist on administering both New Kid's publishing share, and your own. This allows you to issue all the licenses and collect all the income, which you will then distribute. Again, you retain your share for the life of the copyright.

- **Administration:** This is a much more limited structure. In an administration deal, New Kid would hold on to his entire publishing share. You would not have any ownership in the copyrights, but would simply administer them—you issue the licenses and collect the money. For your administration service, you would charge a fee, usually somewhere between 5 and 15 percent of the money you collect. This arrangement lasts only for the duration of the contract (usually three or four years), after which New Kid can take his copyrights somewhere else.

So what sort of deal do you offer?

For a small, independent publisher, there is no question that a full publishing deal is the best of all options. It is very difficult for a modestly sized company to make a sufficient profit with less than 100 percent of a writer's publishing. Remember, if New Kid collaborates, you only own 100 percent of his share of the composition. For instance, if he writes with two other people, you most likely own only 33 percent of the entire publisher's share.

If you then factor in the possibility of reduced mechanical royalty rates, or cut-ins on the income with movie studios or producers, you can see the income dwindling fast. In many cases, a full publishing deal is the only way to make the entire exercise worth your effort. This is particularly true if you work in a genre somewhat outside the commercial mainstream. Publishing is a business built on pennies. You can only split a penny so many ways and still have money in your hand.

But you can't always get what you want. For much of the pop and urban music world, the co-publishing deal has become the industry standard. Many writers are simply unwilling to give up their entire publishing share, and in some instances, for good reason. As I said at the beginning of this book, many of the most successful writers have embraced their role as a publisher, and while they may be willing to share the labor, they are unwilling to step out of the role altogether. If a writer is active in exploiting his or her own work, then it's not unreasonable that he or she should have a piece of the publisher's share.

If we go back then to our New Kid in Town scenario, the question is, how valuable a co-publisher is NKIT Music? If New Kid is genuinely engaged in the business, then a co-pub deal may make sense. Certainly, there will be less money for you, but presumably NKIT Music will be carrying some of the workload in exchange.

But if New Kid is not qualified or interested in taking an active publishing role (at least in the exploitation area) then you can't afford to give up half of the income. Your best solution may be to vary the split, on a song-by-song basis. If NKIT Music gets the song cut, then you split the publishing 50/50. If you get the song cut, then you take 75 percent, and give NKIT Music 25 percent. If you place the song in a movie or a television production, you take the full publishing share of the sync fee. However you structure the percentages, you must make sure that the potential income justifies the labor involved.

For this reason, it rarely makes sense for a small publishing operation to offer an administration deal. In most instances, only a large corporation can achieve the economies of scale necessary to make an admin deal profitable. Think of it this way: If you have one hundred catalogs that you administer, taking on one more increases your workload by 1 percent. If you have only one catalog that you administer, and you add a new one, it increases your workload 100 percent. Large publishers have hundreds of office workers that they already employ and need to keep busy—the cost of administering one more catalog is very low. It's just the opposite for you.

An administration deal would only make sense if New Kid writes exclusively with you or one of your writers. If that were the case, you would be administering those copyrights anyway (on behalf of your writer). It would not be much more work to administer New Kid's share as well. Still, I would suggest a fee in the neighborhood of 15 percent, just to make it worth your time.

Where the Devil Lives: The Details

As you probably suspect, there is much more to any songwriter/publisher contract than just the percentage received by each party. There are a myriad of books available that discuss songwriter agreements in detail and offer samples of the various types of contracts. *This Business of Music* by William Krasilovsky and Sidney Shemel can give you a good idea of how these sorts of deals are structured. For my part, I'm simply going to touch on a few of the terms that will need to be negotiated. This is not a comprehensive list. Just a quick heads-up on issues that can sometimes be contentious:

Term of Contract/Contract Period: Most songwriter agreements are structured as one contract period, plus options. This means that a writer is signed exclusively for the duration of the first period, at the end of which the *publisher*—not the writer—has an option to renew the agreement for additional contract periods (usually three or four).

So what's a contract period? That's the big question. In some contracts, the first period is specified as a calendar year. But in many contracts, particularly co-publishing agreements, the first period ends upon delivery of the minimum commitment requirement. This does not necessarily equal a year.

Minimum Commitment Requirement: This is the specific number of compositions a songwriter is required to write during his or her contract period. The Minimum Commitment can vary wildly for different writers, but in most cases, the number is between eight and twelve. But that number is only a small part of the story.

First of all, the Commitment Requirement refers to whole compositions, owned 100 percent by the writer. A collaboration in which the writer has a 50-percent share only counts as a half a song. So if the minimum commitment is ten songs, and a writer normally writes only 50 percent of any composition, he or she will have to write twenty songs to fulfill the requirement for the contract period. It gets even heavier.

"Record and Release" Requirements: Many contracts will require that at least a portion of the minimum commitment be made up of songs that have not just been written and demo-ed, but have been *recorded and commercially released*. Again, this is particularly common in co-publishing agreements, especially when there is a significant advance being paid by the publisher in each contract period. For instance, a Minimum Commitment might require that five of the ten compositions be recorded and released during the first contract period. Remember, that's five songs owned 100 percent by the writer. If the writer collaborates, that number increases.

For a publisher, the general effect of the "record and release" clause is to lengthen the duration of the contract period. Not even a very successful writer (unless he or she is an artist or producer) is likely to have five songs recorded and released in one year—keeping in mind that many records take a year or more in production. With a "record and release" clause, a contract period can extend up to two or three years, regardless of whether or not the writer has recouped the advance. Multiply that by options for three additional contract periods, and you start to see how long a long-term relationship can be.

Not surprisingly, "record and release" requirements are one of the most contentious subjects between writers and publishers. Personally, as a former writer, I don't like them.

These requirements are largely a reaction by publishers to the insistence of writers on co-publishing deals (which cuts the publisher's income by half), accompanied by exorbitant advance payments. If a writer is willing to agree to a full publishing agreement and a reasonable advance, I think the minimum commitment should be eight to twelve songs, with no "record and release" requirement. If a writer insists on a co-publishing deal and demands a hefty advance, then make the "record and release" requirement commensurate. Fair is fair.

Back to our New Kid story for a second. If New Kid has been offered a deal from a large publisher for what seems like an awful lot of cash, make sure that our young friend understands this concept of "minimum commitment." Upon closer look, he may realize that he's better off taking a much lower advance from you. This way, he writes eight songs during the year and can get another advance twelve months later. If he takes the big money, he better be sure it can last him three or four years.

Advances: So you thought minimum commitment was contentious. Now we're talking real money. Advances are a loan against future earnings, paid by the publisher and then recouped as the writer begins to generate income. For the publisher then, this is not money lost—you should get it back eventually. But, as we said before, there are no guarantees. Very rarely will a publishing deal require a writer to repay the advance if the songs fail to earn back the money. It's a gamble. So how brave are you?

Writer advances vary wildly, from as low as $500 to $1,000 on a single-song deal, to well into seven figures for a superstar writer with a proven catalog. For the purposes of this book, I will assume that few readers are going to find themselves in the middle of a million-dollar bidding war for a writer. Try to come up with a number that is within your financial capabilities, is sufficient to meet the basic needs of the writer, and most importantly, is in line with what you can reasonably expect to earn back. Here's a basic formula:

Pipeline Income: Does the writer already have songs in the market earning income that has not been collected? If so, you need to figure out roughly how much is out there. This means knowing what songs have been released and the share controlled by the writer. You will need to know whether the writer licensed the song at a full or reduced rate. And you'll need an accurate report of the number of records sold—the best method for this is to subscribe to SoundScan.

Projected Income: This is the same exercise, but done on a hypothetical basis. Does the writer have songs that are scheduled to be released? If so, go through the same "pipeline" process, but simply estimate what you think the project can be expected to sell. Be conservative. This is not the time for optimism. If an act sold 300,000 units of their previous album, and the industry buzz says that this record will definitely sell a million—figure on sales of 500,000. If an act sold a million last time, and everyone is nervously assuring you that they'll probably sell a million again—figure on 500,000. Remember to take into account the royalty rate. If the writer is a producer or artist, he or she will almost certainly receive less than full rate. In fact, unless the writer is well established, assume that the rate is between three-quarters and half of the full statutory rate.

Future Income: This one's pure guesswork. What do you think this writer is capable of in the first contract period? One or two cuts? Five or six? Be sure to keep in mind just how long it can take for a song to be written, demoed, shopped, recorded, and released. Other things to consider:

- **Percentages:** How much of each song is the writer likely to have?

- **Output:** How prolific is the writer?

- **Genre:** What are the sales levels for the genre the writer works in?

- **Rates:** Is the writer likely to be "controlled"?

- **Sync and Performance Income:** How likely are you to place songs in a movie? How likely is radio airplay?

- **Full or Co-pub Deal:** What sort of share will you have of the income?

Once you've looked at the numbers for pipeline, and projected future income, you should be able to approximate what you are comfortable offering as a writer advance. But don't get too generous. Only the pipeline number has real substance—everything else is an educated guess.

There's one other essential thing to keep in mind. The advance is recouped from the writer's share of the income, not the gross—after all, part of the gross income already belongs to you. If you pay an advance of $2,000 for a single song, that copyright will have to generate $4,000 in gross income in order to recoup the writer's advance. When you are doing your income estimates, make sure you know what you're calculating:

- the gross income, which is achieved by multiplying 8 cents (if the song is licensed at full rate) by the units sold, or

- the writer's income, which would be half of the gross

In order to be competitive with the other deal offers, you'll probably need to pay the advance upon execution of the contract. If you're really strapped, you could offer to break the advance amount into twelve monthly payments—this sort of "salary" approach can actually be attractive to writers who are used to feast or famine. Or you could offer to pay half the amount upon execution, with the "back end" due when the minimum commitment is fulfilled.

You do need to remember that the writer has financial needs as well. Part of the value of an advance is to offer the writer a certain level of financial stability, allowing him to focus on writing. If the advance is paid out so sporadically that the writer is forced to take a full-time job and a night gig just to make ends meet, you could be hurting your own cause.

Just to warn you, the back-and-forth nature of contract negotiations can be very frustrating. It will likely lead to several crisis points, where you begin to question whether this new, unproven talent is worth the financial risk and the emotional investment. In fact, that's part of the value of the negotiation process. It forces you to continually reassess your initial judgments about the writer and the catalog. As the wheeling and dealing drags on and the stakes keep rising, the weaknesses of the writer, or at least his or her limitations, may become increasingly apparent. Don't be afraid to change your mind. You can walk away at any time.

One of the most interesting aspects of my work in publishing has been the opportunity to observe what qualities go into making a writer successful. Musical talent certainly helps, although there's many different levels of musical skill represented on the Hot 100 each week. And some musical and lyrical talents are more valuable than others. A great sense of melody far outweighs harmonic knowledge; and lyrically, the ability to think conceptually is more useful than a vast knowledge of rhyme schemes.

Ultimately, many of the most important qualities in a songwriter are personal rather than musical. A writer doesn't have to have hit songs to be worth taking a chance on. You just need to believe that he or she has the qualities of a hit songwriter.

What are those qualities?

- **Confidence.** A writer must believe that he or she has something to say that's worth hearing, and be able to convey that confidence to others.

- **Realism.** In show business, most things fail most of the time. A good writer understands the risks, knows the odds, and can accept criticism.

- **Desire.** At Zomba, we call it the "eye of the tiger." Successful songwriters are entirely focused on success, and nothing but.

- **Grace under pressure.** Songwriting is not always a laidback gig. Try sitting in a room, writing with a superstar artist or someone who was once your musical hero. Great writers can raise their game when they have to.

- **Productivity. Writers write.** When a writer explains to me why they haven't been writing, I know he or she isn't really a writer. A great writer can't stop doing it.

- **Savvy.** I call this knowing how to get lucky. Good writers know how to work a room. They know intuitively who can help their career. They know how to make and keep friends.

- **Salesmanship.** Great writers can sell their songs better than any publisher. That's why they are their own best publishers.

- **An inexhaustible supply of positive energy.** Great writers are always up. Up for a challenge. Looking up. Moving up. Up on top of the world. There is no place for cynicism and negativity in this business. As soon as it sets in, the game is lost.

Fortunes are not made in this business by signing proven writers with hits already in their catalogs. Such writers are too expensive for you to ever really make much money with them. Companies like yours become big companies by identifying good writers before they are fully developed. You can't always do that by listening to music, because the hits may not have been written yet. You have to look at writers on a personal level. If you believe in a writer's determination to succeed, that's about as much of a guarantee as this business offers.

No matter how careful you are, entering the pool of talent is always a leap of faith.

Conclusion: The End of the Road

A couple of hundred pages later, we end up back where we started: with that stack of work tapes gathering dust in the closet. At the very least, I hope this tome has empowered you take ownership of your song catalog, and has opened your eyes to how much you can do on your own to transform those songs into money-making assets. Every songwriter needs a publisher—and now you have one. I'd like to think that this book could inspire you to roll up your sleeves and step into the role with confidence.

But I'm not that naïve. I was once a songwriter too. I'm guessing that mixed in with your newfound ambition is another feeling, something a little different . . .

Dread. "Wow man, that's a lot of information. There's a lot to this whole publishing gig . . . ." Yup. The truth is, there's a lot more to it than what's in this book. There was quite a bit I left out, because I just couldn't fit it in. And there's still more that I just don't know anything about. And on top of that, the business is changing all the time.

Question: "So how am I ever gonna deal with all this stuff anyway? Exploitation, administration, protection, collection, acquisition . . . How'm I gonna do all this?"

Answer: Poorly, probably. At first anyway. Then you'll get better. Each day, each week, you'll improve—every time your business moves up to another level, you'll learn a little more. If you start. If you do something to begin the process of building your business, you'll begin to generate some momentum. Things will start to happen. If you don't do anything—nothing will happen.

Something is better than nothing. Do what you can.

You are not alone in feeling overwhelmed. As I mentioned earlier, every

Creative Director in every publishing company feels the same way, every day. There is always one more song that should have been pitched, or tape that should have been sent, or call that should have been returned. Every Administration Department has a pile of split letters that haven't been signed, or registration forms that haven't been submitted. This is not a sign of failure. This is success. This means things are happening.

Of course, some of the paperwork will fall through the cracks. But if you've done the important things—if you've organized your catalog and set up proper systems—you'll be able to spot the mistake and quickly clear up any confusion. Certainly, you will find yourself in situations where you don't know all the answers. If you've set up a solid team to support your business, you'll have experts you can call for advice. Trust me, as one Creative Director to another, no one has ever said that song plugging was easy. But if you've gotten the music right, and if you are tenacious about getting it out to those who need it, you will find opportunities. Step-by-step, you will move your writer up the ladder of success.

The truth about most businesses is that a little success can cover a lot of failures. All of those things you never got around to fade in importance if you get a few big things right. The one thing that you can't afford is inaction. It's not necessary to do all of the things I've suggested in this book. Nor is it necessary to do any of these things perfectly. But you have to do *something*. Don't wait until you think you have the time or the knowledge or the money to start your own publishing company. Just start it. Set the wheels in motion and let momentum take care of the rest.

Once you begin this venture, you'll find there are some areas in which you excel and other areas in which you struggle. If you're a songwriter, you may find that the Creative Director's role comes quite easily to you—while the Administration function always feels like drudgery. Or it could be just the opposite. Perhaps you are highly organized and efficient, but the thought of cold-calling A&R people gives you nightmares. Nobody can do it all equally well. Luckily, nobody has to.

Play to your strengths. Every company has strengths and weaknesses.

Even the largest corporate monoliths are nothing more than collections of human beings. That means they too have their areas of excellence and of vulnerability. If you're frustrated by your inability to handle all the demands of running your company, rest assured that there are managers in other larger, well-established companies, equally frustrated with their employees. Granted, your one-person operation is limited by the fact that you are good at some things and not very good at others. Someone else's company is plagued by the fact that the V.P. of Administration just quit, and the Creative staff in

New York won't speak with the one in London, and the Royalty department is backlogged by an antiquated computer system. Everyone has problems.

Focus on what you do well. Certainly try to fix those things that are holding back your company's progress. As you grow, you'll be able to hire people who can compensate for your own shortcomings. But your business will be built on your strengths. Some companies excel at pitching songs, others focus on acquiring talent, and still others survive by finding niche markets that they can exploit. Some publishers have their success in the film and television world; others find their opportunities in foreign territories. Some people are dealmakers, others are innovators, and some are team-builders. Whatever works. The key is: once you find something that does work, build on it.

The exploitation opportunities and strategies outlined in this book are not a laundry list of tasks to be completed. They are suggestions of what might work and explanations of what has worked for others. Pick the ones you like and use them. Or try them all, and see which ones pay off. As soon as you sense that something is clicking, put your energy into that. A small company can't afford to pursue every possible avenue of opportunity. You need to go where the action is, for as long as it's there. If you can achieve a few small victories, that success will begin to open doors in other areas.

Independence is power. Make them come to you.

It's a funny thing. The more you need people, the less they want to help you. Ignorance, helplessness, and desperation are not big turn-ons. On the other hand, if you can show people that you are able to achieve some success on your own, suddenly everyone wants to be your friend. Any banker will make a loan to a guy who's already got money. Every weasel wants to work with a songwriter who's already got something happening.

The primary purpose of this book is to give songwriters a sense of the power they have over their own career. One of the most difficult aspects of a writer's life is the feeling that one's destiny seems to be in the hands of others. Life is spent always waiting for a phone call or hoping for that big break. Becoming your own publisher means educating yourself about the industry, creating a network of contacts, pursuing opportunities, and managing your own business. It means creating an enterprise that stands on its own. Once you show that you can survive and prosper independently, everyone will be calling, wanting to help you take your business to the next level. It's ironic, don't you think?

As I mentioned in the introduction to this book, I've never intended to suggest that a writer should avoid affiliation with a larger publishing company. There are obvious benefits to having a business partner that can provide a worldwide network through which to administer your copyrights, or access to superstar artists through a well-connected Creative Director. But by establishing some record of success as an independent company, you can make these deals on your terms. You can pick and choose what offer best meets your needs. Most importantly, you will know how to get the most out of such a partnership, should you decide to enter into one.

Many inexperienced writers view the chance to sign with a major publisher as an opportunity to escape responsibility for their own career. Upon inking the deal, all control over their own fate is deposited immediately into the already full hands of their Creative Director. Not surprisingly, the publisher usually drops the ball. Most writers come out of such deals worse off than when they went in. Most publishers have learned to avoid doing these types of deals altogether.

A successful publishing relationship needs to be a partnership—not necessarily between equals, but between two self-sufficient, independent enterprises with a common goal. A large international publishing company can certainly be effective in providing money to help your business grow, or administrative services to alleviate the demands of paperwork, or creative support to bring you into projects otherwise beyond your reach. But such a company cannot afford to provide the day-to-day attention that will keep your business alive. That part is up to you. To ask a major publisher to organize your catalog, collect split letters, or tell you who's looking for songs is to misunderstand the relationship. Your business should already be up and running. You can call on your partner for help with the things that you can't accomplish on your own.

There are no invitations to the big dance. You're going to have to crash the party.

In case you haven't noticed, the music business is not the most welcoming of industries. It's been quite a few years since I came to New York to begin my own career as a songwriter, but this is one aspect of the experience that remains quite vivid in my memory. Just to get someone (anyone) to listen to my songs meant somehow circumventing a thousand closed doors, unreturned phone calls, "no unsolicited material" policies, hostile receptionists, and a teeming mass of other equally frustrated songwriters. I work with enough of today's young writers to know that it hasn't gotten any easier. The entrance to the music industry has not only gatekeepers but armed guards standing watch outside.

If you're waiting for someone to come along, take you under his arm, flash some credentials, and escort you safely through those gates . . . you are waiting in vain. No one is going to discover your songs, hidden away on your shelf, and decide to make you a songwriter. No one is going to ask to hear your music. Nobody will dig through your catalog and offer to put your song on a record—except those cheesy companies in the magazine ads that charge $200 for the privilege.

So stop waiting. The good news is, you don't need someone's permission to become a songwriter or a music publisher. You just need to do it. When someone asks me how I got started as a songwriter, I usually say that I simply started writing songs. Then I had to figure out how to sell them. So I did that too. My story is not unique—it's true of every working songwriter. The only way to enter the music industry is to decide to be a part of it. As soon as you start playing, you're in the game.

I hope this book can provide you with some useful information about the music publishing industry. It should offer a little bit of insight and some strategies to get the ball rolling. It will not teach you everything you need to know—only experience can do that. Most of all, I hope it will inspire you to action. Let this be your official invitation to join the ranks of music publishers everywhere. I hereby declare you a member of the grand fraternal order. Now grab your demos, and get busy.

Happy Weaseling.

About the Author

Eric Beall is a Creative Director for Zomba Music Publishing, as well as a former songwriter and record producer. In his role at Zomba, Eric has signed and developed top writers, including Steve Diamond, KNS Productions, and Riprock and Alex G., and has coordinated and directed Zomba writers in the development of material for Jive Records pop superstars like Backstreet Boys, *NSYNC, Britney Spears and Aaron Carter.

Before joining Zomba, Eric wrote and produced the pop hits "Nothin' My Love Can't Fix" for Joey Lawrence (Top-10 Billboard Hot 100) and "Carry On" by Martha Wash (#1 Billboard Dance Chart), as well as songs for Diana Ross, The Jacksons, Safire, Samantha Fox, Brenda K. Starr, and many others. He also co-founded Class-X Recordings, an independent dance label in New York.

Index